Dare to Repair Your Car

Dare to Repair Your Car

A Do-It-Herself Guide to Maintenance, Safety, Minor Fix-Its, and Talking Shop

Julie Sussman & Stephanie Glakas-Tenet

Illustrations by Gavin Glakas

With additional illustrations by Yeorgos Lampathakis

Collins
An Imprint of HarperCollinsPublishers

HarperCollins books may be purchased for educational, business, or sales promotional use. For information, please write: Special Markets Department, HarperCollins Publishers, 10 East 53rd Street, New York, NY 10022.

FIRST EDITION

Library of Congress Cataloging-in-Publication Data

Sussman, Julie (Julie Ellen)
    Dare to repair your car: a do-it-herself guide to maintenance, safety, minor fix-its, and talking shop/by Julie Sussman and Stephanie Glakas-Tenet; illustrations by Gavin Glakas and Yeorgos Lampathakis.—1st ed.
        p.   cm.
    Includes index.
    ISBN-10: 0-06-057700-2 ISBN-13: 978-0-06-057700-1 (pb)
    1. Automobiles—Maintenance and repair—Amateurs' manuals. 2. Do-it-yourself work. I. Glakas-Tenet, Stephanie. II. Title.

TL152.S8256 2005
629.28'72—dc22   2005045987

05 06 07 08 09 ISPN/RRD 10 9 8 7 6 5 4 3 2 1

We lovingly dedicate this book to our fathers, Warren George Johnson and John Thomas Glakas, two noble men whose strong moral compasses never failed them on their journeys through life. We thank you for being our providers, our protectors, and our North Star.

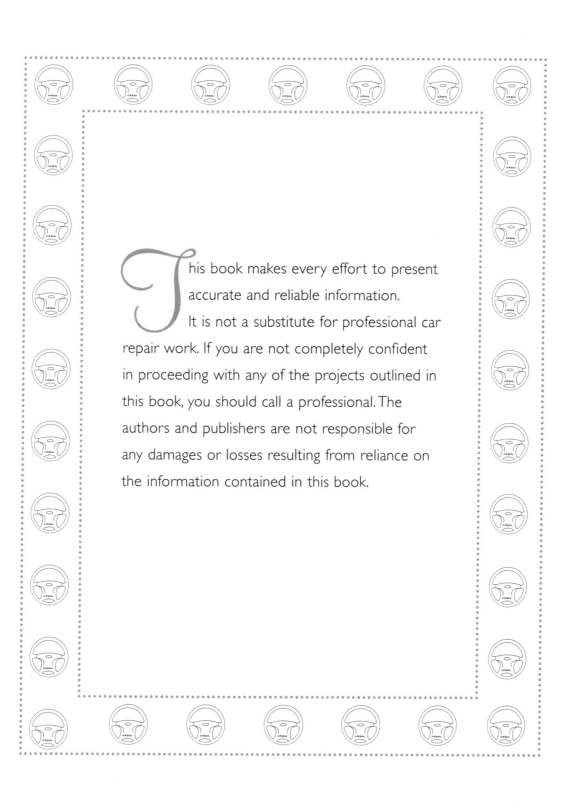

Contents

Acknowledgments

This is our favorite part of *Dare to Repair Your Car* because we get to publicly thank the incredible people (family, friends, coworkers, and technical gurus) whose time, advice, and support enabled us to write this book.

To the wonderful team at HarperCollins. They just don't come any better. First, we want to thank our editor (and friend), Kathy Huck, a woman who successfully combines her innate kindness and patience with her brilliant editorial talent. We love you, Kathy. To Jane Friedman (president and CEO, HarperCollins Publishers), Joe Tessitore (president, Collins), Mary Ellen Curley, Libby Jordan, Keith Pfeffer, and Steve Hanselman—we are truly grateful to you for your continued support of us, our books, and our mission; Paul Olsewski (senior director of publicity), Shelby Meizlik (assistant director of publicity); and Sabrina Ravipinto (publicist)—thank you for handling everything with great humor, patience, and professionalism. You are so delightful to work with. Leah Carlson-Stanisic (design manager), Karen Lumley (associate director, production), and Mareike Paessler (senior production editor)—once again, we thank you for putting your artistic flair from cover to cover; and to Ryu Spaeth (editorial assistant)—we thank you for getting us out of the trenches, time after time.

To our agent, Debra Schneider (Gelfman-Schneider), thank you for your professional wisdom and for always being there for us.

To our artist, Gavin Glakas. Even if you weren't Stephanie's nephew, we would still say that you are one-in-a-million. You have a rare artistic talent, as depicted by the beautiful illustrations throughout the book, but you also have a strong sense of professionalism and accountability, traits that are too rare in today's world. Thank you for gracing the pages with your art, and for gracing our lives.

Speaking of art, we'd be remiss in not thanking our artist from *Dare to Repair*, Yeorgos Lampathakis, for his contributions to the art in *Dare to Repair Your Car*.

To the extraordinary people in our lives who did a lot of heavy lifting for us—our business consultants, Brad Mead (Delta Capital Group, LLC); Diane Gould and Michael Gorski (DH Gould Company); our accountant, Paul Wilner (Grossberg Company, LLP); and our attorneys, Robert Barnett and Deneen Howell (Williams and Connolly, LLP). Thank you for clarifying and rectifying everything for us.

To Julie Valeant Yenichek (Lowe's), our friend and business associate. Everyone should have you in her life. Thank you for believing in us and for constantly promoting our mission. You are an amazing woman.

Stephen Gehring (GM), we were going to thank you with the other technical gurus, but for someone who is as outstanding as you, we thought you should be standing out. We thank you for all the time and effort you put into vetting this book. You are a dear man.

To wonderful Wanda Cockrell—we thank you for not only giving us some technical advice, but also for giving us so many hours of great laughs. How lucky we are to have found you. It must have been divine intervention.

And to Debbie Dingell, a truly extraordinary woman whom we are proud to call our friend. We thank you for always having our backs, for guiding us in the right direction, and for supporting our mission to teach women basic car care.

Now we'd like to single out some of the people who provided us with technical information for *Dare to Repair Your Car*: Chuck Stone (Nationwide Insurance); Larry Kinsel, Nick Richards, Tom Read (GM); Ray Tyson, Kathryn Henry, Essie Wagner, Lou Molino (National Highway Traffic Safety Administration); Justin McNaull, Lon Anderson, Aymee V. Ruiz (AAA); Wendy Wintman (Consumer Reports®); Lorrie Walker, Joe Colella (National SAFE KIDS Campaign); Brian Greenberg, Eleanor Ginsler (AARP); Mark F. Wagner, William Nonnamaker, William Dawson (Johnson Controls, Inc.); Don Goris (Delphi); Dan Zielinski; Leigh

Merino; Greg James and Mark Kuyendall (Bridgestone Firestone North American Tire); Kevin Ferrick and Susan Hahn (American Petroleum Institute); Barry Bronson and Richard Baumgart (Valvoline); Russ Rader (Insurance Institute for Highway Safety); Trish Serratore and Tony Molla (ASE); Mike Cole (National Center for Vehicle Emissions Testing); Mike Thompson (Department of Environmental Quality, Air Check Virginia); John Franklin, Gary McMillen (Oil Dri Corporation of America); Brian Schnell; Richard Roth (AAMCO Transmissions, Inc.); Hank Stocks (AAL-MATIC Transmission Service); Tricia Elwell Singer (Shell Lubricants); Randy Schuetz (Valspar Corporation); Mark Monnet (Thule, Inc); Mike Phillips (Meguiar's, Inc.); Yail Acosta, Brian Lenard (National Tire & Battery); Tom Byrne, Lori Day, Judy Lake (Northwest Federal Credit Union); Michael Fergus Sugrue, Johanna Stefanelli (Montgomery County Department of Police); Donna Honse, Wayne Kennon (Office of the Sheriff, Fairfax County); Sophia Grinnan, Richard Henry, Joseph Vacchio, Dave Kuhar (Fairfax Country Police Department); Gary Burgess (DC Department of Motor Vehicles); Kelly Connolly (The Humane Society of the United States); Monika and Doug Dougherty (Doug's Auto Services and buickfarm.com); Jim Proctor, Geta Wold (Colonial Parking); Tom Inman and Nicholas Greville (Glass Doctor); Joe Lattuca (1-A-Auto); Scott Raughton (Henry's Wrecker Service); Jim Coleman, Greg Raynor, Ivan Adler, and Tom Price, (Jim Coleman Automotive); Scott Peacock, Bobby McIntyre, Scott Brais, Jessica Drakely, Rob Werthman (Pohanka Chevrolet); Christopher Glakas (Herson's Honda); Richard Miller (George Mason University); Dick Spicer (Kenwood Mobil Auto Repair); James Simnick (BP); Robin Ofner (College Admissions Strategies). And a special thanks to the kind and attentive staff at Chantilly National Golf and Country Club: Jeff Avey, Richard Rochford, Tim Tyson, Roberto Fuentes, Jim Summers, Tony Mobasser, and Sean Mooney.

Last but not least, thanks to Steve and Jeryl Oristaglio for giving us seaside shelter to complete this project.

Personal Acknowledgments from Julie Sussman

God has graced me with extraordinary people to accompany me through my life. To my wonderful parents, Warren and Helene Johnson, and my incredible siblings, Ann Walker, Mary Coyle, Chad Johnson, and Amy Marney, who have been my traveling companions the longest: thank you for providing great humor and love along the way.

Next, to my partner-in-writing and dear friend, Stephanie Glakas-Tenet: thank you for always inspiring me to take the road less traveled.

To my children, Chad and Rebecca, whom I love so much: every day with you is a joyful ride.

And to the kindest, gentlest, sweetest man in the world, my husband Jerry: I pray that God grants me the great honor of continuing my life's journey riding shotgun with you.

Personal Acknowledgments from Stephanie Glakas-Tenet

To Julie, a woman with more horsepower than a V-8 engine; without you *Dare to Repair Your Car* would have stalled in the first lap. Thank you, my extraordinary partner and friend, for being the skilled driver and crew chief all-in-one who took us to the finish line.

To my beloved mother, Cleo, whom I lost this past year, my devoted father John, and my loving mother-in-law, Evangelia; thank you for being my green and checkered flags, inspiring me on at every race.

To my wonderful brothers, Nicky and Tommy; my caring sisters-in-law, Katy, Maria Rosa, and Alice; my amazing brother-in-law, Billy; my talented nephews, Christian and Gavin (my "Picasso" who illustrated this book); and my brilliant nieces, Sara, Alexandra, Cristina, Amy, Megan, and Joanna; thank you for keeping me going with the dedication of a NASCAR pit crew.

To my oldest and dearest friends, Jeryl, Patti, Rosemary, and Maureen, without whom every bottleneck would have resulted in a major pileup; thank you for always clearing a safe lane for me to travel.

To my agency family primed with infinite patriotism, dedication, and courage; thank you for being the very best and for allowing me the honor to ride together with you for nine remarkable years.

To my husband, George, and my son, John Michael, the two greatest loves of my life; thank you for teaching me how to maneuver the hazards and the straightaways with equal confidence, for loving me full throttle, and for fueling my every day with eternal optimism, laughter, joy, and loyalty.

And with a grateful heart, I thank God for always being in the driver's seat.

Introduction

n our first book, *Dare to Repair: A Do-It-Herself Guide to Fixing (Almost) Anything in the Home,* we encouraged women to step into the world of basic home repairs—the final frontier for women. Or so we thought.

That was until we asked our female friends, neighbors, family members, and acquaintances to share with us what repairs and maintenance they've done on their own cars. We're still waiting for an answer.

Why do women put the brakes on when it comes to personally caring for their cars? Well, it's part bad habit and part irrational fear. The bad habit is from years of relying on an auto club or the man in their life to come to their rescue. The irrational fear is from continually hearing that cars are too complicated to work on. *Dare to Repair Your Car* will help you overcome your auto-anxiety and turn you from a damsel-in-distress into a do-it-herself diva.

We believe that female car owners can be divided into two categories: (1) women who want to learn how to do basic car care; and (2) women who will *never* open the hood of a car. That's why we've separated most repairs and maintenance projects into Do-It-Yourself (DIY) and Do-It-for-Me (DIFM) sections, so that no matter which side of the road you're on regarding car care, you'll be well informed.

In writing this book, we came to a few roadblocks, one of which was that we're not mechanics. But we think that was to our advantage because we learned basic car care from scratch. And, to make sure that the information was accurate, as well as simple to understand, we had every section vetted by the top authorities in their fields—from a car manufacturer to associations to government agencies to nonprofit organizations.

We encourage you to use *Dare to Repair Your Car* as a vehicle for ending auto-ignorance. It's time that we stop the cycle of taking a back-seat to basic car care and instead willingly get behind the wheel of it.

Use this book to teach yourself everything you need to know about your car, and then share your knowledge with everyone in your life. Make it a rule that your teenager can't get her driver's license until she learns how to change a flat, check the fluids, and jump-start the battery. Make certain that the tires on your parents' car are properly inflated. Go over to your sister's house and teach her how to correctly install her child's car seat. The knowledge you share with your loved ones will provide them greater safety, and give you greater peace of mind.

So buckle up, it's going to be a fun ride.

Pit Stop

Before we wave the flag for you to start learning basic car care, we need you to follow the rules listed below.

Rule #1: Read the car owner's manual.

No one should be allowed to drive her car without first having read her car owner's manual. It's really not as bad as you think. Okay, it won't be your book club's next selection, but all car owner's manuals are simple to read, with lots of illustrations. Think of it this way: you spent $20,000 on your car, so spend 20 minutes reading about what you just bought.

If you don't have the manual, you can purchase one from your local car dealership or online through the manufacturer's Web site.

Rule #2: You must properly maintain your car.
Yes, *you*.

You can't be running to the repair shop for things *you* should be doing. You need to check your tires for air, change your windshield wiper blades, and add oil. Running to the repair shop for every little thing will cost you time and money.

Rule #3: Budget for car maintenance and repairs.
The average annual cost of maintenance and repairs for a new car is $300; for an older car, it's $600. A car is typically the second biggest purchase anyone makes, and therefore you need to protect your investment for better resale value. But the most important reason to put money into your car is for your own safety.

Rule #4: Get over the cost of maintaining your car.
A monthly manicure/pedicure will set you back about $500 per year. Pizza delivered twice a month adds up to more than $300 per year. Neither one will protect your life . . . car maintenance will.

Rule #5: Get over the fact that you may get dirty.
It's a fact that every time you touch anything under the hood, your hands will get dirty. In fact, your hands will get dirty even when you remove the valve cap on a tire. Either wear work gloves or purchase soap (at any auto parts store) specifically made for cleaning off dirt/grime from working on cars.

Rule #6: If there's a problem with the car, check if there has been a recall issued.
The best place to search for recall information is the Web site for the National Highway Transportation Safety Administration at www.nhtsa.gov.

Rule #7: Be aware that car parts do not come with instructions.

That's right. If you decide to try a car repair yourself and need to purchase a part, be aware that the part will not come with instructions. And unlike most manufacturers who supply a Web site or 800 number for customer service, the manufacturers of car parts do not. Therefore, you should either purchase a service manual for your car (typically more than $100) or ask a friendly mechanic/technician for instructions and write them down. You're more likely to get help from where you purchased the part.

Rule #8: We won't wave the white flag.

This doesn't have to be the end of the road for you regarding doing car repairs and maintenance. If you've been inspired to do more, purchase the service manual for your car, sign up for a car repair class through your county, or check with your car dealership to see if it offers any free car care clinics. And share your newfound knowledge with others.

And you're off!

Under the Hood

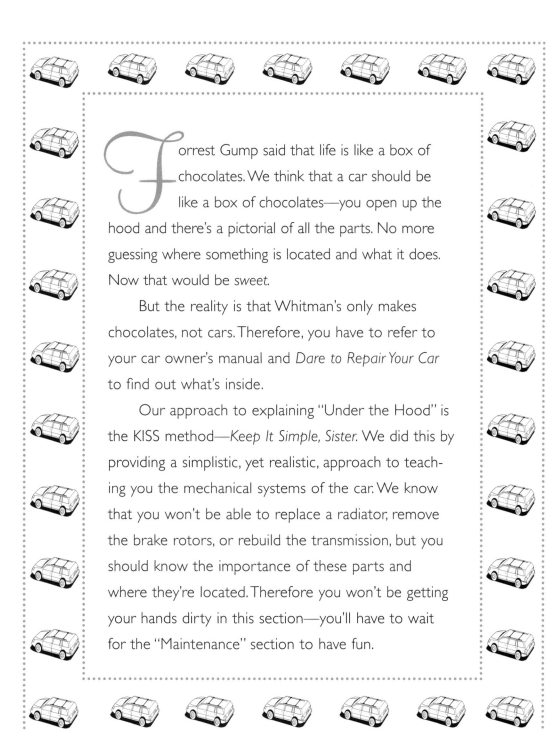

Forrest Gump said that life is like a box of chocolates. We think that a car should be like a box of chocolates—you open up the hood and there's a pictorial of all the parts. No more guessing where something is located and what it does. Now that would be *sweet*.

But the reality is that Whitman's only makes chocolates, not cars. Therefore, you have to refer to your car owner's manual and *Dare to Repair Your Car* to find out what's inside.

Our approach to explaining "Under the Hood" is the KISS method—*Keep It Simple, Sister*. We did this by providing a simplistic, yet realistic, approach to teaching you the mechanical systems of the car. We know that you won't be able to replace a radiator, remove the brake rotors, or rebuild the transmission, but you should know the importance of these parts and where they're located. Therefore you won't be getting your hands dirty in this section—you'll have to wait for the "Maintenance" section to have fun.

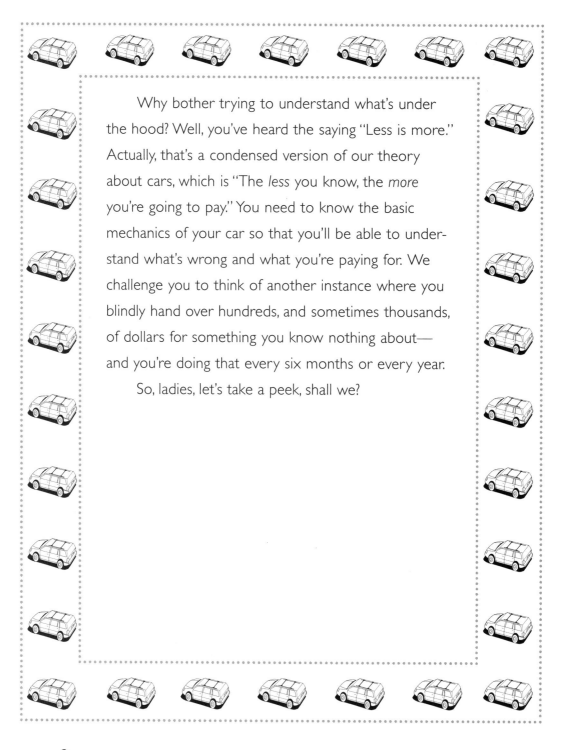

Why bother trying to understand what's under the hood? Well, you've heard the saying "Less is more." Actually, that's a condensed version of our theory about cars, which is "The *less* you know, the *more* you're going to pay." You need to know the basic mechanics of your car so that you'll be able to understand what's wrong and what you're paying for. We challenge you to think of another instance where you blindly hand over hundreds, and sometimes thousands, of dollars for something you know nothing about—and you're doing that every six months or every year.

So, ladies, let's take a peek, shall we?

Hood and Trunk

Popping Open and Closing the Hood and Trunk

You can open a jar of pickles with one twist, a container of crescent rolls with one bang, and plastic packaging with one pull, but you're all thumbs when it comes to opening the car hood. Not anymore.

We can't possibly begin this book without the first basic step—learning how to open the hood and trunk. It may sound (and is) easy, but there are a few things to keep in mind before exploring the great beyond.

Popping Open the Hood

Note: If you're opening the hood after the engine has been running, be careful because the engine and other parts will be very hot.

Exterior Latch

Older cars typically have just one release mechanism for the hood, located on the exterior of the car. The mechanism may not be visible, so stick your fingers under the edge of the hood, in the mid-

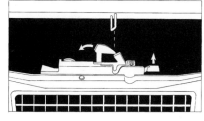
Exterior hood release

dle of the front of the car, and feel for the latch. Move the latch and lift open the hood.

Some cars also have a thin metal prop bar that lays flat on the front of the engine. It acts as a kickstand, so after you've lifted the hood, you just prop up the metal bar and let it rest in its designated spot on the interior of the hood.

Metal prop bar

Interior and Exterior Latches

Note: Some interior hood latches look and feel like the parking brake release mechanism.

Most car manufacturers install two release mechanisms—one interior and one exterior—to act as a theft deterrent, and more important, to prevent the hood from opening while driving.

If your car has two release mechanisms for the hood, you have to release the interior one first, and then the exterior. The interior release mechanism is located on the driver's side, below the steering wheel and to the left of the pedals (typically, there's an illustration of an open hood on it). Pull up on the latch to release. This will only open the hood enough for you to find the exterior release.

The exterior mechanism may not be visible, so stick your fingers under the edge of the hood, in the middle of the front of the car, and feel for the latch. Move the latch and lift open the hood.

Interior hood release

Closing the Hood

There's no need to slam down the hood of the car. Instead, just guide the hood down a few inches above the front of the grille and let it drop. The metal used on newer cars is much thinner than the metal found on its older counterparts; therefore, when you close the hood, be careful not to use the palms of your hands to force it down because you could leave permanent indentations. If your hood uses a metal prop bar for support, be extra cautious once the bar is removed because the hood will come down fast.

Opening and Closing the Trunk

A trunk typically has one release mechanism, which can be opened with a key, a remote entry, or an interior latch. Follow the same guidelines for closing the hood as for closing the trunk so that you don't dent the metal.

Electrical System

People often play a *what*-dunnit game when their car dies. They first assume the *battery* is the culprit, so a new one gets installed. If that doesn't work, then the next suspect is the *alternator,* so that gets replaced. And the last suspicious perp is the *starter.* Oh, and Colonel Mustard has the knife in the library.

Repairs turn into a guessing game for most car owners because no one has a *clue.* You don't have to commit to memory the intricacies of your car's electrical system, but you do need to know the basic mechanics of it so that you get the right part replaced the first time, and not on the third try.

What It Is

The electrical system of the car is kind of like the electrical system of your home—it has circuits and fuses (although most homes have circuit breakers, not fuses), and just like your home, it runs just about everything.

This system can be divided into three circuits: (1) starting; (2) ignition; and (3) charging. To understand these circuits we'll walk, not race, you through them.

How It Works

Starting Circuit
The running of your car all begins with the starting circuit. Here are the main parts.

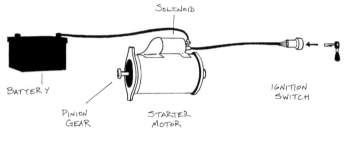

Starting circuit

Ignition Switch

The ignition switch, which is typically located in the steering column or on the dashboard in front of the driver, is where you insert your key to start the car. There are may different types of ignition switches, some with fewer positions than others. Generally, there is an off position; an ignition on/accessory position; and a start/crank position that is designed to spring back to the on position once the car is started.

Battery

A battery has three jobs: (1) start the engine; (2) stabilize the car's charging system; and (3) provide extra power for the lights and radio once the engine is off.

Battery Cables

There are two battery cables: (1) a positive terminal cable, which connects the battery to the starter motor; and (2) a negative terminal cable, which connects the battery to a part of the car frame.

Starter Motor

The starter motor, which is located near the back of the engine, usually engages a flywheel, and uses the electricity from the battery to crank and start the engine.

Starter Solenoid and Starter Relay

Your car has a starter solenoid and a starter relay. The starter solenoid is usually mounted onto the starter. The starter relay is a switch that's located on the firewall underneath the hood. Both work to control the amount of electrical current that goes to the starter motor.

Ignition Circuit

The ignition circuit creates energy to provide sparks needed to ignite the air-fuel mixture in the combustion chamber. Some vehicles have a distributor, while newer cars have a distributorless ignition (look folks, we're not making this up).

Here are the main parts.

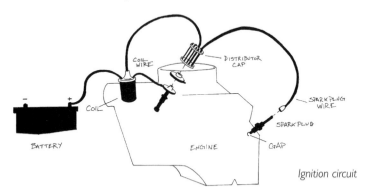

Ignition circuit

Spark Plugs

Spark plugs receive an electrical charge that cause them to spark and ignite the air-fuel mixture in the cylinders. There is one spark plug for every cylinder, so if your car has a V-6 cylinder, then it would have 6 spark plugs. If your car has a V-8 cylinder, then it would have 8 spark plugs.

Each spark plug has an electrode at its base that's inserted into the combustion chamber of the engine (it's kind of like a lightbulb screwed into a light fixture). When the spark plug receives electrical energy, an arc of electricity ignites the compressed air-fuel mixture located in the combustion chamber.

Spark plugs are typically replaced every 30,000 miles along with the spark plug wires, but newer spark plugs—called long-life plugs—are more expensive and are advertised to last up to 100,000 miles.

Ignition Coil

The ignition coil, located on the engine, produces the high instantaneous voltage that creates an arc of electricity that jumps between the spark plug contacts, igniting the air-fuel mixture in the combustion chamber. Newer cars have a separate coil pack for each spark plug.

Distributor and Distributor Cap

The distributor is located in various places under the hood, depending on the car. The distributor *distributes* just the right amount of high electrical voltage at just the right time to each spark plug. Inside the distributor is a rotor that spins when the engine turns, causing the rotor to touch each spark plug wire, via the distributor cap, which then sends the electrical current to each spark plug.

Newer cars often do not have distributors but depend on special sensors to do the job instead.

Charging Circuit

The charging circuit's job is to provide electricity for all parts of the car. Here are the main parts.

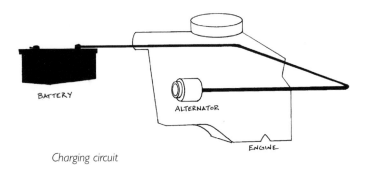

Charging circuit

Alternator

A car's battery provides an electrical current to start the engine. Once the engine has started, the battery's job is done and the alternator takes over. While the car is running, the alternator recharges the battery for the next time you start the engine and generates all the additional power needed to run the lights, the radio, and so on.

Voltage Regulator

The voltage regulator, typically located inside the alternator, protects the alternator from overcharging the battery and other electrical components.

Drive Belt Pulley

The drive belt pulley is located around the alternator and crankshaft pulleys and works to turn the alternator. This is how the current is generated from the alternator.

Fuses

Fuses in a car act just like fuses (or circuit breakers) in your home. They're a safety feature whose job is to keep a circuit from being overloaded by too much electricity. And just like your home, the fuses are located inside a fuse box (some cars have more than one fuse box). Some fuse boxes are located in the front of the inside of the car or under the hood, and some are even located under a backseat! Therefore, you may need to refer to the owner's manual for the location.

Fuses come in different shapes—some are cylindrical glass tubes, some are flat plugs, and others are mini flat plugs. Your fuse box will only have one type. Amperage differs with the circuit it's protecting; for example, a fuse for the radio will have a smaller amp than a fuse that's used for the engine.

Common Problems

You turn the key to start your car and nothing happens. Here's what may be happening behind the scene.

If You Don't See or Hear Anything

If you turn the key and don't see anything (e.g., lights on the dashboard) and hear a clicking noise, the problem could be the battery. The battery could have died from a light or radio being left on, or from old age. If the battery isn't old, the problem could be a loose battery terminal cable (see "Securing the Battery Terminal Cables," pages 146–47) or corroded terminals (see "Cleaning the Battery Terminals," page 147).

The next thing to check is the fuse for the ignition. If it's burned, replace the fuse. If the fuse is in good condition, then try to jump-start the battery or charge it overnight.

If You Hear a Click

If you turn the key and the engine doesn't turn over, but you hear a *click*, the problem could be with the starter. The ignition switch makes the connection with the battery and starter solenoid, which then connects to the starter motor. The starter solenoid always makes a clicking noise, it's just that the noise of the engine starting drowns it out. So, if the starter solenoid isn't able to engage the starter, then the engine won't turn over. Sometimes jump-starting the battery will temporarily engage the starter.

If the Engine Cranks but Won't Start

If the engine cranks but won't start, the cause could be a blown fuse, a faulty spark plug(s), or a fuel or ignition issue.

DIY: Replacing a Fuse

Note: Before replacing a fuse, make sure that all electrical devices and the engine have been turned off.

When you open the fuse box, you'll see that there is a circuit map with lots of abbreviations. The only way you'll know what these correlate to is by referring to the car owner's manual.

The fuse box should contain a few extra fuses as

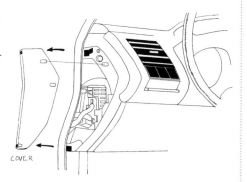

Removing the fuse door panel

Tools Needed

New fuse   **Car owner's manual**

Sometimes the car won't start because you don't have it in the proper gear—park for automatic transmission and neutral for manual transmission—or you're out of fuel.

well as a fuse puller. Don't panic if you don't have a fuse puller because you may be able to use your fingernails to pull out a fuse.

Once you've located the fuse that corresponds to the circuit, pull it out and look for a burned band inside the fuse. If it's damaged, replace it with a new fuse of the same size and amperage. Don't forget to replace the spare, too!

Note: If you're on the road and you need to replace a fuse, but don't have any extras, temporarily remove a fuse from another circuit, such as one that controls the power windows or radio. Be careful that it's the same amperage and replace the borrowed fuse as soon as possible.

Fuel System

The fuel system is quite complex, but we promise not to present a high-octane review of it. No, ladies, our approach is more like *regular* with *no additives*.

What It Is

Your car's fuel system consists of a fuel tank, fuel lines, a fuel pump, a fuel filter, a charcoal canister, and a carburetor or fuel injectors. Fuel (gasoline or diesel) is stored inside the fuel tank, which then travels through the fuel pump into the fuel lines, through the fuel filter, and then into the carburetor or fuel injectors. But transporting the fuel to the right spot is just the half of it. The fuel system is also designed to regulate the right air-and-fuel mixture to guarantee the best performance of the engine.

Since everyone knows what the fuel tank is, we'll start there.

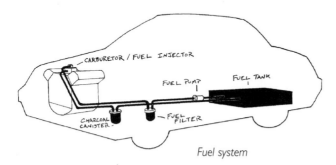

Fuel system

How It Works

Fuel Tank

You know the fuel tank stores the fuel that runs the engine. What you may not know about the fuel tank is that it also keeps harmful fumes from escaping, and it's where the fuel pump is housed in most new cars.

Fuel Pump

The fuel pump is located either inside the fuel tank (many new cars have this feature) or outside the tank. Its job is to provide enough fuel to the engine. As soon as you move the ignition key to the on position, the fuel pump kicks in to prime the fuel system. When the key is moved farther to the start position, the fuel pump provides the right amount of fuel at the correct pressure.

There are two main types of fuel pumps—electric and mechanical. You can find out which type your car has by referring to the car owner's manual or asking your mechanic.

Fuel Lines

The fuel lines carry the fuel from the gas tank to the carburetor or fuel injector.

Fuel Filter

This part filters out harmful contaminants so that they don't enter the engine or the air around us.

Carburetor

Car manufacturers stopped making vehicles with carburetors in the late 1980s because they were not fuel efficient and replaced them with the fuel injection system. But for those of you who have a "classic car," here's what it does: the carburetor, located on the engine, works to regulate the combination of air and fuel that's mixed together to create the proper mixture for the engine.

This mixture moves to the intake manifold and then to the engine block cylinders. It's then compressed through combustion to generate power from the engine. After the spark ignites the compressed air-fuel mixture, the exhaust valve opens up and allows the exhaust gases to exit into the exhaust system.

Fuel Injection System

The fuel injection system (a.k.a. multiport fuel injection) typically consists of one fuel injector per engine cylinder and an electronic control unit (ECU).

The ECU monitors various sensor activities, such as the distance the accelerator pedal has been depressed, the amount of oxygen in the exhaust system, and the engine's speed. Based on this information, the ECU decides the correct amount and timing of fuel that is injected into each cylinder.

Fuel injectors are located at the end of the fuel system and work to provide the correct amount of fuel for the engine to work efficiently. The injectors receive a signal from the ECU to inject a precise amount of fuel spray into the combustion chamber of each cylinder.

Common Problems

Fuel Lines

These can get contaminated with dirt or moisture, which can freeze and prevent your car from starting in the winter. Therefore, during the winter months, it's best to keep the tank filled with fuel so that there's less of a chance of moisture entering, and add dry gas (a fuel additive) to the fuel tank to break up water molecules so they can be burned with the fuel.

Fuel Filter

This filters out the contaminants from the fuel, and therefore can become clogged. It needs to be replaced as recommended by your car's manufacturer.

Fuel Injector

The major problem with fuel injectors is that their gaskets can leak or the injectors can get clogged with carbon. A leaky gasket can cause the engine to idle roughly. If the tip of an injector gets clogged or gummed up, the distribution of fuel into the cylinder will be an uneven or improper amount, which will affect the combustion. It's kind of like the nozzle of a can of hairspray that gets clogged and then won't work until you remove the sticky film.

DIY: Cleaning the Fuel Injectors

To help prevent injectors from clogging, use a premium (higher-octane) gasoline that contains a larger amount of detergent (e.g., BP's Amoco Ultimate). But don't assume that it will only take 1 tank to clean the engine. For example, it will typically take about 5 tanks of Amoco Ultimate to clean the engine.

Another option is to use a fuel system treatment/cleaner. Be sure to read the manufacturer's instructions as well as the car owner's manual before using. But be aware that overusage of a fuel system treatment/cleaner may cause the engine valves to stick, as well as alter the viscosity of the oil.

Note: This needs to be done at a gas station.

Turn the engine off. Pour the fuel system cleaner into a partially empty fuel tank and then add fuel. The force of the fuel entering will mix the two substances together. This should be done as often as recommended by the product and the car manufacturer.

Tools Needed
Funne

Fuel system cleaner

Engine

*L*adies, start your engines. Okay, now we're going to tell you what you just did.

What It Is

We promised to use the KISS (*Keep It Simple, Sister*) method of explaining, so here's our definition of the car's engine: the engine is the part of the car that supplies the energy needed to make it move.

How It Works

An engine needs three things in order for it to work: air, fuel, and spark. If just one of these ingredients is missing, the engine won't start or will stop running.

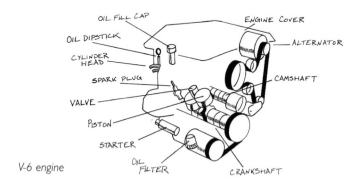

OIL FILL CAP
OIL DIPSTICK
CYLINDER HEAD
SPARK PLUG
VALVE
PISTON
STARTER
OIL FILTER
ENGINE COVER
ALTERNATOR
CAMSHAFT
CRANKSHAFT

V-6 engine

Engine Block (Cylinder Block)

The engine block is the largest part of the engine and contains the cylinders and pistons, the crankshaft, and passages for the oil and the coolant (all of which keep the engine from overheating).

Cylinder

The cylinder is called the core of the engine. It's located in the engine block and houses the pistons. Cars can have 4, 6, 8, or more cylinders, but most have either 6 or 8. You might hear the terms "V-6" or "V-8." These refer to the number of cylinders and how they're positioned in the engine block, either like a "V," in a straight line, or flat.

Each cylinder has a piston with a combustion chamber located at the top.

Pistons and Piston Rings

Pistons are cylindrical metal devices that are located in the cylinders. They move downward to allow air and fuel to flow into the combustion chamber and then move upward to the combustion chamber. A spark ignites the compressed air-fuel mixture, causing it to explode. This explosion pushes the piston down with great force, which helps turn the crankshaft.

A piston ring fits around the piston to provide a protective seal against the explosions in the combustion chamber to maximize power.

Combustion Chamber

The combustion chamber, typically located where the engine block meets the engine head, is where the air-fuel mix compresses and then explodes at the instant the spark plug produces a spark from electrical energy it receives from the ignition coil through the spark plug.

Crankshaft

When the explosion of the air-fuel mixture occurs, it pushes each piston down with great force. The base of each piston is connected to the crankshaft by a connecting rod. The upward and downward movements of all the pistons keeps the crankshaft turning. The front of the rotating crankshaft is used to power the belts located around the alternator, AC compressor, water pump, power steering pump, and so on. The rear of the crankshaft provides power to the transmission, which eventually rotates the wheels.

Spark Plugs

A spark plug provides the electrical spark needed to create the explosion when the piston compresses the air-fuel mixture in the combustion chamber. It produces a spark when it receives a high-voltage current from the ignition coil through the spark plug wire.

Camshaft

The camshaft, which is typically located on top of the engine head, controls the opening and closing of the valves in the combustion chamber.

Valves and Valve Assembly

There are (at a minimum) 2 valves for each combustion chamber: one is an intake valve and the other is an exhaust valve. The intake valve allows the air-fuel mixture to flow into the cylinder, and the exhaust valve opens up the combustion chamber so that the exhaust fumes can be removed through the exhaust system. The valves and combustion chamber are located in the engine head.

Timing System

Timing is everything, especially when it comes to the coordination of all the internal parts of the engine. The timing belt wraps around the camshaft and the crankshaft.

Putting It All Together

The mechanical process of the engine can best be described by referring to the 4 strokes of each piston: (1) intake; (2) compression; (3) combustion/power; and (4) exhaust.

Note: This process is constantly repeating while an engine is running.

Intake Stroke

This is the very beginning of the mechanical process. It requires the piston to be at the top of the cylinder; as it starts to travel downward, the intake valve opens up and allows the air-fuel mixture to be sucked into the cylinder. This mixture is highly flammable, especially when compressed. Read on.

Compression Stroke

Next, the piston moves back up to the top of the cylinder, compressing the air-fuel mixture into the combustion chamber located in the cylinder head just above the cylinders. The air-fuel mixture is now compressed and under pressure.

Combustion Stroke

Now the spark plug releases a spark, igniting the air-fuel mixture causing it to combust, thus forcing the piston to move back down with explosive force.

Exhaust Stroke

During this stroke, the exhaust valve is opened while the piston moves up. The gases that were created during combustion are now being forced into the exhaust system valve and through the exhaust system.

Common Problems

Oil

A common problem for an engine is that the oil and the oil filter are not properly maintained, which leads to the engine being starved of oil, causing it to seize.

Spark Plugs

These can get a carbon build-up due to an improper air-fuel mixture, causing the spark plugs to cease working.

Valves

These can also have carbon buildup on them, causing them to stick, leading to the engine misfiring.

Timing Belt

This can wear and crack over time. Timing belts usually need to be replaced anywhere from 60,000 miles to 100,000 miles. Always refer to the car owner's manual. Luckily, it's not more often than that, because in some cars it's the first belt that gets installed on the engine. Therefore to have it replaced, you need to remove all the other belts, as well as the water pump, the power steering pump, and the air conditioner. So, when you're getting the timing belt replaced, ask your mechanic to check the status of the parts that were removed, because the majority of the cost of replacing parts is the labor, not the part.

CHECK ENGINE TEMP or ENGINE HOT Light

If you see this light, pull over when and where it's safe to do so and turn off the engine to let it cool. Check the level of coolant and fill the coolant reservoir if necessary. Your car may need to be towed.

Diesel Engine

A diesel engine works just about the same as a gasoline-fueled engine—the only significant difference is in the fuel and ignition systems.

Diesel engines use regular diesel fuel, which can be purchased at most gas stations and truck stops along the highway. The air in a diesel engine is compressed to a much higher pressure than in a gasoline engine. After the air is compressed, the diesel fuel is injected into the combustion chamber, which causes the air-fuel mixture to ignite. A gasoline-fueled engine uses spark plugs, but a diesel engine uses glow plugs. On days when the exterior air is too cold, a glow plug will heat up inside the combustion chamber and help cause the air-fuel mixture to ignite.

Cooling System

Radiators seem to only fail when you're far from home ... or a repair shop. Just remember, if your radiator blows its cool, **you need to keep yours and follow the safety rules provided below.**

If you came to this chapter to learn about your car's air-conditioning system, you've come to the wrong place. The cooling system works to keep the car cool ... not you!

What It Is

The cooling system's job is to remove heat from the engine and to keep the car running at its optimal temperature, regardless of the outside temperature. It circulates coolant around the engine block, extracting heat from the engine, and moves the heated coolant to the radiator, where the heat is dissipated. It repeats this process in a cycle.

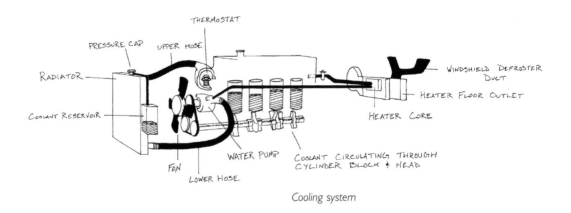

Cooling system

How It Works

Radiator

The main radiator is located at the front of the car (behind the exterior grille) and is connected to the engine by radiator hoses. The radiator uses the fan (if the temperature gets too hot) to cool the heated coolant by dissipating the heat into the outside air.

A smaller radiator, known as the heater core, is located between the engine and the front passenger area and is used to provide interior heat to warm the passengers and to defrost the front windshield. If you're wondering how the back windshield gets defrosted, it's not by a radiator blowing hot air; instead, lines of electrical wiring (the thin lines you see on the back windshield) get turned on and heat the ice or snow that's on it (see "Defrosting a Windshield," page 181).

Coolant

Coolant, which is a mixture of antifreeze and water, is the fluid used in the cooling system to remove heat from the engine and radiator (see "Coolant," page 71).

Water Pump

The water pump, which is connected to the front of the engine, uses the power from the motion of the crankshaft to force coolant through the engine.

It's called a water pump because before the invention of coolant, water was used by itself to cool the engine. However, the water inside the radiator and engine would freeze at 32°F and would crack the radiator—or worse, the engine block!

Heater Core

The heater core is the technical term for your car's heater and defroster. It's actually a smaller version of the main radiator, kind of like a Mini-Me. It does this by using the heat that's been dissipated from the engine. A fan blows air through the heater core to heat the passenger compartment.

The heater core will only work when the engine has heated up, which is why you can't instantly get interior heat when you start your car on a cold morning.

Thermostat

A thermostat, which is typically located between the radiator and the engine, regulates the flow of coolant into the engine. The thermostat has a spring valve that monitors the temperature of the engine, which does not open up to allow coolant to enter the engine until it reaches a predetermined temperature.

Radiator Hoses

There are three radiator hoses—one that connects the engine to the radiator, one that connects the radiator to the water pump, and one that connects the radiator to the coolant reservoir. The hose that's located on the top carries the hot coolant from the engine to the radiator, and the bottom hose carries the cooled coolant in the radiator to the water pump.

Cooling Fan

The cooling fan, located behind the radiator, works to reduce the temperature of the coolant by sucking cool air across the coils of the radiator. This will only turn on if the temperature of the coolant is too high and the outside air cannot cool it on its own.

Caution: This fan can turn on even after a car is turned off. Never touch the fan unless the battery is disconnected.

Coolant Reservoir (Expansion Tank)

The coolant reservoir and the radiator work as a vacuum system. The reservoir, located near the radiator, temporarily stores the overheated coolant that was released by the radiator. When the temperature of the coolant decreases, its volume decreases as well, causing some of it to get sucked back into the radiator, leaving some coolant inside the reservoir.

Radiator Cap (Pressure Cap)

The radiator cap, located on top of the radiator, isn't just an ordinary lid. This cap not only prevents coolant from leaking out, but it also acts to pressurize the coolant inside the radiator. Never remove the cap when the engine is hot or if you see steam, because you will get severely burned.

Common Problems

Overheating

The most common problem caused by a faulty cooling system is the engine overheating. Some signs are if the CHECK ENGINE TEMP warning light is on and/or the temperature gauge is in the red section, or a significant amount of steam is escaping from under the hood. If any of these happen, safely pull off the road as soon as possible, turn the engine off, and call for help. *Never open the hood of the car if you see steam coming from underneath it. And never open the radiator cap when the engine is hot— you can get burned from the steam or from any coolant that may be released.*

Little or No Heat

If the heater isn't working, the problem may be with the heater core, low coolant in the cooling system, or the valve that allows hot coolant to enter the heater core. A sign to look for is coolant leakage on the floor in the front of the car or under the front floor mats.

Radiator Hoses

Hoses, which are made of rubber, can get stiff or crack and tear from wear. You'll need to check these periodically, and if a hose is exhibiting one or all of these conditions, it's always best to replace it as well as the other hoses at the same time.

Have the cooling system checked in the springtime and maintain the coolant according to the manufacturer's recommendation in your owner's manual. It is also a good idea to periodically check that the airflow through the radiator and condenser is not obstructed by leaves, debris, or other objects.

Air-Conditioning System

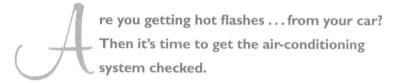

Are you getting hot flashes . . . from your car? Then it's time to get the air-conditioning system checked.

Cars built before 1994 used a refrigerant in the air-conditioning (AC) system called Freon. This substance contained a choroflurocarbon (CFC-12) that contributed to the deterioration of the ozone layer, so in 1990 the Clean Air Act was amended to require all car manufacturers to stop producing vehicles that used Freon and to make cars that use a new refrigerant, R134a, because it doesn't harm the ozone layer. The amended law also states that only a certified technician can work on air-conditioning systems in vehicles.

What It Is

Your car's air-conditioning system cools and dehumidifies the circulating air. To you it's as simple as adjusting a control inside the car, but behind the scene it's a highly technical process at work.

The main parts of the air-conditioning system are the compressor, the condenser, the AC belt, and the evaporator. The compressor is located on the side where the belts are, the AC belt connects the compressor to the crankshaft of the engine, the evaporator is typically located under the dashboard, and the condenser is located in the front of the engine cooling radiator.

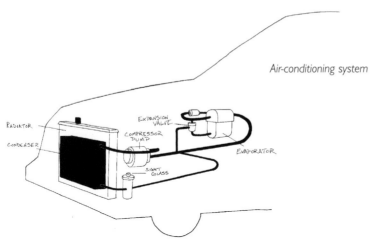

Air-conditioning system

RADIATOR

CONDENSER

EXPANSION VALVE

COMPRESSOR PUMP

SIGHT GLASS

EVAPORATOR

How It Works

Here is a brief overview of how the system works: The compressor is powered by the AC belt, which is connected to the crankshaft of the engine. The compressor *compresses* the refrigerant (R134a) and pushes it through the AC system. During this process, the refrigerant absorbs the heat in the air in the passenger compartment, via the evaporator, and releases the heat outside the car via the condenser.

Common Problems

The Air Isn't Cool Enough

The most common problem with a car's air-conditioning is that the air isn't cool enough. A quick solution is right at your fingertips . . . literally. There's a recirculation control, located with the heating/cooling settings on the dashboard. Its function is to recirculate the air that's inside the car, rather then to bring in air from outside. It's so logical, isn't it— why try to cool the hot air that's outside when you can cool the already cooled air that's inside the car? By doing this, you'll not only be getting the most from your AC, but you'll also be saving fuel because the air conditioner doesn't have to work as hard.

To achieve the maximum performance from your car's air conditioner, turn on the AC control to the coolest setting, and then turn on (depress) the recirculation control. Once the interior temperature is to your liking, turn off the recirculation control or raise the temperature control setting, because failure to do so may lead to the interior windows fogging up.

DIY: Taking the Air Conditioner's Temperature

If you still feel that the air isn't cool enough, you should take its temperature. An air conditioner that's working properly should emit an air temperature that's 20° below the outside temperature.

Note: Make sure the thermometer starts at 0°.

Place a candy thermometer inside a dashboard vent and turn the AC on full blast for 5 minutes while the car is idling. Take a reading. If there is less than a 20° difference from the exterior temperature, then one or more of the following may be the cause, and you'll need to have it serviced:

- Low refrigerant charge
- Loose AC belt
- Slipping compressor clutch or other compressor problem
- Clogged condenser
- Clogged evaporator
- Partially clogged filter or expansion valve

Tool Needed

Candy thermometer

Drivetrain (Transmission)

Have you ever felt that you were going nowhere fast? Literally? If so, then the solution is not getting a life coach, but getting the drivetrain fixed.

You know your car has a transmission, but we bet you don't know that it's part of a mechanical system called the *drivetrain*.

What It Is

The job of the drivetrain is, in simple terms, to transmit the power emitted by the engine to the car's wheels to make them spin. There are three different types of drivetrains: (1) 2-wheel drive (front or rear); (2) 4-wheel drive; and (3) all-wheel drive. Here's how they differ.

2-Wheel Drive

A 2-wheel drive transmission can be either a front-wheel drive or a rear-wheel drive, which means that the power is delivered to the front or rear of the car. Most newer cars have front-wheel drive.

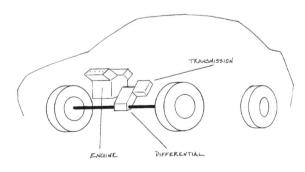

2-wheel drive (front)

4-Wheel Drive

This type of drivetrain offers the driver the ability to select between 4-high (for snowy terrains), 4-low (for off-road terrain), 4x4 (the power goes to all the wheels), or 2-wheel drive (either the front or the rear wheels are driven). As you have probably guessed, many SUVs have 4-wheel drive. Look at the dashboard near the steering wheel to find the control buttons to shift to different selections.

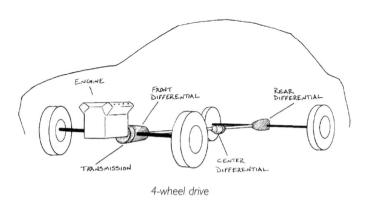

4-wheel drive

All-Wheel Drive

All-wheel drive does not provide the driver with a selection; instead, all the wheels are driven all the time.

How It Works

Every drivetrain runs from the rear of the engine (where it receives its power) to the wheels, but the parts vary depending on the kind of transmission (automatic vs. manual) and drivetrain (2-wheel, 4-wheel, or all-wheel). Here are the main parts for each system.

2-Wheel (Rear) Drive with Automatic Transmission
  - Torque converter
  - Automatic transmission

- Driveshaft
- Differential

2-Wheel (Rear) Drive with Manual Transmission
- Differential
- Driveshaft
- Manual transmission
- Clutch

2-Wheel (Front) Drive with Automatic Transmission
- Transaxle
- 2 drive axles
- Automatic transmission
- Torque converter

2-Wheel (Front) Drive with Manual Transmission
- Transaxle
- 2 drive axles
- Manual transmission
- Clutch

4-Wheel Drive and All-Wheel Drive with Automatic Transmission

The following information is general, and we're only showing this with automatic transmission because the majority of SUVs do *not* have manual transmissions.

- 2 differentials
- 4 half driveshafts
- Automatic transmission
- Transfer case
- Torque converter

Now, we'll try to describe how these parts work together and their common problems, hopefully without *driving* you crazy.

Automatic Transmission

The automatic transmission is connected to the back of the engine, and its job is to convert the power from the engine so that it can be used to move the vehicle. An automatic transmission performs all of the work internally that's necessary to change gears automatically, which changes the speed or rotation of the tires. The torque converter uses the transmission fluid to transfer the power from the engine to the drivetrain.

Manual Transmission

The manual transmission is connected to the back of the engine, and its job is just like the automatic transmission in that it provides gears that change the speed and rotation of the tires. To change gears, the driver presses down on a clutch pedal while using a stick shift to move from one gear to another. Each gear changes the speed or rotation of the tires.

Driveshaft

A driveshaft, found in rear-wheel-drive vehicles and many 4-wheel-drive vehicles, connects the end of the transmission to the differential. Its job is to distribute the power from the transmission to the differential.

Drive Axle

A drive axle is used in front-wheel-drive vehicles, and acts just like the driveshaft, except that it connects the transaxle to the center of the wheel assembly.

Differential

Sounds like a math term, doesn't it? The differential is connected to the driveshaft and is located between the two rear wheels on a rear-wheel-drive car. On 4-wheel-drive and all-wheel-drive vehicles there are two differentials—one located between the front wheels, the other between the rear wheels. The job of a differential is to adjust the wheels' speed when you're making a turn (the outer wheel always turns faster than the inner wheel in a turn).

Transaxle (Drive Axle)

A transaxle is used in a front-wheel drive vehicle as a combination transmission and differential. It performs the same job as the transmission and the differential, but does so combined together in one unit.

Common Problems

The worst thing you can do is to ignore a transmission problem, because it will only make things worse. Don't assume that the problem is going to cost you a lot of money, because it could just be that you're using the wrong transmission fluid or that an electronic part that may cost as little as $50 may need to be replaced.

No Acceleration

If your car won't accelerate, but the engine revs up normally, this could indicate that the transmission or clutch is slipping. You need to have it diagnosed immediately.

Metal Debris

If the mechanic finds metal debris in the transmission fluid or the car won't shift into gears, then the transmission may need to be rebuilt or replaced.

Preventive Maintenance

The best preventive maintenance for your transmission is to properly maintain the fluid, which means to replenish it and to have the fluid flushed according to the manufacturer's recommendations.

Steering and Suspension Systems

wo wrongs don't make a right, but three lefts do. If your car's problem is forcing you in this direction, it's time you steered it toward a mechanic . . . if you can.

What They Are

How about this for a Keep It Simple, Sister (KISS) approach to explaining steering and suspension: the steering system enables your car to make turns and the suspension system provides your car with a smooth ride. *Ta-dah!*

We may have shortened the definition, but we don't want to diminish the importance of these two systems. Without them, your car would still run, but you'd have little control over it.

How They Work

Steering

The steering system allows you to have precise control over the direction in which your car travels. There are two types of steering

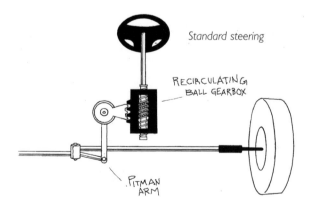

Standard steering

RECIRCULATING BALL GEARBOX

PITMAN ARM

systems: (1) standard, which is manual steering; and (2) power-assisted, which is usually referred to as power steering. The majority of cars have power steering; therefore, we're only going to discuss this system.

The main parts of the power steering system are the steering wheel, the steering column, the steering box (or steering rack if rack and pinion), the power steering pump, the power steering fluid, and the tie-rod ends.

Rack and pinion steering

When you turn the steering wheel, hydraulic pressure (supplied by the power steering pump, driven by an accessory belt from the engine) is converted through the pistons and gears of the rack and pinion or steering box to move the wheels in the direction you are turning.

Suspension

The suspension system does a lot more than just providing shock absorption; in fact, it helps to keep the car level by distributing an equal amount of weight on each tire, as well as keeping the tires firmly on the ground. It also assists in making braking more efficient.

To understand the mechanics of the suspension system, you need to think of the car in layers. The first layer is the wheel assembly (tires, rims, wheels, rotors, wheel bearings, spindles, and steering knuck-

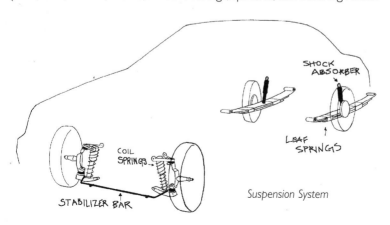

Suspension System

les), and the parts of the car that are closest to the ground. The next layer is the suspension system, which rests between the wheel assemblies and the body frame.

There are two common types of suspension systems used on the front wheels: (1) Twin A-arm (a.k.a. double wishbone); and (2) MacPherson struts. Both of these are independent suspension systems, which means they allow one wheel to move independently of the other.

Twin A-Arm

This suspension system uses either a round coil spring or a torsion bar. Leaf springs are flat and are typically located on the rear wheels. Lead and coil springs and torsion bars do the same thing—they give your car the bounce it needs to manage potholes and bumps in the road. Without them you'd ruin the tires, the wheels, and the frame of your car.

A stabilizer bar is a different type of torsion bar. Instead of providing an up-and-down bounce, the stabilizer bar offers a twisting motion to give better handling and maneuvering around corners. They're additional suspension parts built into the body frame at the front of the car, and are mainly found in SUVs and high-performance cars.

Springs don't just break down instantly; instead, they gradually wear out. One sign is that your car will be riding at a lower height, causing you to bottom out. Another sign is unusual tire tread wear or difficulty steering.

Have the springs checked every time you have the wheels aligned, and replace if necessary.

MacPherson Struts

This suspension system was designed to save space and is therefore found mainly in front-wheel-drive vehicles. The strut assembly combines the coil spring and a cartridge (shock) in a single unit. Because most vehicles today are front-wheel drive, this is the most common suspension system.

MacPherson struts

Shock Absorbers

Shock absorbers are needed to dampen the bouncing action caused by the springs in the suspension system. Without them, a car would continue to bounce indefinitely after hitting a bump.

Shock absorbers

Common Problems

Steering

There's no way of quietly returning home late at night if your power steering is on the fritz. The high-pitched screeching whenever you turn the wheel can wake an entire neighborhood. Dogs from two states away will be howling. The problem could be either from a loose power steering belt, a power steering pump that's gone bad, or a low level of power steering fluid. Check for leaks on the pavement where you park your car at home.

Suspension

Most suspension systems last 70,000 to 100,000 miles or more, depending on the terrain driven, and they'll wear out gradually, rather than break down instantly. Therefore, it can be hard to diagnose exactly when they're about to stop working. Here's an easy way to test their effectiveness.

DIY: Checking the Shocks/Struts

Push down on the back of the car and count how many times it bounces. If it bounces more than once, then it's a sign that the shocks/struts are wearing and may need to be replaced.

If your car is bouncing too much, the problem could be that the shocks/struts are leaking, the shock absorber mounts have been bent or broken, or the bushings are worn.

Coils should be replaced by axle sets, not by the individual wheel.

Brake System

iana may have asked you to "Stop! in the name of love," but can you stop in the name of safety? Don't take your car's brake system for granted—it may be *supremely* vital to saving your life.

What It Is

Every car has either a disc brake system or a drum brake system, or a combination of the two (disc on the front and drum on the back). The majority of cars on the road today have a disc brake system, which includes brake pads, brake lines, calipers, and rotors. A drum brake system includes wheel cylinders, brake lines, brake pads, and brake drums. If you're not sure which brake system your car has, refer to the car owner's manual.

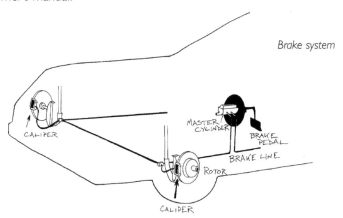

Brake system

CALIPER

MASTER CYLINDER

BRAKE PEDAL

BRAKE LINE

ROTOR

CALIPER

How It Works

If you've never understood how your car's brake system works, just think back to your first mode of transportation—your bicycle. When you engage the brake on your bike, you can see the pads, one on each side of the tire, squeezing the tire to make it stop. It's very similar to what happens on the wheels of your car. There are pads that squeeze either a metal rotor or a drum to stop the wheels from turning.

No matter which type of brake system your car has, each kind has a master cylinder. The master cylinder is located on the driver's side underneath the brake fluid reservoir, near the fire wall. When you press down on the brake pedal, the master cylinder releases brake fluid through the brake lines to the calipers (for disc brakes) or the cylinders (for drum brakes). Brake fluid is a liquid that creates hydraulic pressure to compress and release, and does *not* act as a brake component.

Disc Brake System

If your car has disc brakes, each wheel will have two brake pads (which sit in calipers), one on each side of a rotor (a round metal disc), which press against it to make the wheel stop.

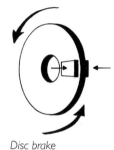

Disc brake

Brake Pads (Friction Pads)

Your mechanic will replace any brake pad that is worn down to $\frac{2}{32}$ inch in thickness, because anything less than that will cause brake failure. You'll know that your pads are worn if you hear a screeching noise either during or after you've braked. You may also hear a high-pitched noise while you're driving if your car is equipped with brake-wear sensors.

Note: Brake pads/shoes are always replaced in pairs.

Rotors

Rotors become worn and even warped over time, but they do not have to be replaced each time with the pads. If the rotors are worn, a mechanic will use a metal lathe to smooth them, so they can be used again.

Note: Rotors should always be replaced in pairs.

Drum Brake System

A drum brake system has two brake shoes, one wheel cylinder, and one brake drum per wheel. When present, drum brakes are most often used on the rear wheels only. Each set of brake shoes has a wheel cylinder that sits in between the shoes and supplies the brake fluid from the brake lines to each wheel. The brake shoes press against a brake drum to make the wheel stop.

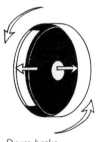

Drum brake

Common problems for a drum brake system are the brake shoes and drums wearing down. Typically, the brake shoes need to be replaced if they're 2/32 inch in thickness. Anything less will cause brake failure.

Brake shoes need to be replaced if they are 2/32 inch in thickness and/or if you notice you have to move the hand brake, or parking brake, farther than normal. This is a sign that the shoes may be too worn.

As is the case with a rotor, a brake drum does not have to be replaced every time with the shoes. A mechanic can use a metal lathe to smooth away any worn areas, increasing the life of the new brake shoes and improving braking efficiency.

Okay, we're almost done!

Antilock Braking System (ABS)

The majority of cars bought today have an antilock braking system as a standard feature, not an option. ABS enables cars to brake without the wheels locking and the car going into a tailspin, which should give the driver better control of the car.

It's a complicated system, but the main thing you need to know is that you should never pump the brakes if your car has ABS because it will just take you longer to stop. Instead, push down firmly on the pedal and allow the ABS to do its job—you may feel the brake pedal pulsate, but that's normal.

Parking Brake (Emergency Brake)

The parking brake (a.k.a. emergency brake) is used to prevent a car from rolling when it's in park and to slow or stop the car when the brakes have failed. Unlike the brake system, the parking brake only uses two of the four wheels—usually the rear wheels. It's controlled by either a handheld or foot device (it's a smaller pedal than the gas and brake) and will be located at the bottom of the driver's side, farthest to the left.

Parking brake

Common Problems

Brake Pads, Brake Shoes, Drums, and Rotors

The common problem for all of these is wear. Be alert to a squishy brake pedal, strange screeching sounds, a steering wheel that vibrates when you brake, and the history of repairs. Have the brake system checked by a certified technician every other oil change or 6,000 miles, or more frequently, if you drive in stop-and-go traffic.

New brake pads/shoes are $^{12}\!/_{32}$ inch in thickness. Most states require that brake pads be replaced when they reach $^{2}\!/_{32}$ inch.

ABS System

The main problem with the ABS is with the motorist failing to apply constant pressure to the brake pedal. If the ABS light stays on while driving, don't panic. Your car's brake system will still work—it's just that the ABS won't. If this happens, get the ABS serviced.

Parking Brake

Be attentive to the range of motion of the parking brake. Do you have to move the handle farther than before? Is the foot brake less resistant

---

Not everyone regularly uses the parking brake, but we recommend that you use it every time you park the car to keep it from getting stuck and becoming unusable, and—more important—to keep the car from moving (this is especially true of vehicles with manual transmissions).

Softer brake pads wear out faster but provide a quieter stop; harder brake pads last longer but provide a noisier stop.

There are many variables that affect the life of the brake parts, such as driving habits, vehicle size, brand of pads/shoes, and whether the car has front-wheel or rear-wheel drive (brake parts wear out faster on the front wheels because the majority of the car's braking is on the front of the car).

to the force of your foot? These are signs of wear. Here's another way to see if the parking brake needs to be serviced.

DIY: Testing the Parking Brake

Put your car on a slight incline (e.g., a sloped driveway) in a controlled environment (no people or cars are within sight). Place the car in neutral and use either the hand or foot parking brake to stop the car from rolling. If the car begins to move, immediately put your foot on the brake pedal and engage the parking brake. This is a sign that your parking brake needs to be serviced. If your car has an automatic transmission, place it in park and turn off the engine. If it has a manual transmission, keep the gear in neutral and turn off the engine.

Exhaust System

If your car could play the starring role in a movie, would it be *The Love Bug* or *Chitty, Chitty, Bang, Bang?* If it's the latter, read on.

Teenage boys are the only ones who aren't humbled by the sound of an exhaust system gone bad. For everyone else, it's probably the *must-repair-immediately* car part.

What It Is

The car's exhaust system is kind of like the exhaust fan above your kitchen stove—it removes the fumes and deposits them outside.

The exhaust system of a car consists of the exhaust manifold, the exhaust pipe, the catalytic converter, the muffler, the resonator (on some vehicles), and the tailpipe. All these parts work together to funnel harmful exhaust fumes away from the car, to silence the noise it

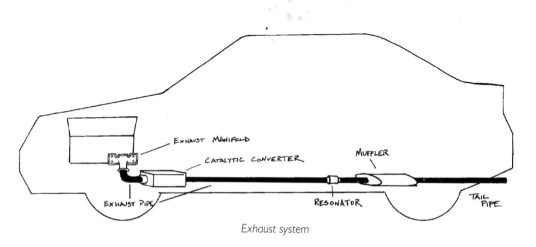

Exhaust system

generates, and to increase the car's fuel-burning capacity and engine performance.

How It Works

We're going to begin at one end of the exhaust system and work our way back, starting with the exhaust manifold.

Exhaust Manifold
The exhaust manifold is located at the beginning of the exhaust system on the engine head. It collects the gasoline fumes discharged by the combustion chamber and sends them to the exhaust pipes.

Exhaust Pipes
There are typically two exhaust pipes—one leading from the exhaust manifold to the catalytic converter and the other leading from the catalytic converter to the muffler. These pipes carry the exhaust fumes away from the car.

Catalytic Converter
A catalytic converter reduces the exhaust gases of environmentally harmful emissions, which are created by the burning of fuel, by converting them into water vapor and less toxic gases.

Note: Catalytic converters get very hot and stay hot for a while after the engine has been turned off. Therefore, never park your car on top of grass, leaves, or any other combustible material.

Muffler
The job of a muffler is to *muffle* the noise produced by the exhaust system. It has an exhaust pipe connected on one end and the tailpipe connected on the other end.

Resonator

Not all cars have a resonator. A resonator, located between the muffler and the tailpipe, is similar to the muffler in that it reduces the noise of the exhaust system. It's kind of like having a double-paned window, instead of a single-paned one.

Tailpipe

The end. Yes, that's exactly what the tailpipe is, the very end of the exhaust system. The end of the tailpipe should extend just past the back end of the car.

Common Problems

Exhaust Manifold

The most common problem for this part is a worn or cracked gasket. This should be taken very seriously because harmful gases can leak inside the car, causing illness or death. How will you know if the gasket is cracked? You'll hear a loud rattle or an even louder engine noise, especially when the engine is cold (the noise lessens as the engine warms up).

Exhaust Pipes

These can become rusted and form holes. Also, the hangers that hold up the pipes and connect them to the car body can fall off if they become rusted or damaged. Once again, it's vital to have the pipes replaced if there are holes or rust because of the risk of carbon monoxide and other harmful exhaust by-products leaking into the car. If the hangers fall off, they can either be repaired or replaced.

Catalytic Converter

This typically lasts about 100,000 miles, but if your car starts to smell like rotten eggs (i.e., sulfur, which is a by-product of burning fuel), it's a sign that your catalytic converter may not be working efficiently, and may need to be replaced. Have your service technician also check the fuel system because it may be allowing too much fuel to be burned at one time.

If you see two tailpipes at the back of your car, your car has a dual exhaust system. Why would you need more than one? A dual exhaust system enhances the car's performance by emitting exhaust faster.

Muffler

The most common problem with a muffler is that it can become rusted, which typically creates holes, or the brackets become loose, causing the muffler to fall off. You'll definitely know when there's a problem with the muffler because the sound will be deafening.

Don't try to tie the muffler up yourself, because you may burn yourself on the catalytic converter. Instead, have the muffler professionally serviced as soon as possible, especially if it's dragging on the ground, which can cause sparks.

Tailpipe

What comes out of the tailpipe is indicative of what's going on inside. Every car emits smoke, but it should only be visible when you start your car, especially on very cold days, and then should dissipate. Here are the different colors of smoke that can be emitted from the tailpipe and what they mean; just note that it can be difficult to distinguish between the colors.

- *White smoke.* If you see thick white smoke after you've driven the car for a while, then coolant may have entered the cylinder and combustion chamber. The problem could be caused by worn head gaskets that have allowed coolant to escape. Check the coolant reservoir to see if it's low and fill it if necessary, and then take the car to a mechanic as soon as possible.
- *Bluish white smoke.* If you notice bluish white smoke, it means that oil is getting into the cylinder and combustion chambers, where it doesn't belong, and is being burned with the air-fuel mixture. A number of different engine problems can cause bluish white smoke, such as worn valve stem seals, worn or cracked head gasket, and/or worn piston rings. Take the car to a mechanic immediately.
- *Black smoke.* If you see black smoke and the car does not use diesel fuel, it's a sign that the engine may have a fuel mixture problem. The solution again is to take the car to your mechanic immediately.

Hybrid Cars

ybrid vehicles have become a power-house seller for car manufacturers. It's not just the rising cost of fuel that's propelled sales; it's also the tough restrictions on car emissions and the ability to ride in high-occupancy vehicle (HOV) lanes while being the only person in the car. These vehicles are evolving as we write; therefore, we are only providing some very generic information about them. For more information about hybrid vehicles, check out the car manufacturers' Web sites.

What They Are

A hybrid vehicle uses two sources of power. A perfect example would be a 2-wheel scooter that has a motor on it—you can use foot power to make it move or turn the engine on and use the battery as the power source.

The main parts of a hybrid car are the gasoline engine, the fuel tank (gasoline), the electric motor, a generator (in a series hybrid), batteries (a.k.a. the battery pack), and the transmission.

How They Work

The main purpose of the hybrid is to reduce tailpipe emissions and to increase fuel efficiency.

A hybrid car uses gasoline and electricity as its two power sources. This means that you don't always have to use gasoline because it has a backup source of power—the batteries and an electric motor.

Another unique feature of hybrids is that they have regenerative braking, which means that when you stop or slow down, the car can store energy from braking to help power the vehicle.

Maintenance

Maintenance for hybrid cars is a little different than for gasoline-powered cars. For example, the batteries and the motors do not require maintenance, and because hybrids have a regenerative braking system (the energy is removed from the brakes when they're engaged and stored for future use), the brake pads may have a longer life. But just like a gasoline-powered car, you must refer to the car owner's manual for the manufacturer's recommended maintenance schedule.

Maintenance

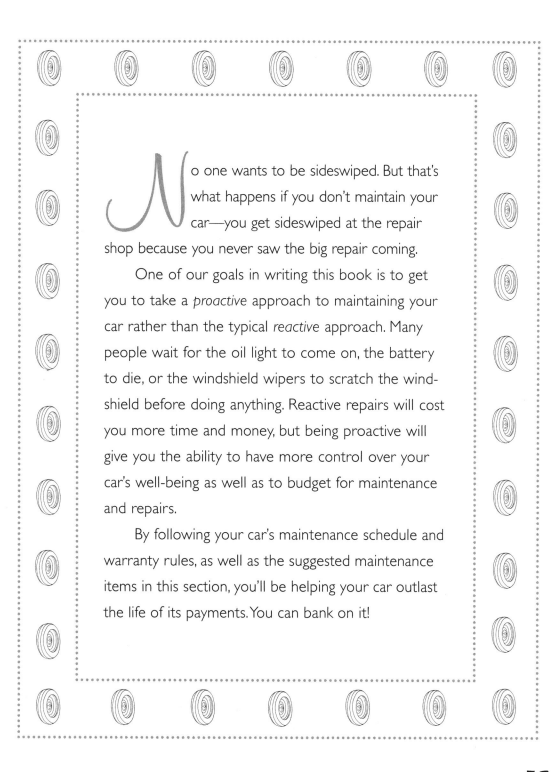

No one wants to be sideswiped. But that's what happens if you don't maintain your car—you get sideswiped at the repair shop because you never saw the big repair coming.

One of our goals in writing this book is to get you to take a *proactive* approach to maintaining your car rather than the typical *reactive* approach. Many people wait for the oil light to come on, the battery to die, or the windshield wipers to scratch the windshield before doing anything. Reactive repairs will cost you more time and money, but being proactive will give you the ability to have more control over your car's well-being as well as to budget for maintenance and repairs.

By following your car's maintenance schedule and warranty rules, as well as the suggested maintenance items in this section, you'll be helping your car outlast the life of its payments. You can bank on it!

Warranties

When you were listening to the salesperson talk about the different warranty packages for your car, did she sound like *Charlie Brown's* teacher: *"Wah, wah, wah"*? All that complicated information just makes you want to say, *"Good grief."*

It's almost impossible to pay full attention to the multitude of offers, when all you want to do is hop in your shiny new car and drive away. Add to that the complexity of the contract and you'll sign just about anything to get out of there.

It's not until you need to have something repaired that you start to think that maybe you need a warranty for the warranty! Here's how to get what you need and know what you're getting.

Factory vs. Factory Extended

Factory Warranty

Every new car comes with a factory warranty, which is a limited manufacturer's guarantee to cover the cost of parts and labor for items specified in the warranty agreement. Most car manufacturers offer a new car factory warranty for 7 years or 100,000 miles. The longest term for a factory warranty is 10 years or 100,000 miles. Of course, the most crucial element is often not the length of the deal, but what's being covered—and perhaps even more important, what's not.

Warranty

Factory-Extended Warranty or Vehicle Service Agreement

A factory-extended warranty kicks in *after* the life of the factory warranty has expired and guarantees parts and labor for items specified in the agreement. This is a must-have for people who buy a used car and intend to keep the car for a period of time or mileage that exceeds the factory warranty.

A factory-extended warranty (i.e, GM, Ford, Toyota) is honored by all dealerships selling those brands of cars. Warranties sold by other companies (Geico, GE) are *not* honored by all dealerships and therefore you may be directed to a specific garage.

If you are leasing a car, you may not need to purchase an extended warranty. A typical lease is for 3 years, and a factory warranty covers a car for at least the first 3 years or 36,000 miles, whichever comes first. However, if somehow you ended up with a long lease, or you know that you will probably exceed the mileage limit of the warranty, then purchase an extended warranty.

If you're the type of car owner that does not like to keep a new car for more than 2 or 3 years, don't buy an extended warranty, unless you're able to purchase one that follows the car and not the owner (this should be stated in the warranty as "transferable"). This can be a big bargaining chip when it comes to selling the vehicle.

Another reason for not needing to purchase an extended warranty is if the used car you're buying already has close to 100,000 miles on it. The typical extended warranty will only cover an additional 50,000 miles, up to a total of 100,000 miles.

Before Buying an Extended Warranty

You should start learning about factory and extended warranties *before* you buy a car, *not* after negotiating a deal for one. You're too emotional, too anxious to move the process forward, and too happy to be getting a new car. Vulnerability equals dollar signs to a salesperson.

Don't assume that a car dealership is the only place that you can purchase an extended warranty. In fact, you may find a much better deal elsewhere, such as your credit union.

There are lots of companies that specialize in selling automobile warranties; you just have to be willing to do some research. A good place to start is on the Web. Do a search for companies that sell automobile extended warranties. You want to make sure that the company is properly licensed and possesses a strong financial rating. Another option, if you belong to a credit union that sells car loans, is to ask for a list of reputable warranty companies.

If you'll be buying a car from a dealership, request a copy of the factory warranty for that vehicle and a copy of the extended warranty packages. Or go online and obtain that information at the manufacturer's Web site.

No matter what company you use to purchase the extended warranty, most will not cover mechanical failure *and* wear and tear, such as wiper motor breaking or brake pads wearing out. Check the warranty for this type of coverage.

The best time to purchase an extended warranty is right after purchasing the car, because that's when you'll get the best deal. After you buy it, you typically have 30 days to decline it.

Buying an Extended Warranty

An extended warranty doesn't have to be purchased through a car dealership. In fact, there are financial institutions online that can offer much better deals. It is important to purchase it when you buy your car, or as soon as possible thereafter, to get the best rate.

Typical Coverage

You've probably heard the term "bumper to bumper warranty," but in reality, there's no warranty that covers everything from bumper to bumper. In fact, here's what is usually covered and what is usually not.

Covered

- Starter
- Alternator
- AC compressor
- Transmission
- Air conditioner
- Brake master cylinder
- Power window and door lock (master switch)
- Towing reimbursement
- Rental-car reimbursement

Note: Some extended warranties will even cover towing and rental cars.

Not Covered

- Exhaust system
- Air bags
- Windows, windshields, and mirrors
- Lights
- Carpeting, mats, and upholstery
- Brake pads
- Disc brakes
- Tires

- Paint
- Any preexisting problem on a used car
- Fluids

Understanding the Warranty

When you purchase an extended warranty for your car, check to see if you are under a contractual obligation to have the car dealership or a licensed repair facility with an approved mechanic—i.e., one who is ASE (National Institute for Automotive Service Excellence) certified—perform repairs authorized under the warranty.

Before the mechanic at the dealership or repair shop can do any repairs on your car she has to contact the warranty company to explain what work needs to be done and to get an official authorization in order to proceed. *It's like an HMO for your car!*

The good side of this is that the warranty company can immediately tell if you're being overcharged for an item; the bad side is that the warranty company has the right to refuse to pay more than what they deem is reasonable. Here's what may be the biggest annoyance when dealing with a warranty company: if a mechanic needs to remove Part B to get to Part A and only Part A is under warranty, then the warranty company will not pay the labor cost for the mechanic to remove Part B. Oh, and by the way, labor is billed by the hour, not the minute.

Upholding Your End of the Deal

You know that you have to use a car dealership or a licensed repair facility with an approved mechanic and get the repairs authorized before having the work done, or else it won't be covered. But there's something else that can nullify your warranty, too. You have to follow the manufacturer's maintenance schedule and use parts recommended by the manufacturer.

You can do all the maintenance work on your car and it will be validated by the warranty company as long as you have receipts from all the parts you purchased. The best way to protect your car's warranty is to keep a designated folder with dates, receipts of purchases, and receipts of any repair work done by you or a certified technician. And check out the following section.

Maintenance Schedule

When you schedule a health checkup for yourself, don't forget to schedule one for your car. Think of it as giving your car a shot in the arm.

Car manufacturers have different suggested maintenance schedules. So do auto repair shops and dealerships. So how do you know who's right? The best thing to do is to gather information from all the sources, including the Internet, so you can make a well-informed decision.

Scheduling a maintenance checkup

Note: If your car is under warranty, follow the maintenance schedule provided in order for your car to remain under warranty.

Car Owner's Manual

Every car owner's manual has a maintenance schedule divided either by miles or months. The National Institute for Automotive Service Excellence (ASE) recommends that instead of thinking "3,000 miles or 3 months, whichever comes first" you should think, "3,000 miles or 3 months, whichever comes second." You're going to have to decide which system works best for the type of car you own and the amount of miles you put on it.

Just remember, it's always better to err on the side of more maintenance rather than less, especially if your car is under warranty.

Online

If you don't have your car owner's manual (*tsk, tsk*), then you can go online to the car manufacturer's Web site for the maintenance schedule. Not only can you obtain a printout of the car owner's manual and warranty, but you can also sign up to receive e-mail service reminders and vehicle-specific recall notices; view vehicle operation, maintenance, and safety videos; and access online service and maintenance records.

Another option is to go to www.edmunds.com. Just plug in the required information about your vehicle and it will show you not only the maintenance schedule, but also the suggested cost of parts and labor.

Mechanic

Because you're dealing with a checkup for your car instead of an unexpected repair, you'll have time to do some comparison shopping. Then ask your mechanic or dealership for a printout of everything that will be done on the car, as well as an estimate. Compare it with the online estimate. If there's a vast difference, call around to other repair shops and dealerships for more price quotes. We guarantee that you'll be shocked at the differences you'll find in prices and services.

DIY

Just because we told you how to formulate the right service checkups for your car, it doesn't mean that there's nothing left for you to do. In fact, any maintenance you do on your car will lessen the to-do list for the mechanic, which will lessen your bill.

Weekly

- Check the air pressure in all the tires, and add air if necessary.
- Look for any nicks, dents, or scratches on the car.
- Check for fluid leaks.

Monthly

- Check the oil, coolant, and windshield washer fluid and replenish if necessary.
- Check the tire treads for tread depth, uneven wear, and blisters.
- Remove the spare tire and check the air pressure. Fill, if necessary.
- Check all the exterior lamps.
- Wash your car (you may need to do this more often, depending on the weather conditions).
- Inspect the battery terminals for corrosion and clean if necessary. Make sure that the cables are properly connected.
- Look for any worn or frayed belts and brittle or cracked hoses and have them replaced, if necessary.
- Clean the wiper blades (twice a month) and replace if necessary.
- Look for any damage to the tailpipe and muffler and check that they're properly secured.

Quarterly (or 3,000 Miles)

- Change the oil and oil filter.
- Change the air filter, if necesssary.
- Check the brake and transmission fluids, and replenish if necessary.
- Detail the exterior and interior of your car (including waxing).

Maintaining Fluids

Introduction

Being a responsible driver doesn't just mean that you stay within the speed limit, or that you always use your turn signals, or that you don't drive aggressively. It also means that you take responsibility for properly caring for your car.

The first step is to maintain its fluids (we'll get to the others later). Every car has 7 fluids: brake, coolant, fuel, oil, power steering, transmission, and windshield washer. *You* need to regularly check their levels, replenish them, and look for leaks. It's so simple to do that you'll wonder why you never did it before. Heck, you may even be inspired to change the oil, and that's why we've included instructions for that, too.

Fluids get contaminated and therefore need to be professionally flushed (with the exception of oil and windshield washer) by your mechanic and replaced with new fluids. This should be done every other year, or as recommended by your car's manufacturer.

One more thing we'd like to suggest is that you purchase separate funnels for each fluid to prevent contamination and use lint-free rags for doing any work around fluids.

Brake Fluid

We've all seen the bumper stickers on cars that read, "I Brake for Animals" and "I Brake for Garage Sales." Maybe there should be a bumper sticker that says, "I Brake Because I Maintain the Brake Fluid." Catchy, huh?

Would you believe that 1 out of 3 cars needs maintenance or repairs on its brake system? That's a frightening statistic, especially when you think that the only thing keeping cars from running into each other are their brakes!

Brake fluid is the easiest of the fluids to maintain, yet it's probably the most neglected. Hopefully the following information will keep you from putting the brakes on when it comes to maintaining them.

What It Is

Brake fluid is an amber-colored oil that lubricates the brake system. It's stored in a reservoir that sits on top of the master brake cylinder.

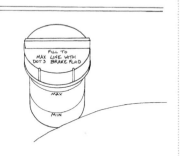

Brake fluid reservoir

There are three classifications for brake fluid set by the U.S. Department of Transportation (DOT): DOT-3, DOT-4, and DOT-5. The difference between the three types is the boiling point for the fluid. The most common type for passenger vehicles is DOT-3, but there's no need to guess because the information is located in the car manual.

Brake fluid is hydroscopic (now there's an SAT word for you), which means that it absorbs moisture from the air. Moisture is very bad for brake fluid because it decreases the boiling temperature, contributes to the deterioration of the fluid, and causes rusting in the brake system.

IY

Checking the Fluid

You only have to check the brake fluid every 3,000 miles, or every time you change the oil. In fact, the hardest thing you need to do for this job is to park the car on level ground.

The brake fluid reservoir, typically found at the rear of the engine, has a cap on top that reads BRAKE FLUID and either DOT-3, DOT-4, or DOT-5.

The reservoir is translucent and because there's no dipstick, you'll have to eyeball the fluid in the reservoir against the markings on the container; FULL and ADD, or MAX and MIN. The difference between the markings is less than a pint of brake fluid.

When you're looking at the level of brake fluid in the reservoir, also look at its color. Brake fluid begins as an amber-colored oil, but darkens over time. If the fluid looks very dark, or if it looks like there is metal debris in it, then you need to have the system flushed by a mechanic.

Adding Fluid

As we stated above, brake fluid absorbs moisture from the air; therefore, whenever you're going to add brake fluid to the reservoir, you

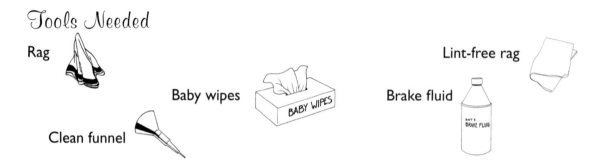

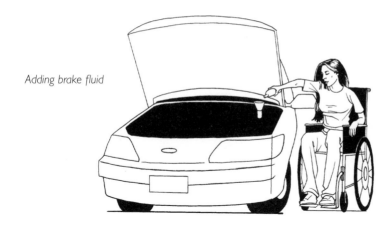
Adding brake fluid

must use an unopened (i.e., sealed) bottle. This also means that you won't be able to store any that's left over. Luckily, brake fluid is inexpensive and you rarely have to add it. But you will need to contact your county government to see if it recycles brake fluid; if not, ask your car dealership or mechanic to recycle it for you.

Wait … one more word of caution. Be very careful not to spill any brake fluid on the paint of the car because it will cause the paint to bubble and peel. If you have a spill, quickly wipe it off with a lint-free rag. If you're doing this at a gas station, get the squeegee that's sitting in the windshield washer fluid near the fuel pumps and use it to clean off the brake fluid.

We've told you that moisture is harmful to brake fluid, but so is dirt. Therefore, before you begin adding brake fluid, use a baby wipe or clean rag to clean around the reservoir cap to prevent any dirt from entering.

Turn the reservoir cap counterclockwise to remove. Remove the foil seal and throw it out—you don't want it falling into the reservoir. Place the cap in a place so that it won't roll under the car and get dirty.

Insert the funnel into the reservoir. Remove the cap and seal from the brake fluid container and pour the fluid into the reservoir, making sure not to overfill it.

Remove the funnel and replace the reservoir cap, turning it clockwise to tighten. Drive the car for about 10 miles and recheck the level.

Checking for Leaks

If you can push the brake pedal all the way down, the cause may be a fluid leak, low fluid level, master cylinder failure, or worn pads/shoes. If the brake pedal seems squishy when you press it, it may be due to moisture diminishing the boiling point of the fluid, and you'll need to get the brake fluid flushed.

If there is a pool of dark fluid under your car, dip a corner of the paper towel into it. If the fluid is brown and located near any of the tires, it may be brake fluid. Leaks rarely happen, but if you have one it's probably from a leaking brake cylinder. Check the brake fluid level and add fluid if necessary. Have the brakes serviced immediately.

DIFM

Brake fluid begins as a clear amber color, but over time it darkens. To keep the brake system running smoothly and effectively, it's important to have the brake fluid flushed one year and drained the next year, or as recommended by the vehicle's manufacturer. Check the car owner's manual for more information.

Tool Needed

White paper towel

Coolant

*J*o Anne left the cold of Maine for the warmth of Florida, leaving behind all reminders of frigid weather—snowblower, ski pants, and the container of antifreeze for her car. When her car's engine eventually overheated, she blamed her costly mistake on brain-freeze.

What It Is

Coolant, which is a mixture of antifreeze and water, is used by the car's cooling system to disperse heat in order to prevent the engine and the radiator from overheating in the summer and freezing in the winter.

No matter if you live in the Snowbelt or the Sunbelt, every car needs coolant and not just water or just antifreeze. In fact, car manufacturers typically recommend a 50-50 ratio of antifreeze to water (70-30 ratio for extremely cold climates). Why? Because too much water can cause the engine and/or radiator to freeze and crack in the wintertime, and using only antifreeze can cause the engine to overheat on hot days. And, of course, using no coolant at all will destroy the engine, too.

Note: Repairs will not be covered by your car's warranty if you did not use the proper coolant ratio.

DIY

Signs of Trouble

If the coolant warning light comes on, it doesn't mean that the reservoir is out of coolant, but it does mean that you need to check the level immediately and add fluid if necessary.

If you notice the engine temperature gauge is climbing into the red range, it's a sign that the engine is operating too hot and will stop running. Turn off the car, wait for the engine to cool, and then check the coolant level.

Note: Never open the hood of the car if you see steam coming from underneath it. And never open the radiator cap when the engine is hot—you can get burned from the steam or from any coolant that may be released. Also use caution when pouring coolant into the reservoir, because if you spill any on a hot engine part it can spatter onto you, causing a burn.

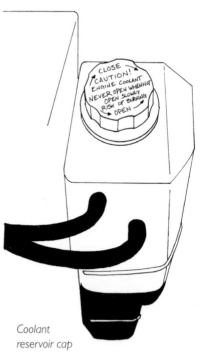

Coolant reservoir cap

Checking Coolant

Checking the level of coolant is as easy as looking at a clear plastic container, also known as a coolant reservoir, overflow bottle, or coolant surge tank. You should do this every time you fill your car up with fuel—and, of course, if the coolant warning light appears.

The coolant reservoir and the radiator work as a vacuum system. The reservoir, located near the radiator, temporarily stores the overheated coolant that was released by the radiator. When the temperature of the coolant decreases, its volume decreases as well, causing it to get sucked back into the radiator. So if you see coolant in the reservoir then there's coolant in the radiator, and vice versa.

Park the car on a level surface and let the engine cool. Pop open the hood of the car, locate the reservoir, and note the level of coolant in it.

The reservoir will have a COLD reading and *maybe* a HOT reading too, both of which refer to the temperature of the engine. It will also have a marking for FULL. Some reservoirs also have a marking for FILL.

Don't assume that the markings will be facing you, because they may be on a different side of the reservoir. If the coolant reservoir is empty, and you happen to have the ready-made coolant in your car, add it now. If you don't have any coolant, you'll have to get your car towed.

Buying Antifreeze

Antifreeze is commonly sold in gallon containers, and it comes in bright colors, the difference being that some are standard and some are long-life. Before purchasing either one, refer to the car owner's manual to see which one is right for your car.

You can even buy ready-made coolant, which is a convenient alternative to mixing antifreeze and water. If your home has hard water (which contains minerals), you should either use ready-made coolant or filtered water to mix with the antifreeze.

Getting the Mixture Right

If your car requires a 50-50 mixture, fill the empty (and clean) gallon container halfway with water and place it inside the dishpan to prevent spillage. Insert the funnel into the container and fill it to the top with antifreeze. Remove the funnel and place the caps securely on both containers.

Getting the mixture right

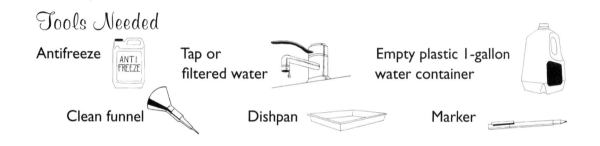

𝒯ools 𝒩eeded

Antifreeze ANTI FREEZE   Tap or filtered water   Empty plastic 1-gallon water container

Clean funnel   Dishpan   Marker

Adding Coolant

Before you do this repair, the car must be parked on a level surface and the engine must be completely cool.

Pop open the hood of the car and locate the coolant reservoir. With the rag in one hand, slowly turn the cap counterclockwise. If you hear a hissing sound, it

Adding the ready-made coolant

means that there is still some pressure built up inside the container, so stop and wait a few minutes. Once the hissing sound has stopped, it's safe to continue. If the cap won't turn, push down on it and continue to slowly turn it counterclockwise. Remove the cap and put it in a safe place so it won't roll under the car.

Place the funnel in the opening of the reservoir and pour in the coolant until it reaches the COLD FULL mark. Wait—you're not done quite yet. Remember, it's a vacuum system, so you'll need to have the engine warm to get an accurate reading of your handiwork.

To test your handiwork, turn the engine on and look to see if the ENGINE COOLANT light is off. If it's off . . . good job! If the light is still on and there's no leak, then the problem could be with the sensor or with the engine. Have a mechanic take a look.

Properly store the remaining coolant inside the garage (see "Safely Storing Items," page 317).

Tools Needed

Rag

Coolant

Clean funnel

DIFM

Coolant needs to be drained one year and flushed the next. Beware of antifreeze that states it lasts over 100,000 miles. Antifreeze contains chemicals that break down over time (and miles) and will collect sludge and deposits. Because coolant is so vital to your car, we recommend that you maintain it according to the car owner's manual, and not what's on the back of the antifreeze container.

Coolant Leak

If you see a puddle of fluid on the driveway that's a bright color and has a sweet smell, it's probably coolant. A coolant leak is typically the result of a problem with a radiator hose, the radiator, or the reservoir container. Have the problem fixed immediately.

50/50 coolant has a freezing point of –34°. 70/30 coolant has a freezing point of –84°.

Fuel

Gasoline and diesel fuels are regulated at the pump by your state's Department of Agriculture.

Are you afraid of the tiger in your tank? The following information will help tame your fears by providing *grrrrr-eat* safety tips.

What It Is

Fuel is defined as "something that is burned to provide power or heat." Vehicles are either powered by gasoline, diesel, or a combination of gasoline and battery power (hybrid).

The majority of cars in the United States are fueled by gasoline, and in Europe the majority are powered by diesel. But there is no car that can use both, which is why the nozzle on a diesel pump will not fit into a car that uses gasoline, and vice versa. It's a great design that keeps you from destroying the engine.

Diesel fuel can be purchased at most service stations and is pumped into a car the same as gasoline, only there's usually just one pump per service station—unless you fill up at a truck stop.

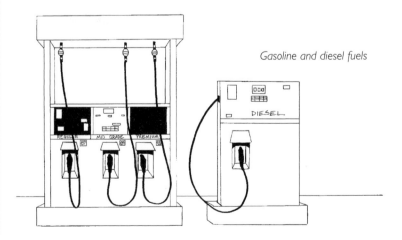

Gasoline and diesel fuels

Gasoline Grades

Regular, Plus (Mid-grade), and *Premium.* We're not talking about sizes of McDonald's french fries. No, these are the typical choices of grades of gasoline at the pump. What's the difference between them, other than the price? The difference is the level of octane, which is the measurement of a fuel's resistance to engine knock. The American Petroleum Institute defines engine knock as the "uncontrolled combustion associated with using gasoline with too little octane." The only thing we can relate it to is your stomach growling because it doesn't have what it needs. The level of octane is represented by a number, for example: 87 (Regular), 89 (Plus), and 93 (Premium). The higher the number the higher the octane.

Since the mid-1990s, all grades of gasoline contain a minimum amount of detergent, which aids in cleaning the engine and, therefore, the environment. Depending on the gasoline manufacturer, each grade of gasoline can have a different level of detergent added—the higher the grade, the more detergent. For example, BP's Amoco Ultimate Premium gasoline has several times more than its Regular grade.

How do you know which grade of gasoline your car needs? Always refer to the car owner's manual. But even if the manual recommends Regular gasoline, you need to consider the age of your car, your car's performance, your driving habits, and your personal preference. Even if you don't hear your car's engine knocking, it doesn't mean that it's not happening. Most of the cars on the road today have knock sensors that adjust the spark timing upon detecting engine knock. This adjustment can reduce fuel efficiency; therefore you may be saving money in the long run by using Premium gasoline.

Name-Brand vs. No-Name-Brand Gasoline

The lesser-known gas stations obtain fuel from the same refineries that the big-name gas stations use. The reason they can charge less is because they have a lower overhead than the others, but you're more likely to get bad gasoline—and here's why. The problem with using gasoline from a lesser-known gas station is that gasoline breaks down over time, so the less-used gas stations may have gasoline that's not as new as the better-known stations. The choice is up to you, but we suggest that you only fill up at a name-brand station.

> Premium gasoline can prevent the knock and restore engine performance by allowing the knock sensor technology to retune the engine.

DIY

Pumping Gas

We wondered whether to provide instructions for pumping gas, because let's face it, everyone knows how to pump gas. Of course, there are some of you who pay the extra money for full service because you're afraid to do it (hopefully, after reading this section, you'll *dare* to pump gas) or because you live in New Jersey, where all gas stations are full service only.

So why are we writing about pumping gas? Because what most of you may not be aware of are the safety procedures that should be followed every time you fill 'er up.

Static Electricity

Did you know that you should never get back into your car during refueling? Getting in and out of your car can create static electricity, which, when combined with the vapors emitted from gasoline at the fill site, can create a flash fire. This rarely happens, but there's an easy way to prevent it from occurring. If you absolutely must get back into the car, use your bare hand to touch a metal spot on the car (not near the pump) to discharge any static electricity before getting inside.

If you have a cell phone, turn it off. Even though there is no empirical data that supports the theory that cell phones can produce static electricity, it's best to assume that they can. So cut the cord with your cell phone for the few minutes you're at the pump.

And don't even think about smoking at a gas station or anywhere near gasoline. You can't smoke in your car, either, because you're not suppose to be in it while refueling, remember?

Staying at the Pump

Not only should you not get back inside the car while refueling, you should also never leave the pump unattended. This means no running to the restroom or going inside the convenience mart to buy a Krispy Kreme while filling the tank. Why? Because sometimes the pump may

If you can't stand the smell of gasoline on your hands, then fill up at gas stations that offer free disposable gloves, or keep some in your car.

not click off when the tank is full or the nozzle may fall out of the gas tank while filling, spilling fuel on the ground.

Never let your child under driving age pump the gas for you.

Fire at the Pump

Gas stations are required to have an emergency shutoff button for the pumps, either outside the station or mart for motorists and/or inside for the attendant to operate. The exterior shutoff button is typically located underneath a sign that says "Emergency" or "Emergency Shutoff."

If a fire occurs at the pump while refueling, there a few things you should and should not do. Do *not* remove the nozzle from the car. If you do, you'll spill gasoline, which will only increase the size of the fire. Instead, leave the pump, go to the other side of the car to remove any passengers, and *run* to the service area to notify the attendant. If you know where the emergency shutoff button is, push it.

Emergency shutoff

Every gas station is required by law to have fire extinguishers located at the fuel pumps, but it's up to each gas station to maintain them; therefore, you can't be guaranteed that they will work. The safest thing to do is to get away from the fire.

Fill 'er Up

Pull up your car so that the fuel cap is facing the pump. Place the car in park if your car has an automatic transmission and *neutral* if it's a manual transmission. Turn off the engine and engage the parking brake.

Note: Always turn the engine off before refueling.

Follow the instructions on the pump to determine the method of payment and grade of gasoline you want.

Pumping gas

While you're waiting for your car to fill up, check the motor oil and windshield washer fluid levels, and refill if necessary.

Open the fuel door and remove the fuel cap by slowly twisting it counterclockwise, allowing air to escape. Newer cars have fuel caps that are tethered so they won't get lost, whereas older cars typically have fuel caps that come completely off, in which case it's important to put the cap in a place where you won't forget it. Some cars have a fuel cap holder located on the inside of the fuel door.

Note: Some fuel doors are released by depressing a button inside the car on the dashboard, on the driver's door panel, or inside the glove compartment. .

Remove the nozzle and place it into the fuel tank and squeeze the trigger handle. If you don't want to hold it the entire time, engage the refueling latch. If the latch is broken or missing, do not substitute an object in its place. Some gas stations have removed the latches to ensure that motorists won't leave the pump unattended.

The fuel nozzle is designed to cut off when the tank is full. Never top off your tank because you need to leave space for the gasoline to expand.

Replace the nozzle in the fuel pump. Twist on the fuel cap, making sure that it's tight. In fact, you'll hear a *click* when it's tight. Close the fuel door.

If you've spilled any gasoline on your car, wipe it off immediately using the squeegee that's sitting in the windshield washer fluid located near the pumps. And if you spilled a large amount of gasoline on the ground, notify an attendant.

Fuel Cap

You've heard the saying "Big things come in small packages." Well, that's absolutely true about the fuel cap. If you think its only job is to cover the fuel tank filler, you are wrong. Would you believe that the fuel cap helps to protect the environment and saves you up to 30 gallons of gasoline a year? Wait, there's more. The fuel cap also keeps gasoline from spilling out in case of an accident or a rollover. We think it deserves a little *r-e-s-p-e-c-t!*

A fuel cap (made of plastic or metal) is located behind the fuel tank filler door and inserts into the neck of the fuel tank filler. Remove the fuel cap by slowly turn-

Fuel cap

ing it counterclockwise to allow any gases to escape. You'll know that you've properly closed the fuel cap when you hear it *click*. If you don't close the fuel cap correctly, the CHECK ENGINE light on the dashboard will most likely turn on (see "Emissions Tests and Safety Inspections," page 222). Simply remove and retighten the fuel cap.

If you've lost the fuel cap, replace it as soon as possible. Almost 20 percent of the vehicles on the road have either missing, broken, or loose fuel caps, which equates to about 150 million gallons of gas that's vaporized into the air. Don't be a part of that statistic. You can purchase a new one at a dealership or an auto parts store, with prices ranging from $5 to $20. Make sure that you get the right one for the make and model of your car—and don't buy a cheap one, because it may not pass the emissions test.

An alternative to purchasing a replacement fuel cap is to receive one for free! Some states have created alliances with associations, corporations, and oil companies to provide fuel cap exchange programs for motorists. The motorist turns in her old fuel cap in exchange for a new one that meets the emissions test standards. Contact your state EPA for more information.

Out of Gas

There are those who like to live on the edge of life, and then there are those who like to live on the edge of the fuel gauge. For all you easy riders, we recommend that you get your kicks on Route 66 without running out of gas, because not only can it be dangerous for you, it can also be harmful to your car's engine. You see, most cars have the fuel pump inside the fuel tank; therefore, if there's no fuel inside the tank, the fuel pump can burn up. So if you love the rush of having the needle in the red, you need to know what to do when the inevitable happens.

Gasoline Container

Never leave a filled container of gasoline in your car because the container may spill or leak and pose a fire hazard. Another important reason is that if your car is involved in a crash, it can cause a very dangerous situation.

Gasoline containers are made of either plastic or metal, but no matter which kind you buy, it must be vented to prevent the buildup of pressure and greater potential of spilling while filling.

If you have to walk to a gas station, only do so if it's light outside and walk as far away from the street or highway as you can. If you don't have a gasoline container in your car, don't panic, because gas stations usually sell them.

Filling a Gasoline Container

Place the container on the ground and remove the lid. *Never fill a gasoline container while it is on or in a car or in the back of a truck. Only fill a container while it's on the ground to avoid static electricity and spills.*

Select the grade of gasoline and payment method. Remove the gas pump nozzle and fill the container slowly to prevent overfilling and static electricity. Do not use the refueling latch because the container will fill up quickly and you'll end up spilling gasoline.

The common gasoline container can hold 1 to 5 gallons of gasoline, but don't fill it to the top because you need to leave space for the gas to expand, and you only need enough gasoline to get you back to the gas station in your car (a full container of gasoline can be heavy to carry, especially if you're walking a great distance). The average car gets around 18 miles to the gallon, so if you know the distance between your car and the gas station, you can figure out how much you'll need to drive back to the station to fill the tank up completely.

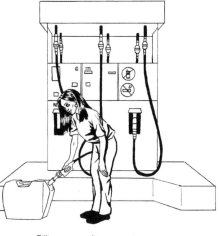

Filling a gasoline container

Return the nozzle to the pump and place the lid on the container making sure that it is really tight. You don't want to be leaving a trail of gasoline behind you!

If you spilled any gasoline, use a paper towel (typically located at the pumps) to wipe it up; and if it was a big spill, notify the attendant. If you are putting the filled container into a car, be sure to secure it so that it won't tip over.

Calling for Help

If you had to call for a tow truck, there are things you can do while you wait: set up safety triangles behind your car, pop open the hood, and wait up on a hill, behind a metal guardrail, or, if in the city, wait on the sidewalk. *Never, never, never* get in a car with a stranger. If a stranger really wants to be helpful, have him or her bring back a container of gasoline to you.

If you belong to an auto service, don't just say that your car needs to be towed. Instead, request that some fuel be brought to you—but remember, some auto services provide this service and oth-

If your car is burning a lot of fuel, it could be a sign of a problem with the engine, fuel, or exhaust systems. Bring your car to a mechanic as soon as possible.

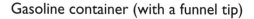

𝒯ool 𝒩eeded

Gasoline container (with a funnel tip)

GASOLINE
2½ GALLON
9½ LITER

ers do not. If a tow truck driver hands you a gasoline container, make sure that he stays until you fill the car with fuel and start the engine.

If the towing company is only allowed to tow you, request that the car be towed to a gas station instead of a repair shop. Once again, don't let the driver leave until you fill the car with fuel and start the engine.

Saving Fuel

Your car owner's manual says that you should be getting 18 miles to the gallon, but you find you're frequenting the gas station more than Starbucks! It's time for you to calculate the mileage yourself.

Calculating Actual Fuel Mileage
There are five easy steps to this task.

1. Fill up the gas tank.
2. Reset the trip odometer so that it reads all zeros.
3. The next time you go to the gas station (and it doesn't have to be when the tank is almost empty), fill up the tank and get the receipt. The receipt will tell you how many gallons you put into the tank.
4. Write on the receipt the miles on the trip odometer.
5. Divide the total mileage (driven between fill-ups) by the total gallons used and you have the answer to how many miles per gallon your car is getting.

Write this information and the date into the car owner's manual for future reference. After doing that hard math, you deserve a Frappuccino.

Tools Needed

Car owner's manual   Pen

Calculator, if necessary

Fuel-Saving Tips

We all know that the bigger the car, the bigger the bill at the pump. But did you know that driving conditions, tires, tire pressure, speed, and proper maintenance also play a major role in fuel consumption? Even having a luggage carrier on top of your car causes you to use more gas (the carrier creates wind resistance, or drag, which makes the car work a little harder while moving).

In these times of high fuel prices, every penny—oops, every *dollar*—counts. Therefore, learn and practice the following tips.

- Drive the speed limit.
- Don't warm up your car for more than 2 to 3 minutes in the winter and a minute in the summer—it just wastes fuel. A car's engine doesn't warm up until it's been on the road for 10 miles.
- Don't speed up to a red light or stop sign and don't put the pedal to the metal after the light changes to green. Quick starts and stops wreak havoc on your brakes and tires and waste fuel.
- Keep your tires properly inflated, rotated, and balanced, and have your wheels aligned.
- Change the air filter regularly.
- Follow the guidelines in the car owner's manual for regular maintenance checkups.
- Change the oil and replace the oil filter every 3,000 miles, or as recommended by the car manufacturer.
- If your car has a manual transmission, shift properly to avoid straining the gears and engine.
- Carpool.
- Get organized. Don't just run one errand at a time; instead, try to do several errands at once. You'll save both time and money by making your trip more efficient.
- Visit www.gasbuddy.com or AAA's www.fuelcostcalculator.com to find the cheapest gas in your area.
- Don't drive around with a trunk filled with items you don't need to keep there, such as lawn chairs, bags of mulch, athletic gear, and the like. The extra weight your car is carrying around causes it to use more fuel.

Oil

re you afraid to ask the gas station attendant where the dipstick is because you
know he'll be thinking that he's looking at
one? If so, help is on the way.

Changing oil requires you to go underneath your car, but we know that some of you would never, ever—and we'll throw in another *ever*—do that, not even if Denzel Washington was under there waiting for you. And that's okay. But even if you choose to pay someone to change the oil, you still need to know how to locate the dipstick, check the level of oil, add oil, and detect an oil spill. Here's why.

What It Is

Most people think that gasoline is the lifeblood of a car, but it's really the motor oil. Oil not only lubricates and cools the engine parts, thus reducing friction and wear, but it also helps to remove contaminants from the engine. And unlike gasoline, you can't just add oil to an empty oil pan and expect the car to start running again. Once the engine is damaged from driving without oil, or with oil that's never been changed, the engine cannot be resuscitated.

The average cost of a new engine: $5,000.

The cost of a quart of motor oil: $2.50.

The cost of being car smart: Priceless.

How It Works

We just gave you the reasons why oil is vital to your car; now here's a brief description of how it works. Oil is poured into the oil filler and then deposits into the oil pan. The oil pump forces the oil through the oil filter, which takes out impurities, and then into the engine, where it lubricates and cools all the moving metal parts. The oil then flows back into the oil pan.

DIY

Checking the Oil

Where and When

You need to check your car's oil once a week. Most drivers check the oil while they're pumping fuel, but it's actually better to wait until *after* the fuel tank is full so that the oil has time to flow back down to the oil pan.

The optimal time to check the oil is in the morning, when the engine and oil are cold and the oil is in the oil pan. To ensure an accurate reading, have the car parked on a level surface.

Oil Dipstick

An oil dipstick is a long thin piece of metal with a round pull handle at the top, and an end that sits in the oil pan. Its sole purpose is to measure the level of oil in the oil pan.

The oil dipstick's handle is usually painted a color, such as yellow or red, that makes it easier to locate. The dipstick will have words imprinted on it, such as FULL or ADD, or it will have crosshatch markings to indicate the level of oil.

The oil dipstick is typically found near the front of the engine near the side of the car—but be careful, because the transmission fluid dipstick can be easily confused with the oil dipstick. So if you're not 100 percent sure, refer to the car owner's manual for a diagram of the engine parts.

Note: Do not pour oil into where the dipstick rests. The only place to add oil is the oil filler hole. More on that later.

You've probably seen a gas station attendant remove the oil dipstick, wipe it off with a rag, and then put the dipstick back in, only to take it out again, and wondered why he didn't just read it the first time. There's a reason to this madness—you need to clean the dipstick first because hot oil can splash up on the dipstick, giving you an inaccurate reading.

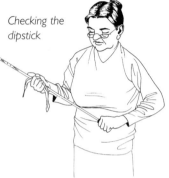

Checking the dipstick

Note: Never check the oil while the engine is on. If the engine is hot, be careful not to touch any part of the engine and use one rag to pull out the dipstick and another to wipe the oil off the end. Be careful, because the dipstick may be hot, too.

Open the hood of the car. Pull out the oil dipstick and wipe the end with a rag to remove the oil. Push it completely back in and pull it out again. Look to see where the oil has reached on the dipstick.

If the oil reaches the FULL mark, then you're good to go; but if it's at the ADD mark, then you need to add just enough oil to get it to the FULL mark or close to it. The difference between FULL and ADD is usually about one quart.

If the oil is at or below the crosshatch (the part closest to the end of the dipstick), you'll need to add at least one quart. If you're unsure, refer to the diagram of the dipstick in your car owner's manual to see how many quarts are needed. Never overfill your engine with oil because damage may occur.

If you don't see any oil on the dipstick, the engine may be two quarts low. If you're not sure, have your car serviced.

Tools Needed

Rags or paper towels

Types of Motor Oil

There's lots to tell you about motor oil, but we can hear you shouting *TMI, TMI!* So we'll just stick to the need-to-know items.

A quart of motor oil has numbers that depict the viscosity, or thickness, and rate of flow of oil at varying temperatures. Oil viscosity changes with temperature—in hot weather, the oil gets very thin, and in cold weather it gets very thick.

The car owner's manual may or may not tell you which brand of motor oil to buy for your vehicle, but it will tell you exactly what numbers to look for. We recommend that you only purchase name-brand motor oil and stick with it because different manufacturers add different detergents and additives.

You can purchase motor oil in auto supply stores and gas stations, as well as places you'd never expect, such as grocery stores, convenience stores, and even wholesale warehouses.

Adding Oil

Note: Never add oil with the engine on.

Now it's time to locate the oil filler, which is typically located at the front of the engine close to the side. Some cars will have the word OIL imprinted on the cap of the oil filler, some will have a picture of an oilcan, and others may not have anything.

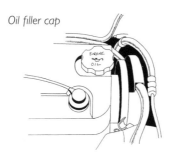

Oil filler cap

Don't bother opening up another quart of oil just so that the oil reaches the FULL mark. As long as it's in-between ADD and FULL, it's fine to drive your car.

Before you add oil, you need to understand the importance of not overfilling the oil pan. Too much oil may permit parts of the crankshaft to dip into the oil and churn air into it, causing foaming and oil pressure fluctuation.

Don't add oil without using a funnel or a paper cup, and not just for the obvious reason of avoiding spillage. Another advantage to this method: when you remove the cap from the oil container, a plastic ring is left on it (just like with a gallon milk container), which can fall right into the oil fill/oil pan. We know because this happened to a friend, who had to get the car towed and then pay a mechanic to remove the plastic ring from the engine.

Some gas stations have paper funnels available for use, but we suggest that you buy a funnel *and* keep it in your car. You can also use a paper cup with a hole punched in the bottom. Don't use a funnel that's been used for pouring other fluids such as transmission, brake, or steering, because you may contaminate the oil.

Pop open the hood of the car. Twist off the cap of the oil fill and put it in a safe spot. Place the funnel into the oil fill.

Remove the cap from the quart of oil and peel off the protective seal, or use a pen to punch a hole in it.

Pour the oil into the funnel, adding the amount recommended by the car owner's manual and the marking on the dipstick. *Remember, do not overfill.* Check the level by using the dipstick.

If you used a paper cup, throw it out. If you used a funnel, wipe it

clean with a rag or paper towel and place it inside a plastic bag. Write the word OIL on the bag so you won't confuse it with another funnel.

Changing the Oil and Replacing the Oil Filter

Every time the oil is changed and the oil filter is replaced, you're adding years to the life of your car, possibly doubling or tripling its life expectancy. Therefore, we can't stress enough the importance of changing the oil and oil filter regularly. What's regularly? Well, some experts say that it should be done every 3,000 miles or 3 months. Others say that's a bit excessive. We say that you can never hurt your car by changing the oil that often, but you should refer to the car manufacturer's recommendations, as well as take into account your driving habits.

Low Mileage

Don't assume that just because you only drive your car to church on Sundays that you can wait a year or more to change the oil. Actually, it's just the opposite. If your car isn't getting driven much, then the oil is sitting there unused, breaking down into sludge, and is not lubricating the parts as well as it should. Therefore, if you don't drive much, stick to the 3-month plan for changing the oil and replacing the oil filter.

Oil Warning Light

Cars have oil warning lights that come on when the engine oil pressure is too low, which means that there's not enough oil in the engine. If your oil pressure warning light comes on, pull over to safe spot and check the oil level.

Some cars also have lights that tell you when to change your oil (CHANGE OIL). The downside of an oil change sensor is that it bases its information on miles driven, not conditions, and not time. You could be driving on the streets of Manhattan, New York, or the streets of Manhattan, Kansas, or you could be driving 3,000 miles in 1 month or in 3 years. It also doesn't take into account your style of driving—whether you are a quick-start-and-stop person or a slow-lane-only kind of driver—or weather conditions.

Getting Ready

Before you begin the task, you need to use a flashlight and look under the car (on your back) to locate the oil filter and the oil plug. These parts can be located in the middle or on one of the sides in the front of the car, depending on the make and model. If they're located in the middle, you may have to lift the entire front of the car using a hydraulic jack along with jack stands.

If you have an SUV or lightweight truck and the oil filter and oil plug are on the side, you may not have to lift the car to reach these parts. It may just take you sliding your arm and part of your body under the side of the car.

Note: It's best to change the oil when the engine is warm or hot because the contaminants are suspended in the oil and are removed more easily. It is also important to note that oil filter wrenches come in different types, so refer to the car owner's manual for the correct oil filter and oil filter wrench for your car.

The car should be on level surface, in park (or neutral, if manual transmission), with the parking brake engaged and the engine off.

Remove the cap to the oil fill. There are two reasons for removing it now: (1) it acts as a reminder to add oil afterward (you can't believe how often even mechanics forget); and (2) it aids in quickening the flow of oil because the air acts to help push the oil down.

Tools Needed

New oil (most cars take 5 quarts; some take as much as 7)

New oil filter

Oil funnel

Oil filter wrench (cup-shaped)

Ratchet wrench (to use with oil filter wrench)

Socket wrench (to use with oil plug)

Work gloves

Old, long-sleeve shirt

Line up the tools next to the side of the car where the oil pan is located for easy access. If you have a friend helping you, she can hand you the tools as you need them. Put on the old shirt, the safety goggles, and the work gloves.

Using a Car Jack

A car jack is a device that lifts a vehicle off the ground. There are lots of different kinds of jacks— a bottle jack, which is usually the smallest of the three and looks like it doesn't have the power to lift the car, but does; a scissor jack, an X-shaped device; and a

Using a scissor jack

hydraulic jack. Your car probably came equipped either with a scissor jack or a bottle jack. A scissor jack is operated by rotating a metal hand crank, and a pumping bar is used on bottle and hydraulic jacks.

Note: Never put any part of your body, not even a hand, under a car that is only supported by a car jack.

The purpose of a car jack is to *temporarily* lift the car so that the jack stands can support the weight of the car. People are injured or killed by not following this important safety information.

When working under a car it's best to wear safety goggles and work gloves.

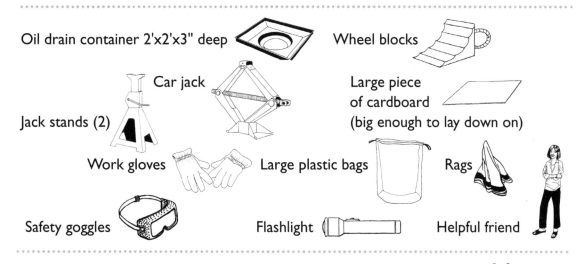

Oil drain container 2'x2'x3" deep

Wheel blocks

Car jack

Large piece of cardboard (big enough to lay down on)

Jack stands (2)

Work gloves

Large plastic bags

Rags

Safety goggles

Flashlight

Helpful friend

You'll need the car owner's manual to know where to place the jack. There are four lift points located underneath the frame of your vehicle, one near each tire. Some vehicles may have the word JACK imprinted at the lift sites. Putting the jack in the wrong spot can really damage your car; therefore, if your car doesn't have any markings, we recommend that you put a piece of duct tape on all four locations so you'll never have to wonder again.

Now that you know where the oil filter and oil plug are located, place the jack under the lift site on the same side. Use the jack to raise the car high enough to get a jack stand underneath the car. Once the jack stand is in place, remove the car jack. Place the wood blocks behind the two rear tires to keep the car from rolling backward.

Note: If the oil filter and oil plug are located in the middle, you'll need to use a hydraulic jack on both sides of the car and place the jack stands underneath, one on each side of the car.

If the car is not stable or is moving, try jacking it up again, or if you're feeling uncomfortable, then stop. Nothing is worth your safety.

Draining the Oil

Note: So that you don't get confused, the oil pan is a part of the car and the oil drain container is what you place underneath the oil pan to catch the oil that's being emptied.

Never start a car if the oil has been drained.

Push the oil drain container under the oil pan. Now push the cardboard under the car below the hood and shimmy onto it.

Feel for the drain plug on the side of the oil pan. (Be careful that you're not touch-

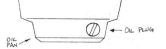

Placing the oil drain container under the oil pan

ing the transmission plug instead of the oil plug. They're pretty close, so just remember that the transmission plug is larger than the oil plug.)

Use a socket wrench to loosen the drain plug, turning it counterclockwise. Once you've gotten it loose, you can untwist it completely with your fingers. Be careful because the oil will shoot out, especially if it is more hot than cold. Wipe off the drain plug with a rag and put it in a safe place.

Depending on the amount of oil, it may take anywhere from 5 to 10 minutes to drain. So come back out and wipe off the drain plug and drain plug gasket and check them for wear and tear. If the threads on the plug look worn or bent, and/or the gasket is cracked, you'll need to replace them.

Attaching the oil filter wrench onto the oil filter

Get back onto the cardboard and push the oil filter wrench onto the oil filter. Attach the ratchet to the oil filter wrench and turn it counterclockwise to loosen. Don't remove the oil filter yet because there's oil in it. To prevent a big mess, just let it drain a bit.

If this is your first time changing the oil and oil filter in your car and you're feeling nervous, ask a friend to help.

Removing and Installing the Filter

Carefully remove the oil filter and pour it into the oil drain container. Let it sit there for a bit until all the oil is drained. For environmental reasons, never throw out an oil filter until it is completely drained. Place the oil filter into a plastic bag.

Before installing the new oil filter, make sure that the seal from the original filter is not stuck on the surface where it attaches. If it's there, you need to peel it off with your fingers, because the two seals won't adhere and you'll have leakage. Another thing you should do is to take a rag and wipe around the inside of the engine oil filter seat.

Adding Oil

Open one of the new quarts of oil and rub a little of it onto the new seal of the filter (this provides a better fit). Insert the new filter into place and hand-tighten it. Place the oil filter wrench onto the oil filter and tighten using the ratchet. You don't want to overtighten the filter, so the rule of thumb is give it ⅔ to 1 full turn after you've hand-tightened it. Use the label on the oil filter as a reference point for the correct position after tightening.

Twist on the drain plug and tighten by hand. Then use the socket wrench to tighten, *but not too tight.*

You can remove the oil drain container, but leave the cardboard for a little bit longer.

Now it's time to add the oil. Insert the funnel into the oil filler and pour in 1 quart of oil at a time. Remember, it's very important not to overfill. Place the oil cap back on and hand-tighten.

Use the car jack to lift the car up a bit so that you can remove the jack stand and lower the car. If you had to use both jack stands, follow this step on one side, and then repeat on the other side. Remove both wheel blocks.

Let the oil work its way down into the oil pan—it should take about 5 minutes. Remove the dipstick and check the oil level. Turn the engine on, letting it run for a minute or two to let the oil heat up. Turn the engine off and check to see if any oil has spilled onto the cardboard. If you see any leaks, you may need to check that the drain plug and oil filter are on properly.

Refer to the car owner's manual to learn how to reset the oil change light.

Proper Disposal

Stand on the cardboard and have your friend hold the water container while you slowly pour the oil into it. Repeat until you've emptied the oil drain pan.

Proper disposal of the used oil will require you to contact your state EPA or your local recycling center.

Tools Needed

Empty plastic 1-gallon containers   Helpful friend

Power Steering Fluid

*I*f you want to get rid of that unsightly arm flab, just start driving your grandmother's car. You know, the one that doesn't have power steering. And you thought she was doing Pilates!

Anyone who is too young to remember driving a car without power steering can't truly appreciate the wonder of it. All cars now come equipped with it, so the only way to understand what we're talking about is if you drive your car when it has run out of power steering fluid. That's when your upper-body strength is truly put to the test.

What It Is

Power steering fluid (under pressure) transmits power to the steering system. A low level of power steering fluid can cause excessive (whining) noise, difficulty in maneuvering the steering wheel, and increased wear on parts.

Another sign of a power steering problem is that the steering wheel will be difficult to move. This is typically due to a loss of power steering fluid.

DIY

Checking the Fluid

The power steering fluid reservoir is typically located near the front of the engine on the driver's side. Look for a cap that either says POWER STEERING or has a picture of a steering wheel on it. If in doubt, refer to the owner's manual.

Power steering fluid can be checked when the engine is hot or cold, but a warm engine provides a more accurate reading. So, go run an errand to warm up the engine, or let the engine idle for a few minutes (outside, of course) and turn the steering wheel to the left and right a few times while

Power steering fluid reservoir

the engine is running (with the parking brake engaged).

With the car parked on a level surface, turn the engine off, engage the parking brake, and pop open the hood. Wearing the safety goggles and gloves, remove the reservoir cap by turning it counter-clockwise. Don't put the cap down because the dipstick is usually attached to the cap.

Dab some of the fluid from the dipstick onto the paper towel and look for any metal particles. If the fluid, which is typically clear or red, looks silver or gray, that's a sign that there's too much wear and tear on the system, and it will need to be checked and flushed by a qualified technician.

The dipstick will have a hot reading on one side and a cold reading on the other. Because the engine is warm, look at the hot reading and see if the fluid is at the FULL or ADD (or MIN or MAX) mark. (If the engine is cold, refer to the cold reading side of the dipstick). The difference between the two is usually a pint. If you don't need to add fluid, replace the reservoir cap, turning it clockwise to tighten. If you need to add fluid, place the reservoir cap in a safe place so that it won't roll under the car.

Tool Needed

White paper towel

Adding the Fluid

Before purchasing power steering fluid, be sure to refer to the car owner's manual for the type recommended by the car manufacturer. This fluid is typically sold in pints, but you will usually only need to add a few ounces.

Remove the cap and seal from the power steering fluid container. Place the funnel into the reservoir and add enough fluid to bring the level between the ADD and FULL (or MIN MAX) marks. Be very careful not to overfill.

Replace the cap and then remove it to check the level on the dipstick. Add more fluid if necessary. Put the reservoir cap back on, turning it clockwise to tighten.

Wipe the funnel with a paper towel and place it inside a plastic bag marked "Power Steering."

Recycling or Storing

If you have power steering fluid left over, place the cap back on tightly and either properly store it inside the garage (see "Safely Storing Items," page 317) or check with your local recycling center or state EPA to see if it is recyclable.

Power steering fluid, just like all other fluids, breaks down over time. Therefore, it's important to have the entire system flushed and drained every other year or according to the car owner's manual.

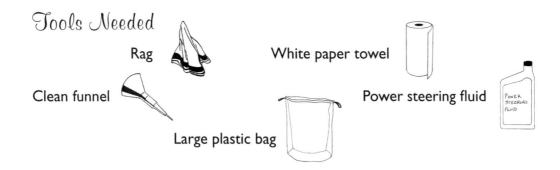

Tools Needed

Rag

White paper towel

Clean funnel

Power steering fluid

Large plastic bag

Transmission Fluid

*C*an't get it into gear? Feel like you're a quart low? These may be car metaphors for how we're feeling—but for a car, one is actually the solution for the other.

You're having a difficult time shifting gears and you immediately think the worst: your car's transmission is dying. Don't think doom and gloom just yet. Typically, the problem is just that your car is low on transmission fluid. Phew!

What It Is

As you know, your car either has an automatic or a manual transmission. And just as the transmissions are different, so are their fluids, as well as the way you service them. Both fluids work to lubricate the transmission; therefore, it's vital to maintain the proper level of transmission fluid, because if there's not enough fluid, the transmission will slip and burn, requiring you to have it rebuilt or buy a new one.

It's also equally important to use the proper transmission fluid for your car because using the wrong type can change how your car runs. Therefore, before purchasing transmission fluid, refer to the car owner's manual for capacity, fluid type, and service intervals.

Automatic Transmission Fluid

Checking the transmission fluid in an automatic transmission is a little bit like checking the oil—both sytems have dipsticks that are located under the hood of the car. But that's where the similarities end. To check the automatic transmission fluid, the engine needs to be warm and running, and the fluid is added into the same container that houses the dipstick.

Manual Transmission Fluid

Checking the manual transmission fluid is difficult because there's no dipstick and the reservoir is located under the car, not the hood. Not only does it require you to have the car jacked up, but you also need to have the car as level as possible, and the engine *off*. You also have to remove a plug, which requires using tools.

Because of the complexity involved in checking manual transmission fluid, we recommend that you have it serviced by a certified mechanic. Therefore, we're only providing instructions for checking and adding automatic transmission fluid.

Automatic Transmission Fluid

Because the transmission system is a sealed system, if you're regularly low on transmission fluid, then there's a leak and you need to get it fixed immediately.

Checking Fluid Level

In order to get an accurate reading of the transmission fluid, the car must be parked on level ground and the engine must be warm. For the engine to be warm, you need to have driven about 10 miles. If the engine is really hot because you were towing a trailer, or you were driving at a high speed, let the engine sit for about 30 minutes before checking the fluid.

With the engine running and the parking brake engaged, move the gear selector to each position (PARK, REVERSE, NEUTRAL, DRIVE, 3, 2, 1, or as equipped), waiting about 3 seconds in between each gear change. Return to PARK and keep the engine running.

Note: Some car manufacturers require that the vehicle be placed in neutral to test the level of fluid. You can find this information in the car owner's manual, or sometimes it is noted on the transmission dipstick.

Pop open the hood and locate the transmission fluid cap. It should be located at the back of the engine and will probably have the label TRANS FLUID on it. If in doubt, consult the car owner's manual.

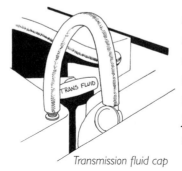
Transmission fluid cap

Note: The engine is running, which means that parts are moving, so it's critical to your safety that if you have long hair you put it up, and that you remove any scarves, loose clothing, or jewelry that may get entangled in a moving part.

The transmission fluid cap may be warm or hot to the touch, so you'll want to use a rag to remove it. Pull out the dipstick and wipe it clean with the lint-free rag. Note the color and odor of the fluid, referring to the information below. Push the dipstick completely into its tube, wait 3 seconds, and remove it again. Look at the markings on both sides of the dipstick (on some cars, one side is for a hot reading and the other is for a cold reading) and read the lower level. The optimal mark is when the fluid is in the crosshatched or "hot" area. If it's in the FILL area, you need to add transmission fluid immediately. The difference between a low fluid level and an acceptable level is typically one pint of fluid.

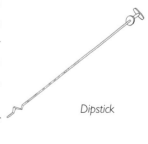
Dipstick

If the fluid level is fine on the dipstick, push the dipstick completely into its tube. Turn the engine off.

ome cars with automatic transmissions do not have a dipstick, such as certain Volkswagen, and BMW models.

Tools Needed

Lint-free rag(s)   Car owner's manual

Adding Fluid

Transmission fluid is sold in quarts, but you'll probably never need to add the entire quart. In fact, you'll probably only need to add a pint or less.

Typically, a car can hold from 6 to 12 quarts of transmission fluid; pickup trucks and SUVs can hold up to 16 quarts. The transmission needs only to be 1 pint low for it to start exhibiting problems.

Note: It is critical not to overfill the reservoir with transmission fluid because if its level is too high it will get into the rotating parts of the transmission and possibly cause problems in the transmission's pump assembly.

Use the rag to remove the transmission dipstick and place it on the rag.

Insert the funnel into the tube that houses the dipstick. Remove the top of the automatic transmission fluid container.

Slowly pour the fluid into the funnel. Remember that you'll probably only need a pint and that you don't want to overfill the reservoir. Insert the dipstick completely inside its tube.

Wipe the funnel with a paper towel and place it inside a plastic bag marked "Transmission."

Recycling or Storing

If you have transmission fluid left inside the container, you can choose to store it or recycle it. Some recycling centers take transmission fluid if it's unused and in its original container.

Adding transmission fluid

> **U**se lint-free rags when working with transmission fluid because you don't want any particles getting into the transmission.

Tools Needed

Long-neck funnel (clean)

Paper Towels

Automatic transmission fluid

Large plastic bag

Lint-free rag

Common Problems (Automatic and Manual)

No matter which type of transmission your car has, they both exhibit similar signs of problems, such as a change in the color or odor of the transmission fluid, leaks, and a hesitation in gear shifting called "slipping." Any of these problems can cause major damage if not treated timely.

Change in Color

When first poured out of its container, transmission fluid has a strong sweet petroleum scent and is pink, but it doesn't stay that color for very long. As soon as you ride around in your car and the fluid has had a chance to lubricate the transmission, the fluid will turn from pink to dark red. Red is good. Here are some colors that are not:

- *Reddish brown.* This indicates that the transmission fluid needs to be flushed.
- *Brown.* This means that you haven't been maintaining the transmission fluid and you need to have the transmission fluid flushed and the transmission serviced before it's too late.
- *Black.* This is not good. You're looking at replacing the transmission.
- *Milky brown or pink.* This signifies that there's coolant or water inside the transmission and the transmission will need to be rebuilt. There is no way to reverse the damage with a fluid change or flush. In addition, you may need to have the radiator replaced.

Remove the dipstick as described above and dip the edge of the paper towel into the spillage and observe the color of the transmission fluid. Refer to the above list of colors and causes.

Tool Needed
White paper towel

Checking for Leaks

A leak is typically caused by a faulty gasket in the transmission. If you notice red fluid on the driveway under the front of your car, it's probably transmission fluid (but it could also be power steering fluid). First, check the fluid level and add if necessary. Next, call for an appointment to get your car into a repair shop as soon as possible. If the level is really low (as in there's no fluid on the dipstick) you shouldn't drive it at all. Instead, call to have it towed to a repair shop.

DIFM

Having the Fluid Flushed

No matter if your car has an automatic or manual transmission, the transmission fluid needs to be maintained as outlined in the car owner's manual. In fact, some manufacturers use 100,000-mile transmission fluid in new cars. Depending on the make and model of your car and your driving conditions, you should have the transmission screen/filter replaced or cleaned when the fluid is flushed. The only way to know how often is to refer to the car owner's manual.

Flushing the fluid out of the transmission is really important because it's the only way for all of the fluid to be almost completely changed. When the transmission fluid is drained, just ⅓ of the fluid is actually removed because the rest of it is dispersed throughout the transmission. But if you have it flushed, you're getting rid of over 90 percent of the old fluid.

If a mechanic finds metal debris in the transmission fluid or the car won't shift into different gears, the transmission needs to be serviced immediately.

Windshield Washer Fluid

n a clear day, you can see forever." **But is your windshield singing a different tune? If so, here's an easy** *solution.*

What It Is

Windshield washer fluid is used to clean dirt and debris from the windshield. Some vehicles have a wiper system for the rear window, too, which also uses windshield washer. No matter if you have 1 or 2 wiper systems, there's only 1 windshield washer reservoir.

The reservoir is a plastic container that is typically located in the front of the engine compartment. If you can't find it, look for a container with a washer symbol on it, or refer to the car owner's manual.

What to Buy

Windshield washer fluid comes in a regular formula, a concentrated form, and a deicer. If you use the standard fluid, never mix it with water because you may cause the mixture to freeze. If you choose to use the concentrate, follow the manufacturer's instructions for adding water. And if you live in an area where the temperature frequently drops below 32°F, purchase deicer, a winter formula, which has an additive that keeps it from freezing in temperatures as low as −34°F. (But if you're living in that kind of weather, you probably own a dogsled, not a car.)

Washer fluid can be purchased at auto supply stores, gas stations, and even in grocery stores.

DIY

Filling the Washer Fluid Reservoir

Pop open the hood of the car and find the washer fluid reservoir. Be careful not to confuse the washer reservoir with the engine coolant reservoir, which can be located near it.

Sometimes you can see the amount of fluid in the reservoir because its blue liquid is visible through the plastic (if you see green or orange, then you're looking at the coolant reservoir). If the fluid level is low, open the lid and place a clean funnel inside. Pour the washer fluid into the funnel, making sure not to overfill it. If the outdoor tempera-

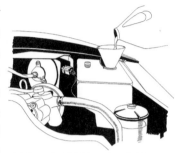

Adding windshield washer fluid

ture is very cold, only fill up the reservoir ¾ of the way so that there's room for the fluid to expand.

Remove the funnel and replace the lid on the reservoir.

Never use water instead of windshield washer fluid because it can freeze and crack the reservoir.

Tools Needed

Clean funnel or paper cup

Windshield washer fluid

Cleaning Up Leaks

We've all heard that you shouldn't cry over spilled milk. Well, there's no need to shed a tear over a fluid spill on your driveway, either. We have a simple solution to this problem, so save your hankies for a good chick flick instead.

You probably already know that cat litter is great for providing traction for your tires if there's snow or ice on the ground. But what you might not know is how effective it is at removing fluid spills from the floor of your garage or driveway.

Note: Cat litter will not work effectively on removing a coolant spill or stain because the litter will turn to mud. Therefore, use an oil absorbent for this type of spill instead.

Spreading cat litter

Removing a Spill

Generously spread enough cat litter or oil absorbent over the spill and pat it down with your foot. Let it sit for a few minutes—this will depend on the size and amount of

Tools Needed

Broom

Dust pan

Clay-based cat litter or oil absorbent

the spill, of course. Sweep up the absorbent or cat litter and remember to dispose of it according to your state's EPA requirements.

Removing a Stain

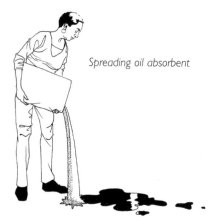
Spreading oil absorbent

The best way to remove a transmission fluid stain from your driveway or garage is to use a degreaser—but you need to act quickly. The longer you let it sit, the more time it has to seep deeper into the asphalt or concrete.

First, cover the stain with the degreaser. Next, pour the cat litter or oil absorbent over the stain (about ¼ inch deep) and pat it down with your foot. Let it sit for about 24 hours so that it will absorb the degreaser and the stain. Sweep it up, and remember to dispose of it according to your state's EPA requirements.

Tools Needed

Biodegradable degreaser (Simple Green or Spray 9)

Clay-based cat litter or oil absorbent

Broom

Dustpan

Changing an Engine Air Filter

id you know that every car has a dirty little secret? It's an air filter, and it's time to come clean and deal with it.

What It Is

Every car has an engine air filter, which is typically located between the front grill and the engine (for older cars, it's located on top of the carburetor). Depending on the type of car, the filter can be flat, like the air filter in your home's furnace, or round, like an old slide carousel (okay, we just dated ourselves).

What It Does

An engine air filter is very similar to the air filter in your home's furnace, in that its job is to filter out dirt and dust from the air so that it doesn't enter the engine (or furnace, for a home). An engine air filter also helps to keep any flames, which may occur from an engine backfiring, away from the engine or causing you burns.

Just like your home's air filter, you need to regularly maintain it. The difference is that for a furnace you can clean *or* replace the filter, but for a car you *have* to replace the filter.

It's important to change the engine air filter regularly because a dirty air filter allows particles to enter the engine, causing possible damage. It's also important to do because a clean air filter allows the engine to run more efficiently, which is good for your wallet and the environment.

How will you know when you need to replace the engine air filter? The frequency can vary from every time you change your oil to once a year to once every 150,000 miles, depending on the air filter, your car, and your driving conditions. Therefore you should refer to the car owner's manual for the manufacturer's suggestion. Some vehicles have an indicator on the air filter's housing that signals when the filter needs to be replaced. Or you can simply remove the filter, hold it up to the sun, and look to see if it's clogged. Of course, when in doubt, it's always best to err on the side of changing it.

DIY

This may be the easiest repair to do on your car, and it may be the most cost-effective, too. Typically the cost of an air filter is around $20, and you won't need more than 10 minutes to replace it.

Place the car in park (if automatic) or neutral (if manual), turn off the engine, engage the parking brake, and let the engine cool. Pop open the hood of the car and locate the engine air filter (refer to the car owner's manual if necessary).

Remove the fasteners (e.g., screws, clips, or wing nuts) that secure the cover to the housing of the air filter, and lift or remove the cover. Pull out the air filter, deposit it into the bag, and dispose of it properly.

Note: Never, never, never start the car's engine without the engine air filter in place. You may get burned if the engine backfires.

Now that the old filter is out, use the rag to clean the interior of the housing. Insert the new filter and replace the cover and fasteners.

Note: If the air filter is not inserted correctly or the cover is not replaced properly, the engine warning light may be triggered, resulting in a $75 charge to have it reset. Remove the cover and the filter, and check that the filter is the correct size before inserting it again.

Tools Needed

New air filter   Phillips screwdriver, if necessary

Rag   Car owner's manual   Large plastic or paper bag

Tires and Wheels

Introduction

The wheels on the bus go round and round . . . but so do tires! A lot of people unknowingly interchange the word "tire" for "wheel," and vice versa, but they're actually two different things. Tires are made of rubber and are secured to the wheel by a tire bead. Wheels, which are made of aluminum, steel, or an alloy, attach to the car with lug nuts. If you're still confused, just remember that no one ever said they had a flat *wheel*! (The exception to this is when we discuss changing a flat tire. Here, the two terms will be used interchangeably, because even though you're actually changing the wheel, everyone describes it as changing a flat tire.)

We won't *tread* lightly in this section. In fact, we're going to teach you how to inflate a flat tire and change one, as well as how to buy new tires and properly maintain them. So enough of this *idle* chat; let's burn some rubber, baby!

Buying Tires

"Tires for $200, please."

It smells of rubber, the television is always on the wrong channel, and there's 1 *People* magazine for every 6 *Popular Mechanics*.

"What is . . . the waiting area of a tire store?"

Maybe a better game show question would be "Where won't you find an aromatherapy candle?"

Our friends waiting in the tire shop

Well, we have good news and bad news for you about this section. The good news is that you'll learn how to choose the right tire for your car and probably save money, too. The bad news is that we can't get you out of the waiting area any faster.

Tires are the only parts of the car that touch the ground; therefore, your safety is truly riding on them. Which means that when it's time to buy new tires, be pound smart, not penny foolish (*take that, Ben!*).

No one wants to buy new tires because it always seems like they just did, and they're so darn expensive, right? But let's put this all into perspective, shall we? Tires range in price anywhere from $11 to $500 per tire, with the average customer paying about $80 for each. Tires, with proper maintenance, have a tread life of about 40,000 to 80,000 miles. A haircut with highlights is about $150 without tip, and it only lasts about 3 months (*at least that's what we've been told*).

So think of buying tires as investing in your safety. And you can't put a price on that, can you? But before we tell you how to buy tires, we need to tell you what you're buying.

Types of Tires

Tires are classified by their internal and external construction.

Internal Construction
Radial refers to the internal construction of the tire. Radial tires have belt plies that are laid diagonally under the tread to stabilize the tread and reinforce the tread area. The majority of tires are radial.

External Construction
There are three categories: (1) all-season performance; (2) high-performance; and (3) winter/snow. The main differences between these are tread, stiffness in sidewall, speed ratings, cost, and noise level while driving.

All-Season Performance Tire (Mass Market)
The all-season performance tire is the most basic and the least expensive of the three categories of tires. It uses a combination of treads: one for highway use (straight ribs) and one for snow use (arranged blocks). This means that it is designed for acceptable traction for winter snow and slush driving conditions, without excessively compromising dry and wet traction.

High-Performance Tires
If you want to feel the road, this is the tire for you. High-performance tires have stiff sidewalls and high traction, which means that the

emphasis is on gripping the road and not on getting the most mileage from the tires, or comfort.

Winter/Snow Tires

Winter/snow tires are different from other tires because they have little grooves cut into the treads, called sipes, which allow for better handling on snow and ice. These tires, which may be marked with a mountain snowflake symbol on the sidewall, are more expensive than regular tires. To provide the best vehicle mobility and control, install the winter/snow tires on all four wheels.

Studded winter/snow tires have metal studs imbedded in them, which provide even better grip on icy roads. Never have used tires fitted with studs, even if the tires are relatively new. To provide the best vehicle mobility and control, install studded winter/snow tires on all four wheels.

Studded winter/snow tires are harder on pavement than regular tires, and therefore cause more wear and tear on the roads. So before you have studded winter/snow tires mounted, check with your local police department or your state's Department of Motor Vehicles (DMV) to find out if there are driving restrictions.

When Do You Need New Tires?

No matter which type of tires you use, they'll probably need to be replaced sooner than you'd like. Most tires last about 2 years.

Telltale Signs of Tire Wear

How do you know if a tire needs to be replaced? There are telltale signs to look for, and you can perform a simple tread test (see "Testing the Tire's Tread," page 116) as well.

The best way to start checking your tires is by making it a habit. In the mornings, take the long way around your car to the driver's side and look at all four tires to see if there is a flat or if a tire is low. And when you check the air pressure in your tires every week, also look for any problems on the treads and sidewalls.

Sidewall

Be aware of any blisters, cuts, tears, or bumps in the sidewall, which can be caused from contact with foreign objects, such as hitting a curb or a pothole you didn't know existed, or from improper mounting. Any of these deformities may cause a tire to have a blowout or a flat.

Tire Treads

The tread of a tire is like the tread of your sneaker—it's the first part that hits the pavement. The tire tread looks so sturdy and rock-solid that it seems there's no way it could ever wear out, but it does. You need to check the 3 sections of the tread (both sides and near the center) for uneven wear, bald spots, bubbles, and nails or other foreign objects stuck in it.

If the tread shows uneven wear, the cause could be that the tires are not properly inflated, that they haven't been rotated or balanced, that the suspension is off a bit, or that the wheels were not properly aligned. Be sure to talk to the serviceperson about checking the suspension and aligning the wheels while the new tires are being mounted.

Note: If you discover that a tire is losing air, it must be removed from the wheel by a qualified technician for a complete internal inspection.

Testing the Tire's Tread

There are two ways to test the tread of a tire. The first is to look for the treadwear indicator bars located every so often on the treads of the tires. When the tread is worn down to the same height as the bar, which is $\frac{2}{32}$ inch, then by law the tire must be replaced.

Note: Tire tread depths are measured in $\frac{1}{32}$-inch increments.

The other way to test the tread is by measuring its depth. To measure the tread depth, you can purchase a tread gauge, but we suggest using some plain "cents"—actually, just one penny.

Take a penny and turn it upside down so that Abraham Lincoln's head is facing the ground. Put the penny into groove of the tread with Abe's head going in first.

If any part of Abe's head is covered by the tread, then the tire's tread is good. If you can see all of Abe's head, then the tread is too low and you will need to have the tire replaced.

Checking the tire's tread

Don't just check the tread on one tire or in one tread location. Be sure to check all the tires, including the spare, in various spots (of course, you'll only need to check the tread on the spare if it's been used).

One, Two, Three, or Four?

Question: If you have a flat or a very worn tire that needs to be replaced, but the other tires are fine, can you just replace the one or do you always have to replace tires in pairs?

The rule of thumb is that you should never replace just one tire because it could have a negative effect on the car's suspension and transmission systems, as well as the tires' treadwear. If it can't be avoided, then pair the new tire with the tire with the deepest tread on the rear axle. If you're replacing 2 tires, have them installed on the rear axle. Of course, before doing anything, you need to refer to the car owner's manual.

If you have an all-wheel-drive car and you need to have a tire replaced, you may be in for quite a shock when the tire technician tells you that your car's manufacturer requires that all four tires be replaced or the warranty will be nullified. Refer to the car owner's manual for more information.

When you're visiting your parents, perform the penny test on the tires of their cars to make sure that their tires are safe!

Tool Needed

Penny (American, use Abe's head)

Doing Your Homework

You can test-drive a car, but you can't test-drive tires, so how do you know which tire will work best for your car? There are actually a lot of things that need to be factored into the decision-making process, but luckily it's all been done for you. You just need to know where to look and how to decipher the information.

Car Owner's Manual

Always refer to the car owner's manual before buying tires because it will state the car manufacturer's recommendations and restrictions for replacement tires, such as tire size, inflation pressure, load-carrying capacity, and tire maintenance schedule.

Sidewall Information

You've heard the saying "The writing's on the wall"? Well, for tires, the writing is actually on the wall ... the sidewall. The sidewall of a tire has a lot of information on it, called the Uniform Tire Quality Grading System (UTQGS). It consists of the tire manufacturer's name, the tire's brand name, the tire size, the tire

Sidewall information

identification number, and the grades for tire treadwear, traction, and temperature.

Here's an example of a UTQGS decoded for a typical passenger tire P215/65R15.

- The first letter will either be a "P," for p-metric or passenger vehicle, or "LT," for light truck or SUV.
- The first set of numbers (215) represents the width of the tire, measured in millimeters from sidewall to sidewall. In general, the larger the number, the larger the tire.
- The next two digits (65) represent the ratio of the tire's

height to its width; therefore, the height of the tire is 65 percent of it's width.

- The next letter stands for the construction of the tire. "R" stands for radial.
- The next two numbers (15) indicate the wheel or rim diameter in inches.
- If there is an additional number, it is for the speed rating.

Wasn't that fun?

Treadwear Grade

The treadwear grades are an indication of a tire's relative wear rate. There is a "control tire" that is given a treadwear grade of 100. All tires are compared to that control tire and are given a grade. For example, if a tire has a treadwear grade of 200, that means the tire should wear twice as long as the control tire. Therefore, the higher the number, the better the tirewear rate.

Traction Grade

The traction grades are an indication of a tire's ability to stop on wet pavement. A higher-graded tire should allow a car to stop in a shorter distance on wet roads than a tire with a lower grade. The highest grade is AA and the lowest is C.

Temperature Grade

Temperature grades are an indication of a tire's resistance to heat. The highest grade is A and the lowest is C.

Age

Look for the letters DOT and the numbers next to it. The numbers will tell you the week and the year the tires were made. Here's some examples: DOT169 means that the tire was manufactured during the 16th week of 1999. DOT705 means that the tire was manufactured during the 7th week of 2005. This information is particularly important if you are purchasing tires from a used-tire store.

Maximum Inflation Pressure

This is probably the number one mistake people make with their tires. They assume that the pounds per square inch (psi) number listed on the sidewall is the correct psi for their vehicle's tires, and so they keep their tires at that level. The maximum inflation pressure imprinted on the sidewall is the maximum pressure at which the tire will run safely at normal operating temperature, not its *optimal* tire pressure. For normal operation, follow the inflation pressure recommendations found either on the vehicle tire information placard or in the car owner's manual.

Brands

Okay, so now you know the specs of the tires you need, and you know that they only come in one color (hee-hee), so the last decision to make is the manufacturer. Some of the top-selling brands are Firestone, Goodyear, Dunlop, Bridgestone, BFGoodrich, Michelin, Uniroyal, Pirelli, Yokohoma, Kumho, and tires sold under the Sears name. There are also generic brands, which can cost as little as $11 per tire. We recommend that you only purchase a well-known brand because of quality control, warranties, and recall alerts.

Before buying a tire, refer to (and follow) the car manufacturer's replacement tire restrictions, recommendations, and warranty compliance. Don't rely on a friend's or family member's suggestion for a particular brand of tire because everyone has a different style of driving—quick-start-and-stop driver, likes-to-feel-the-road vs. quiet-ride driver. Also, a tire may perform well on one vehicle but not on another. Therefore, it's better to stick with your own experience, as well as rely on any research you've done.

Tires for a Used Car

If you're not the original owner of the car, and you need to buy new tires, don't assume that the ones on the car are the correct type. The previous owner may have put on tires that were wrong for the car and/or may have put on cheaper tires and kept the original ones for herself.

So if you're driving a previously owned vehicle, and therefore can't rely on the sidewall information, where do you turn? You know that we'd normally say "the car owner's manual," but unfortunately not all manuals will give you the specifics. The best place to look is on the vehicle information placard, located either on the doorjamb, the glove box door, or the fuel tank filler door. The placard lists the recommended cold inflation pressures for the tires (including the spare) and tire size. (Some placards even state the vehicle's seating capacity and its combined weight with occupants and cargo.)

If you have any questions, contact your local dealership with the VIN of your car and ask for the correct specs for new tires. Or go to a tire center and ask to see a reference book in which customers can find the manufacturer's suggested tires. Write down the information in the car owner's manual so you'll always have it handy.

Where Can You Purchase Tires?

A tire store will offer the widest choice of brands and sales; discount clubs (like Costco) offer fewer brand choices, but the prices are usually lower and constant; car dealerships can be expensive; and buying online may be cheap, but the hassle of trying to locate a mechanic who will mount the tires and then schlepping the tires to his shop may not be worth it.

If you can only afford to buy from a used-tire store, be sure to test the tread on the tire, as well as to check the date it was manufactured. Some of the used tires are actually spare tires that may have good treadwear, but they also may be quite old. Any tire that is 6 years or older is not worth buying for safety reasons.

Warranties

Some vehicle manufacturers warranty tires that are sold with new cars as well as replacement tires sold through some car dealerships. And some tire dealers provide a warranty (a.k.a. tire protection plan) if there is a problem with a tire that's not for general use—such as for trailers, RVs, and so on—and offer a warranty that will cover tire cuts and sidewall damage, flat repairs, lifetime wheel balancing, and tire rotation. So, before buying tires, shop around for the best price and warranty package.

If you live in an area with a lot of home or road construction and/or rural roads, consider purchasing a warranty for your tires.

Some warranties are prorated according to tread depth. Therefore, if there's a problem early in the life of the tire, the warranty may cover it.

When you purchase new tires, ask for the manufacturer's registration card. It's worth filling out because in case of a recall of the tires, the manufacturer will be able to contact you.

But wait, there's more!

Additional Costs

So you've found the right tires for your car and the price is reasonable. But before you pay, you need to ask about the extra cost of mounting, balancing, valves, stems, and aligning—and if you're just replacing one or two tires, then you also need to figure in the cost of rotation. Plus, there's normally a fee for used-tire disposal and possibly a state environmental fee. Ask the mechanic to add up all the line items and see if it's still affordable. If not, you may need to choose a comparable tire at a lower price. Just be aware that lower-priced tires can equate to handling and noise issues.

Tire Maintenance

Maintaining your car's tires is vital to your safety on the road. And we're not *inflating* its importance one bit.

Maintaining a Tire's Air Pressure

What if we told you that there is one simple thing you could do to increase your car's gas mileage, help the environment, prevent accidents, and extend the life of your tires—and it only takes about 10 minutes to do? Curious? It's keeping your tires properly inflated. This is probably the quickest and easiest maintenance you can do on your car, but would you believe that most people don't have properly inflated tires?

Notice we used the term "properly inflated"—that's because both under- and overinflated tires can be hazardous. Underinflated tires wear out more quickly, negatively affect the way the car handles, and increase fuel consumption. If your tires squeal when you turn a corner, it could be a sign of underinflated tires. Overinflated tires create a harsher ride, bad handling, and can be damaged easily from potholes. With all the benefits of keeping your tires properly inflated, it's just a no-brainer to do this weekly and absolutely before any long trips.

PSI

How do you know how much air your tires need? The unit of measurement for air in tires is psi (pounds per square inch). Okay, that's as scientific as we're going to get. Most passenger car tires have anywhere from 26 to 42 psi. To find out the psi for your tires, look for the vehicle's certification tire label located inside the driver's doorjamb, glove compartment, or fuel filler door, or you may find more information in the owner's manual. You may think that the information is on the sidewall of the tire, but the psi listed on the tire is the maximum pressure. An easier way to understand this is that the tire is designed to fit a vehicle and the psi is what carries the load.

Vehicle's certification tire label

For some cars, the psi for the front tires may be different than the psi for the back tires. Refer to the car owner's manual for correct inflation pressures.

Another important thing to know about the psi rating is that it is based only on a "cold" reading. *Huh?* Okay, a little more science. Driving your car causes the air in the tire to heat up and expand. Therefore, if you test the air in your tires after you've been driving around, you will get a higher psi reading than if the tires were cold. That's part of the reason why so many people drive around with underinflated tires.

Tire Gauge

You only need one tool to measure psi, and that's a tire gauge. We suggest buying your own, because a gauge at a service station is overused and exposed to the elements, and therefore will probably give you a false reading. You can purchase a tire gauge at any auto supply store; in fact, buy one for every car in your household. The best place to store the gauge is in the glove compartment.

There are two types of tire gauges: (1) electronic/digital, and (2) mechanical (stick or dial). A digital gauge is more expensive and runs on batteries, but it is typically more accurate. A mechanical gauge may not be as reliable as the digital one because the stick can become bent or dirty with residue and not release completely; therefore, we recommend that you buy a digital gauge because it's a small price to pay for reliability. When looking for a digital gauge, find one that has a notch for air release, too—it's easier to use than your nail or a key (you'll understand as you read along).

Checking Tire Pressure

Note: Remember to check tire pressure only when the tires are cold, which means that the vehicle has been parked for at least 3 hours and/or has been driven less than a mile.

A valve cap is important to the tire because it keeps dust, dirt, and water from entering into the valve stem and tire, which could result in air loss and tire damage. It doesn't matter if the valve cap is rubber or metal, but there should be a valve cap on every tire. If not, then you need to purchase one immediately.

Remove the valve cap by turning it counterclockwise with your fingers.

Some digital tire gauges require you to press a button to activate them; if so, do it now. Whether you're using a digital or a mechanical tire gauge, the process is the same—press it straight and firmly onto the valve stem.

If the cold psi reading is *lower* than the tire's recommended psi, you'll need to add air to the tire. If the cold psi is *higher* than the tire's recommended psi, than there is too much air in the tire and you'll need to release some

Checking the tire's air pressure

of it. Use the notched part of the gauge and gently press down on the metal stem in the center of the valve to release some air. You'll know you're doing it when you hear a hissing sound. But don't overdo it! In

Tools Needed

Car owner's manual

Digital or mechanical tire gauge

Pen

fact, it's best to release some air, check the psi, and then repeat the step, rather than releasing too much. Replace the valve cap and tighten.

Repeat this process on the remaining tires, including the spare. (Check the car owner's manual for the correct psi for the spare, because it's common for the spare to need a higher psi than the other tires.)

Write in the back of the owner's manual the cold psi reading for each tire and the date. Keeping a written record of your tires' psi readings will enable you to keep track if a tire is losing more air than the others, which will give you a heads-up on any leaks.

Adding Air to Tires

Very few people have air compressors in their garages, so the majority of us need to go to a service station to put air in our tires. Don't assume that every service station has an air pump and that using it will be free. Some stations charge for air—of course, we never thought we'd be paying for bottled water, right?

Pull your car up to the air pump and turn it *off*. Remember, you're going to add the difference between the *cold* psi reading and the recommended psi for your tires. Refer to your notes if necessary.

Before you put the air into your tire, you need to release some air from the hose by depressing the notched part of the tire gauge onto the air valve. Why? Some air hoses get water inside just from being exposed to the elements, so by doing this you won't get moisture in your tire.

Note: Air compressor systems may vary from service station to service station; therefore, if you have any questions, ask the attendant for help.

Depress the air hose nozzle onto the valve stem, making sure that the air is entering and not escaping from the tire. (If you hear a

Tool Needed

Digital or mechanical tire gauge

hissing sound, then air is escaping.) Squeeze the handle and hold for just a few seconds.

Adding air to the tire

Now use the tire gauge to take another psi reading. Did you add the right amount? If you've added too much air, just release some by using the notched end of the tire gauge to depress the metal stem in the center of the valve. If you need more air, depress the air hose nozzle over the stem valve and add more air. Check the psi again. If it's right, replace the valve cover and tighten. Repeat with each tire.

Note: Never exceed the maximum inflation pressure stated on the tire's sidewall.

Releasing some air

Adding Nitrogen to Tires

If you're a NASCAR fan, you may already know that racecar drivers have been filling their tires with nitrogen instead of air. It sounds so strange, doesn't it? But nitrogen makes up about 80 percent of the air we breathe (and the air in our tires), so it's not dangerous.

In fact, nitrogen has been proven to extend the life of the tires because unlike oxygen (a.k.a. air) there is no moisture in it—and moisture can cause a tire to deteriorate prematurely. Also, oxygen escapes 3 to 4 times faster than nitrogen. This means that there will be less loss of pressure, thereby providing better handling of the car, greater fuel efficiency, and extended life for the tires.

There are some downsides to using nitrogen. First, you need to take the car to a mechanic who has a machine that can completely remove the air that's in the tires before filling them with nitrogen. (Mixing the two gases won't ruin the tires; you just won't get the benefits from the pure nitrogen.) Second, you'll have to find a gas station that has a nitrogen filling tank. And you'll have to pay for the nitrogen, unlike air, which is (usually) free.

Aligning and Rotating Wheels and Balancing Tires

Alignment, balance, and rotation are the ABCs of tire maintenance. Well, okay, maybe they're the ABRs, but no matter which acronym you attach, they are the basic steps in keeping your tires properly maintained. Each of these steps extends the life of the tires, conserves fuel, and provides better steering. What's not to love?

Normally, we would give you DIY instructions, but not this time. For those of you who cringe at handing over your car to a mechanic, we love your can-do spirit and certainly don't want to *deflate* it one little bit (*hee-hee*). However, the alignment of the wheels and the balancing of the tires has to be done professionally, and we think that rotating wheels is not worth your time since it can cost less than a movie ticket. (Some tire centers even offer free balancing and rotation for the life of the tires if you purchase the tires from them.) A mechanic will also be able to look for irregular treadwear patterns on the tires and diagnose any unusual problems.

Rotating Wheels

Having said all that, if you still want to rotate the wheels yourself, do it while you're changing the oil because the car will already be jacked up. *And then move yourself to the head of the class!*

Whether you choose DIY (Do It Yourself) or DIFM (Do It For Me), you should refer to the car owner's manual because on some cars the front set of wheels are a different size than the rear set.

What It Is

Rotating wheels means that the wheels are moved to different positions on the car. Most of the car's braking power is in the front; therefore, the front tires typically wear out faster than the rear tires. So if you rotate the wheels, you'll be able to get more life out of *all* your tires. Always refer to the car owner's manual for rotation recommendations. If there are none, then the wheels should be rotated every 6,000 miles, or twice a year.

Rotation Patterns

When you think of wheels being rotated, you probably assume that it's done in either a clockwise or counterclockwise movement. But it's not that simple. In fact, there are multiple rotation patterns based on multiple factors.

- The front and rear tires are different sizes.
- A full-size spare can be added to the rotation.
- Your car's high-performance tires are either unidirectional or asymmetrical. These tires are marketed as excellent wet-weather tires because of their tread patterns. These tires must be rotated correctly or they may hydroplane more than regular tires. The tires should be rotated according to the direction of the arrows on the sidewalls.
- Your car has 2-wheel, 4-wheel, or all-wheel drive.
- There are one or two new replacement tires.

See the illustration for the correct rotation patterns for each tire.

If you are the original owner of your car, the first wheel rotation is very important because all future rotations (with the original tires) will depend on it.

There are three things you can do to ensure that a rotation is done correctly every time: (1) have it serviced by a reputable mechanic; (2) know the rotation pattern that's right for your car (located in the car owner's manual); and (3) use chalk to mark on the sidewalls the current location of each tire *before* the wheels are rotated.

DIY

Using the chalk, mark FR for front right, FL for front left, RR for right rear, and LR for left rear. Check the markings on each tire *after* the rotation is

It's often much cheaper to purchase a lifetime (of the tire) rotation and alignment service than to pay as you go.

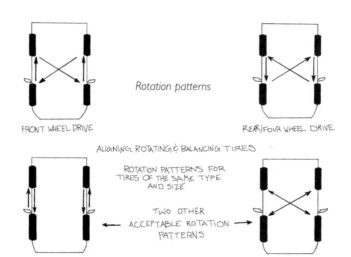

Rotation patterns

FRONT WHEEL DRIVE

REAR/FOUR WHEEL DRIVE

ALIGNING, ROTATING & BALANCING TIRES

ROTATION PATTERNS FOR
TIRES OF THE SAME TYPE
AND SIZE

TWO OTHER
← ACCEPTABLE ROTATION →
PATTERNS

done to see if the mechanic used the correct rotation pattern for your car; if not, talk to the service manager about the problem.

Balancing Tires

Balancing tires is not a DIY project. In fact, a highly sensitive machine is used to calculate if the weight is evenly distributed across each tire, and if not, where and how much weight is needed. If a tire's weight is spread unevenly, the tread will not wear properly, causing the car to vibrate.

What It Is

If you're told that a tire needs to be balanced, it means that it is heavier in one part than another. To fix the problem, the mechanic will add some weights to the wheel. Tires come balanced on new cars, and really only need to be balanced again if you buy new tires, or if you notice your car is vibrating.

Common Problems

If the front of your car shakes at a certain speed (typically between 50 and 70 mph), it could mean that one or more tires need to be balanced. If you feel the vibration in the driver's seat, the rear tires may need to be balanced. If the front of the car vibrates at any speed, then one of the tires may be out-of-round, which means that it needs to be replaced, or there is an alignment problem.

Tool Needed **Piece of chalk**

Aligning Wheels

Driving a car that's out of alignment is kind of like using a grocery cart that has one evil wheel that won't let you push it straight. You can go get a different cart, but with a car, it's much more practical to get the tires aligned.

What It Is

Proper alignment of wheels requires positioning them so that they're each lined up in the same direction, are perpendicular to the ground, and are parallel to each other and to the center of the car.

Your car is either going to require a front-wheel alignment or a 4-wheel alignment. The difference is exactly what you would assume it is—either just the two front wheels are aligned or all four wheels are aligned. It seems that it is just common sense to have all of them aligned, but some cars do not have adjustable rear-alignment settings. Most cars, as well as 4-wheel-drive and all-wheel-drive vehicles, can have a 4-wheel alignment. If you're not sure, refer to the car owner's manual or contact the dealership or car manufacturer.

Common Problems

Sometimes it's really obvious when your car's wheels need to be aligned, like when the car pulls to one side or starts to shimmy while you're driving. A less-obvious sign that you won't notice unless you're looking for it is uneven treadwear.

To check for uneven wear, use the treadwear test (see "Testing the Tire's Tread," page 116). If you notice either or both of these patterns of wear on your tires, these are signs that your car's wheels need an alignment.

You don't need to wait for any problems to arise to get an alignment. A good preventive maintenance tip is to have the wheels aligned every 12,000 miles or after the tires are rotated. And be sure to have them aligned immediately after hitting a pothole or running over a curb.

If a tire is vibrating, and it's not flat, it could be that the wheel is not aligned, the tire is not properly balanced, or the wheel is bent. You need to get the problem fixed immediately.

Avoid potholes if possible because they can throw off an alignment, bend a wheel, blow out a tire, and damage the suspension. If you must drive through a pothole, drive slowly but don't hit the brakes.

Flat Tire

Fiona had taken her three children out for Sunday brunch as a special *treat,* but the day turned out to be more like a *trick* when she came out of the restaurant to find one of her tires as flat as the pancakes they just ate. She had never changed a tire in her life, but luckily there was a *great* Samaritan ready to help.

Don't wait for a flat tire to happen to learn how to change it. If there is one repair you learn from this book, this should be it.

Another reason (which you probably never thought of) for learning to do this project ahead of time is that you need to know *if* you *can* lift one of your car's tires. A tire from Fiona's SUV weighs almost 100 pounds. Fiona weighs 110 pounds. How many of us can lift our own weight, especially if it's an awkward shape and you're removing it from your car? Being stuck on the side of the road with a flat is *not* the time to discover your lack of upper-arm strength!

So even though it looks like an awful lot of information, the steps for changing a tire are simple and easy to remember. And once you've changed a tire, you'll never forget how to do it.

Be Prepared

You can't prevent your tires from getting a flat, but you can be more aware of when a problem is brewing. Do a quick visible check of the tires before you start the car in the morning by walking the long way around to the driver's door to get a look at all four tires. If you see one that looks lower than the others, check that tire's air pressure, as well as the other three, and fill with air, if necessary. A tire that is worn or low on air is more likely to get a flat or have a blowout.

Also, have the following items in your car, and try to keep them together so that you're not looking all over your car for them. You may wonder why we suggest you have work gloves, a towel, and an old shirt on hand. You'll understand after you've replaced a tire!

- Car owner's manual
- Spare tire (properly inflated)
- Flashlight (with new batteries) or 12-volt work light
- Car jack
- Cheater bar
- Crowbar
- Cross-shaft lug wrench (looks like a big X)
- Wheel blocks/chocks
- Safety triangles
- Reflective outerwear (vest)
- Work gloves
- Old shirt
- Towel
- Lubricating spray
- *Dare to Repair Your Car*

Getting Off the Road

The American Automobile Association (AAA) strongly recommends that if you have a flat tire, do *not* pull off onto the shoulder of the highway. Instead, turn on the emergency flashers, decrease your speed, and drive in the slow lane to the next exit. Don't stop your car until you've found a safe place to park, even if it means that you have to drive on a flat tire and ruin your wheel. Why? Many die each year after pulling onto a shoulder—a shoulder that they *thought* was safe. But more densely populated cities are allowing the shoulders to be used as traffic lanes during rush hours, leaving no area for breakdowns. If you must get off onto a shoulder, leave your car for a safer area, such as a hill or behind a guardrail until help arrives.

Park your car on pavement and nothing else—not dirt and not grass, because your car, and or jack, could sink into them and the heat from your catalytic converter (located underneath your car) could cause grass to catch on fire. And the spot where you park must be flat. No slope, no hill. If your car has air suspension, turn it off by flipping the switch (check the car owner's manual for the location). Turn the engine off and *firmly engage the parking brake!*

Making Yourself and Your Car Visible

Now you need to let motorists know that you're having car trouble—not so much because you want help, but (more important) because you want them to see you and drive carefully past you.

Making your car visible

Put on the old shirt and the reflective gear (if it's dark outside). Remove the safety triangles from the trunk and place them at least 200 feet from the car in the direction of traffic.

Pop open the hood of the car and turn on the emergency flashers—two more signals that you're giving to motorists that you're having car problems.

Take out the car jack, wheel block(s), lug wrench, lubricating spray, towel, and work gloves and place them on the ground near the flat tire.

Spare Tire

The spare tire is typically hidden out of sight, and therefore it's out of mind, too. But don't forget about this very important tire, because it can *spare* you a lot of grief.

Types of Spares

A spare tire is typically smaller than a regular tire because it needs to fit into a storage compartment. Your spare may be one of three kinds: (1) a temporary spare (a.k.a. doughnut), which is small and compact; (2) a folding spare that needs to be inflated; or (3) a full-size spare that is the same size as the other tires on the vehicle. If you car does not have a spare or you want to upgrade the doughnut to a full-size spare, you can purchase one at any tire shop. Just make sure that it meets the correct specs for your vehicle and that you can safely store the spare in your vehicle.

Locating the Spare

Depending on the type of car you own, the spare can be found in the trunk, on the outside of the rear door (e.g., on some Jeeps), or underneath the car (on some minivans and SUVs). This is when the car owner's manual comes in very handy.

Removing the Spare

If the spare tire is located in the trunk, it may be concealed. Simply remove the cover, unbolt the spare, and take it out. If the spare tire is located on the exterior of the rear of the car, it typically has a tire cover over it. Remove the cover, unbolt the spare, and take it out. If the spare tire is located underneath the car, you'll need to refer to the car owner's manual to locate the tools needed to release the stored tire. Some cars have a lock for the hoist system to prevent theft (the ignition key is normally used to unlock it).

Make certain that the spare is properly inflated because you don't want to replace a flat tire with another flat (hopefully you've been checking it every month).

Place the spare tire near where you'll be working for quick access. You don't want the car to be on a jack any longer than necessary.

Before calling an auto membership service or towing company, check that you have a spare tire *and* that it's not flat. If your spare is flat or is missing in action, ask the auto club to bring a spare and be sure to include the make or VIN of your car.

Keep in mind that temporary (compact) spare tires are designed to get you to the auto shop, not across the country. Check the information written on the sidewall of the spare for the maximum speed and mileage restrictions. Typically, you should not drive faster than 50 mph.

Removing the Wheel Cover

Place the wheel block behind the tire that is diagonally across from the tire that needs to be removed. The wheel block will help to keep the car from moving when you jack it up. If you don't have one, use a brick or a thick block of wood.

If your tire has a wheel cover (a.k.a. hubcap), remove it by using the flat side of the lug wrench (a.k.a. tire iron, which looks like a flathead screwdriver) to pry it off. Lay the wheel cover on the ground near the car. (If the wheel cover is secured in place with lug nuts, you'll remove the wheel cover when you remove the lug nuts later.)

Loosening the Lug Nuts

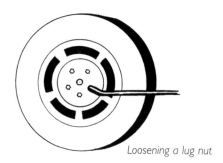
Loosening a lug nut

Lug nuts are what secure the wheel to the car. Depending on the size of the wheel, there will be 4, 5, or 6 of these hexagonal nuts. Use the lug wrench to loosen (not remove) each nut by placing the open end of the lug wrench over the nut and turning it counterclockwise. (Remember, *righty-tighty, lefty-loosie.*) All you need is to be able to loosen each nut one turn around, because you don't want to remove them just yet. If you're having a hard time budging the lug nuts, apply some lubricating spray to them, wait a few minutes, and try again. If you're still not able to budge them, put the cheater bar onto the end of the lug wrench and pull the cheater bar in an upward motion. This will minimize the stress on the stud where the lug nut rests. Repeat with the other nuts. If you're still not successful, get yourself to a safe area and wait for help.

It's important to have the car owner's manual because you may need it to locate the car jack, the lug wrench, and the spare tire.

Using a Car Jack

Using a scissor jack

A car jack is a device that lifts a vehicle off the ground. There are lots of different kinds of jacks—a bottle jack, which is usually the smallest of the three and looks like it doesn't have the power to lift the car, but does; a scissor jack, which is an X-shaped device; and a hydraulic floor jack, which is the largest and heaviest of the three and is typically stored in a garage. Your car probably came equipped with either a scissor jack or a bottle jack. A scissor jack is operated by rotating a metal hand crank, and a pumping bar is used on bottle and hydraulic jacks.

You'll need the car owner's manual to know where to place the jack. The lift points are located underneath the frame of your vehicle, one near each tire. Some vehicles may have the word JACK imprinted at the lift sites. Putting the jack in the wrong spot can really damage your car; therefore, if your car doesn't have any markings, we recommend that you put a piece of duct tape on all four locations so you'll never have to wonder again.

Use the jack to raise the flat tire about 2 inches off the ground. This may seem a little high, but you have to remember that the tire is flat and the spare will need the extra space because it's fully inflated.

Note: Never get under a car that is supported only by a jack. If the car is not stable or is moving, try jacking it up again, or call for help.

Car with scissor jack and tire block

Lug nuts can be very difficult to remove if they've become rusted or they were over-tightened. Therefore, whenever a wheel is being put onto a car, ask the technician to use an anti-seize lubricant on the lug nuts so that you'll be able to remove them more easily.

Replacing the Flat Tire

Now that the car is raised, remove all of the loosened lug nuts by hand. Place the nuts inside the wheel cover to prevent the nuts from rolling away.

Grab hold of the flat tire and pull it off. Roll it to the back of the car and lay it down.

Note: Be careful to place the spare with the writing on the outside, facing you.

This is the most difficult part—lifting the spare. If it's too heavy, use a crowbar and wedge it under the spare, pushing the handle down to lift it up just high enough for you to place it on the studs. Align the holes on the spare with the protruding studs on the car's brake rotor or drum.

Once the spare is on the car, put on the lug nuts, making sure that the tapered side of each nut is facing the car. Hand-tighten each nut as much as you can, being careful not to cross-thread them.

Slowly lower the jack until the spare is touching the ground. Remove the jack and place it on the ground nearby.

Use the lug wrench and tighten the nuts in either a crisscross pattern (if you have four lug nuts), a star pattern (if you have five lug nuts), or a crisscross sequence (if there are six lug nuts). This ensures that the tire is centered correctly.

Put the jack and wheel blocks inside the car. Replace the hubcap/wheel cover, if so equipped. Don't forget to remove the safety triangles and the flat tire and put them away, too. To save time, put the tire inside the car or in the trunk, instead of putting it in the spare's usual location.

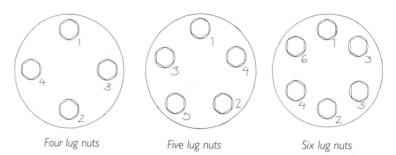

Four lug nuts   Five lug nuts   Six lug nuts

Cleaning Up

Even though the wheel is on, you can't leave just yet! If your spare is stored underneath the car, don't forget to raise the retaining cable. And if your car has air suspension, be sure to turn it back on *before* you turn on the car.

Get the flat fixed or replaced as soon as possible.

Quick Fix for a Tire

Don't get deflated just because your tire's gone flat. Both you and your tire can be riding high in no time.

We told you how to change a flat, but you may not be in a safe place to do it, or have all the tools you need. Therefore, we suggest two products that can get you back on the road—a portable air compressor or a tire inflator (e.g., Fix-A-Flat), both of which can be purchased at an auto parts store. The beauty of using either of these items is that you don't have to jack up the car and you won't have to remove the tire.

No matter which product you use, you should only drive a short distance and only in the slow lane afterward. If possible, drive immediately to a mechanic to have the tire patched or replaced.

Do not use these products together; it's one or the other. Also, do not use either of these products if the tire has separated from the rim. If this happens, you'll need to change the tire or call for a tow truck.

Tire Inflator

Note: There are a number of tire inflator products on the market. Be sure to purchase one that is nonflammable.

A tire inflator is a great quick remedy for a flat tire because it can be easily stored inside your car. The product is inexpensive, and it does work in a pinch. When the contents are injected into the flat tire, it

If your custom wheel covers have locking lug nuts, consult the owner's manual for the location of the keyed wrench to loosen the nuts. It's best to keep the keyed wrench in an accessible place like the glove compartment.

The manufacturer of Fix-A-Flat states that a tire does not have to be replaced after using its product. However, not all tire inflator products can make that claim. Therefore, before purchasing a tire inflator, read the instructions and/or contact the manufacturer for more information.

coats the inside, providing a protective sealant that will temporarily make the tire drivable.

Here are some other things you need to know before using this product.

- No matter which type of tire sealant you use, you must alert the technician who will be repairing/replacing the tire that you have used the product. Some tire sealants can be explosive.
- The tire inflator is good for only one use.
- You must drive immediately after using this product to allow it to coat the entire inside of the tire and build pressure.
- This product is for emergency use only.
- This is a temporary quick fix, not a permanent solution.
- You cannot use this product if the hole is in the sidewall of the tire.
- Tire inflators come in two sizes—one for regular passenger tires and the other for SUV and lightweight trucks.
- After using the product, notify the tire mechanic before the tire is serviced.

Note: Before using, be sure to read the manufacturer's instructions, and remember to use the same safety rules as for changing a flat.

First, see where the tire valve is located. The optimal position of the tire valve for this repair is either at 4 o'clock or 8 o'clock, so if you have to move the car a tiny bit, do so.

Tools Needed

Tire inflator
(such as Fix-A-Flat)

Safety goggles

Flashlight,
if necessary

Plastic bag

Remove the valve stem cap and place it in your pocket for safekeeping. Put on the safety goggles and shake the can vigorously for 30 seconds and then remove its cap.

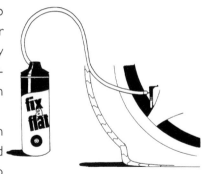

Inflating a tire with Fix-A-Flat

Place the can upright on the ground in front of the tire and attach the hose (which is clear, so you can see through it) to the valve stem. Push the button and hold it down until you no longer see any of the contents moving through the hose. Unscrew the hose, replace the valve cap, and put the can and the cap into the plastic bag.

For the tire inflator to work properly, you must drive your car immediately after so that the contents will spread throughout the tire—usually about 2 to 4 miles—so drive yourself right to a repair shop! And if you can't, fill the tire up to its recommended psi.

Note: The tire inflator is only adding a little air (not the recommended psi) to your tire while plugging the hole.

Portable Air Compressor

A portable air compressor works by adding enough air to a low or flat tire to enable to get you back on the road until you can get it replaced. The upside is that it won't ruin the tire. Also, it's super easy—it's just like filling the tire up at the gas station. The downside to using this method is that it can take up to 20 minutes to fill a flat tire.

Before using the air compressor, you'll need to read the manufacturer's directions, as well as knowing the correct air pressure for your tire (refer to the car owner's manual or the vehicle's certification label located on the doorjamb on the driver's side).

Note: Remember to use the same safety rules for changing a flat.

The first thing you need to do is to check the air pressure in the low or flat tire (see "Checking Tire Pressure," pages 125–26). Based on the reading, you'll know how much air you should be adding. Typically, for a flat tire, you won't need more than 35 to 40 psi.

Insert the 12-volt plug of the air compressor into the cigarette lighter inside your car (you'll need to leave the car door open). Remove the cap from the valve stem and place it in your pocket for safekeeping.

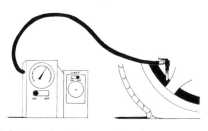

Inflating a tire with a portable air compressor

Place the valve/tire adapter over the valve stem and push down on the valve lock lever to secure it.

On the air compressor box, you'll see an "on/off" switch. Turn it "on" and watch the gauge. When the dial reaches the correct psi number needed, turn it "off." Release the adapter from the tire valve and remove the plug from the lighter. Replace the valve cap.

Note: The portable air compressor can get hot, so do not put it back inside its casing until it has cooled, which will probably take about 10 minutes. Drive to the nearest repair shop to get the tire fixed or replaced.

Tools Needed

Portable air compressor

Flashlight (if necessary)

Digital or mechanical tire gauge

DIFM

Calling for Help

It's raining cats and dogs, you have your two young children in the car, and you get a flat. There's no way you're going outside to change the tire, so you decide to call for roadside assistance. And we completely agree with your decision. Sometimes, it's just not worth the hassle.

There are a few things that you need to do prior to contacting your auto club service or a towing company so that everything will run smoothly ... a lot smoother than the flat tire.

First, check the condition of the spare. A tow truck does not carry spare tires, so if you're spare is missing, or it's flat, you'll need to let them know. (For more information on what to tell the auto club service or towing company, see "Towing," page 299.) Second, be sure to follow the safety rules for getting off the road (see "Getting Off the Road," pages 133–34).

Battery

What It Is

A battery has three jobs: (1) start the engine; (2) stabilize the car's charging system; and (3) provide extra power for the lights and radio once the engine is off.

We toyed with the idea of going into detail about how it works and that's when we realized that's the perfect way to explain it.

How It Works

A battery in a toy provides the electrical current needed to make the toy operate, and if the battery is removed or dies, the toy ceases to work. A car's battery is somewhat similar in that its primary job is to provide an electrical current to start the engine. The difference is that once the engine has started, the battery's job is done and the alternator takes over. As the car runs, the alternator recharges the battery for the next time you start the engine and provides electrical power for the car.

Cause of Death

No one wants to believe that a car battery is mortal. For the majority of motorists, the death of a battery comes unexpectedly. But the truth is that a battery gives signs of its demise *before* it dies, such as difficulty in starting the engine, or the battery warning light stays on. Most drivers don't know what to look for or they don't *want* to see it.

Listed below are the most common reasons a battery will lose its charge.

Lights/Radio

If you leave the lights or radio on (with the engine off) for an hour and a half or more, chances are the battery will be DOA (dead on arrival). Batteries have about a 2- to 3-hour reserve capacity if the headlamps are left on (6 to 7 hours if the dome light is left on).

Most new cars have an annoying alarm that sounds if you are exiting your car and the lights are left on (of course, it's more annoying to come back to a car that won't start). Some cars are so smart they'll even turn the lights off for you after the engine has been turned off. And then there are cars that expect *you* to remember to do it ... *geez!*

Weather

Freezing cold temperatures can play a role in the premature death of a battery because it takes more power to start an engine in temperatures below 32°F. If you live in a cold climate, be sure to purchase a battery that has high cold cranking amps and/or a battery charger.

While battery ads always depict someone trying to start a car on a freezing cold day with 2 feet of snow, what they don't show you is the other climate that wreaks havoc on a car battery—excessive heat. High heat under the hood is actually the number one reason for a battery to die because the battery loses water through evaporation.

Age

A battery only lasts 4 to 5 years, on average. Every battery has either a label or an imprint that states the month and the year the battery was manufactured. For example, if you see A04, then the battery was manufactured in January 2004; and if it's F05, then it was built in June 2005. So, whenever you're purchasing a new battery, or you're buying a used car, be sure to check its birthday!

Voltage Regulator

An alternator produces electricity when the engine runs, and it recharges the battery with this electricity. But if the engine is running really hard, then the alternator generates a lot of electricity, which can overcharge a battery and damage it. That's where the voltage regulator comes in. The voltage regulator, typically located inside the alternator, works to control the amount of electrical current the battery receives from the alternator, as well as to prevent the other electrical components in the car from being overcharged. If the voltage regulator is faulty, then the battery can become overloaded and die.

Before Calling for Help

You're stressing out because your car won't start, and, of course, the first thing you do is assume that the battery is dead. A good way to test your assumption is by turning on the ignition and looking to see if the warning lights are lit on the dashboard. If not, then the battery is the likely source of the problem. However, if you do see the warning lights, it could be that the battery has enough power to turn on the warning lights, but not to turn over the engine. But wait, it still may not be the battery.

There are a few things you can do to possibly prevent from having to get your car jump-started or towed. First, check that the car is in the proper gear (park for automatic and neutral for manual); next, rule out lack of gasoline; make sure that the battery terminal cables are properly secured to the terminals; and remove any oxidation that may be corroding the battery terminals.

Securing the Battery Terminal Cables

A tow truck driver told us that the biggest mistake a motorist can make is not checking that the battery cables (not jumper cables) are securely attached to the battery terminals. Battery cables (there are two, one for

Tools Needed

Flashlight (if necessary)

Work gloves

Safety goggles

Wrench

each terminal) have to be tightly connected to the battery terminals, otherwise the battery will not receive enough power to operate.

Note: Use caution not to overtighten the battery cables, which could damage the battery or cause it to explode.

Wearing safety goggles, pop open the hood of the car and find the battery and battery cables. If the cables are loosely connected to the battery terminals, use the wrench to tighten (remember, do not overtighten).

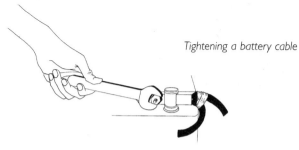

Tightening a battery cable

Cleaning the Battery Terminals

We've all heard that battery acid leaks out of the battery and collects around the terminals, causing them to corrode. Well, we're here to put a stop to that urban myth. Every battery contains acid inside its casing. The acid creates vapors that can escape and collect around the terminals, causing the terminals to corrode. The substance, which is a white powder, should be removed immediately (see "Cleaning a Battery," pages 157–59). Once the terminals have been cleaned, tighten the battery terminal cables and get back into the car and try to start the engine.

If the engine still won't start, then you'll need to have the battery jump-started or have the car towed.

Jump-Starting the Battery

Before we teach you the steps to jump-start a battery, there are some safety tips you need to know.

Clothing, Jewelry, and Long Hair

Whenever you are working near an engine that's running, do not wear loose clothing, and if you have long hair be sure to put it up so that it doesn't get caught in any moving parts. Also, remove any rings and bracelets. Metal jewelry can cause a short circuit between two electrical contacts, creating a spark that will burn the area of skin where the jewelry is worn.

Tools

Be very careful when working with any metal tools, such as a wrench. If the wrench touches the positive terminal while also touching the metal on the engine or frame of the car at the same time, you will create a short circuit and the electrical current may go through your body, as well as possibly igniting the acidic fumes from the battery.

Protective Eyewear

The organization Prevent Blindness America states that thousands of people each year are seriously injured or blinded by sulfuric acid that's released when a battery explodes.

To prevent this from happening you need to use protective eyewear, and we don't mean sunglasses. Regular glasses and sunglasses are not designed to keep flying fragments or caustic fluids from entering your eyes. The best eyewear for automotive use is a pair of safety goggles, which protect the eyes on all sides. They can be purchased at most hardware or auto parts stores.

If an accident happens and you get sulfuric acid in your eye, immediately rinse your eye with a drinkable liquid—water, milk, or even soda—for about 15 minutes and call 911 for help.

If you get a flying fragment in your eye, do *not* flush the eye. If the eye is punctured, you don't want to lose any fluids in the eye that are protecting it. Call 911 for help.

Prevent Blindness America provides at no cost (but a donation is welcome) a sticker that's an informative step-by-step guide to jump-starting a battery. This is great because you can attach it under the hood of your car for easy reference.

Don't Jump-Start a Battery If . . .

- The battery is frozen, cracked, or has a bulge, because it will explode.
- The jumper cables are rusted, or have exposed wires, because it may cause severe burns or the battery to explode.
- You don't have safety goggles to wear. It's not worth risking your eyesight.
- You're smoking or you've lit a match.

Jump-Starting Using Another Vehicle

Note: We will be referring to the car with the dead battery as the "bad car" and the other car as the "good car." It just makes it easier to understand. And as always, refer to the car owner's manual for specific information on jump-starting a battery.

Turn off all electrical accessories, such as lights, radio, air-conditioning, or heater, on both cars.

Have the *good car* pull up as close as possible to the *bad car*, being sure to leave at least 18 inches in between them. You never want the two cars to touch because it could damage the electrical systems in both cars. Both cars should be placed in park (or neutral if they have a manual transmission) with parking brakes engaged and radios and lights turned off. Both engines should be turned off now and the hoods popped open. Put on the safety goggles to protect your eyes, but be sure to shield your entire face as well.

Making the Right Connection

Take a look at both batteries to find the positive and negative terminals located on the top of the batteries. The positive terminal will be

If the radio and lights are not turned off before jump-starting the car, the electrical system of the car may get damaged.

Tools Needed

Jumper cables

Safety goggles

Flashlight (if necessary)

Car owner's manual

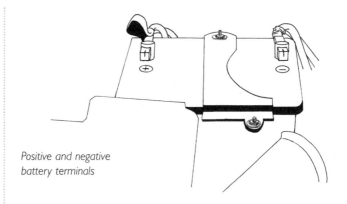

Positive and negative battery terminals

marked with a + sign, and the negative terminal will be marked with a − sign. If you don't see any terminals, don't panic. Some batteries have plastic caps that cover the terminals to protect them against corrosion. Just don't assume that the caps were put on correctly and that the positive and negative markings on them correspond to the markings on the battery. The only markings you should care about are the ones imprinted on the battery.

If there are caps covering the terminals, pry them off with your fingers. They should pop off easily.

Note: There is only one right (safe) way to hook up the jumper cables and to remove them. You must follow these instructions to the letter or you can damage the alternator or cause the battery to explode. The trick is to remember that you're going to start with the bad car and end with the bad car.

Remote Battery Terminals

Some cars have a remote battery terminal, which is a safety device to protect the car's electrical system in case of a problem caused by jump-starting. If you're not sure if your car has this feature, refer to the car owner's manual. Also, check the manual for information on jump-starting using the remote terminals.

You may need to rock the jumper cables back and forth to get a solid connection.

Make sure that the jumper cables are not near any belts, fans, or moving parts. Also make sure that the jumper cable ends are not touching one another.

Take one of the red cables (positive/+)—it doesn't matter which one—and connect it onto the positive terminal of the bad car. Now take the other red cable (positive/+) and connect it onto the positive terminal of the good car.

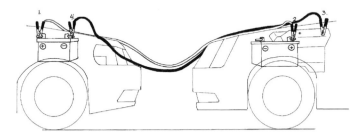

Connecting the jumper cables

Next, take one of the black cables (negative/–) and connect it onto the negative terminal of the good car. Now, here's the part you may not understand at first. Take the other black cable and clamp it onto an unpainted metal part of the bad car, such as the engine block on the side away from the battery. Some cars have a designated place to attach the last negative cable and will have the word GROUND and an arrow imprinted next to it.

Whatever you do, *do not connect the last cable to the battery.* If you connect every cable to a terminal, the circuit of electricity will be complete. If that happens, a spark may occur near the battery and ignite the vapor coming from the battery, which may cause the battery to explode.

Both drivers need to get into their cars, but the motors should not be started until no one is standing near the engines. Have the motorist of the good car start the engine and let the engine idle for 2 minutes, but don't rev it.

If Your Car Starts

Now turn the ignition in the bad car. If the engine starts, don't turn it off. It's okay to remove the jumper cables from both cars now (see

"Safely Removing Cables" below for correct method). Now drive the car, with a friend following, to a battery shop or your mechanic.

If Your Car Doesn't Start

If, however, the bad car did not start, turn off the good car's engine and make sure that the cables are securely attached on the bad car. If one fell off, hook it back on and try again, repeating the steps above. If the engine still has not started after several attempts, then it's time to stop and call a towing service.

Safely Removing Cables

To do this, you need to *reverse* the order that you put them on, while making sure that they don't touch because they'll create a spark. So, first remove the black cable from the engine block or metal part of the bad car, and then the black cable from the negative terminal of the good car. Then remove the red cable from the positive terminal of the good car and then the red cable from the positive terminal of the bad car.

If you were unsuccessful at getting the engine to start and you're home, you can hook the battery up to a battery charger.

Jump-Starting Using a Battery Charger/Starter

A great alternative to using another car to jump-start your battery is to use a battery charger/starter. You can use it at home, and it gives you the option of charging your battery over a few hours or instantly.

Check in the car owner's manual for specific instructions prior to using a battery charger/starter.

Buying a Battery Charger/Starter

Battery chargers/starters can usually be purchased anywhere auto parts are sold, but not every place where batteries are sold. When you go to purchase a battery charger/starter, you need to make sure that:

- It's specifically made for a car battery.
- It's an automatic charger, not a manual (an automatic turns

off once the battery has been charged; with a manual, you have to physically turn it off).

- It comes with easy-to-understand instructions.
- It has at least a 3-year warranty.
- The manufacturer supplies a customer service number.

Preparing the Car Battery for Using a Battery Charger/Starter

Getting a car battery ready for using a battery charger/starter will require you to clean the battery terminals as well as to check that the battery is in good condition.

Remove any oxidation on the terminals, the top of the battery, and the battery terminal cables. Also, check the exterior of the battery to see if it has any cracks or bulges. If any of these conditions exist, or the acid inside the battery is frozen, then you *cannot* charge the battery. You'll have to replace it instead.

Safety Tips

The oxidation around the terminals is extremely caustic if it gets on your skin or in your eyes, so follow the safety guidelines listed in the manufacturer's manual and below. And if you don't feel comfortable doing either, then don't—just call a tow truck.

- Remove any jewelry on your hands and wrists. If a spark hits your jewelry, it will burn your finger or hand.
- Have plenty of clean water and towels nearby in case of an accident with the battery acid.
- If you are using a manual battery charger, refer to the voltmeter so you don't overcharge it.

Tools Needed

Battery charger/starter

Extension cord, if necessary

Manual for battery charger/starter

Safety goggles

- If you've charged the battery for the recommended time suggested by the manufacturer, and the battery still won't work, do *not* try charging it again. Replace the battery.
- If the battery becomes hot to the touch, unplug the charger.
- Never use a battery charger that is damaged, has been exposed to moisture (e.g., rain or snow), or has a damaged cord.
- Always charge the battery in a well-ventilated area—outdoors is preferable.
- Never smoke near the battery and battery charger.
- Wear safety goggles.

Charging or Quick-Starting the Battery

The first thing you need to do is to read the manual for the battery charger/starter and have a clear understanding of the directions and the safety precautions recommended by the manufacturer.

Note: Do not plug in the battery charger before attaching it to the battery. It's best not to use an extension cord for the battery charger/starter, but if there's no alternative, then make sure to use an extension cord that is grounded (3-prong) and in excellent condition (i.e., no tears or exposed wires).

Don't remove the battery from the car—there's no need. However, you should have the battery charger/starter as far away from the battery as possible. And never, ever place one on top of the other because it may cause an explosion.

Wearing the safety goggles, connect the positive clamp (red with a + sign) of the battery charger to the positive battery terminal, rocking it back and forth a bit to make sure that you have a solid connection. Attach the negative clamp (black with a − sign) of the battery charger to the engine block or another unpainted metal piece of the engine.

The battery charger/starter will have different settings for the charge rate and the battery type. The charge rate is typically either 2 amps for a slow charge that can take up to 4 to 6 hours; 10 amps for a quicker charge, about 45 minutes; or it may even have an option for

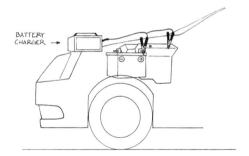

Connecting the battery charger to the car's battery

Depending on the length of your cables and the size of your car, you may need to rest the charger on the car itself. Place it on a flat surface away from the battery.

50 amps for what's called an *engine start.* Flip the switch to the size of the charge that's appropriate for your need. (We recommend that you use the slow charge, if possible, to minimize risk to the battery and other electrical parts and not leave home while it's charging.)

Next, flip the other switch to whichever battery type you have—conventional/low maintenance or maintenance-free. Most cars have the maintenance-free battery.

Now you can plug the battery charger/starter into a grounded electrical outlet (i.e., 3 prongs).

If you're charging the battery: How will you know when it's completely charged? Most battery chargers have a green light that turns on and there are words imprinted on the charger saying "full charge." You can also refer to the amp meter. If the battery is charged, the arrow will point to the lower amperage, such as 2 amps. But remember that you don't have to babysit it because an automatic battery charger will shut itself off when the battery is charged, but don't leave home.

If you're using the engine-start setting: Put the key into the ignition and try to start the car. Set the battery charger switch to the 50-amp setting.

Note: Leaving the charger in the 50-amp setting for more than a few minutes may cause electrical damage to your car's ignition system or cause a fire.

If you're having to charge the battery every day or even a couple of times a week, then it's time to buy a new battery!

Most batteries are 12 volt. Some new hybrid vehicles have special batteries. Check the car owner's manual.

DIFM

Do It For Me, in this case, means having the car towed. Be sure to follow the safety guidelines for towing and remember that the towing company will probably not jump-start the battery; instead, it will tow your car to a repair shop or a dealership.

Buying a New Battery

One of the biggest mistakes a car owner can make is thinking that you shouldn't buy a new battery *until* the old one dies. That attitude may work for a toaster, but when your safety is at risk, it's time to shift the old paradigm. Just remember, it's always much easier if *you* make the choice of when to replace the battery instead of the battery choosing the time for you.

Signs

The most common sign that a battery needs to be replaced is when it takes more than one try to start the engine and it's happened more than once. There's no set amount of time from when you first notice a sign and when the battery will stop working (although it can be just a day or two). You can use a battery charger in a pinch, but it's not a permanent solution.

If the battery warning light on the dashboard is lit, it's usually not the first sign, but it may be the last. It could mean that the battery does not have enough cold cranking amps or there's a problem with the alternator.

Before You Buy

Even though you won't be installing the battery yourself, *you* need to be the one who decides which battery goes in your car. If you go into a shop to buy a battery without knowing what type is required for your car, then you're as powerless as your car's dead battery. You may accidentally be sold a battery that has been sitting around the shop for too long, or you may be pushed to buy one that's on sale even though it's not the correct type for your car.

Two primary bits of information are needed in order to get the right battery for your car, both of which can be found on a sticker on the driver's doorjamb or in the car owner's manual: (1) the cold cranking amps; and, (2) the casing size.

Cranking and Cold Cranking Amps

Cranking amps (CA) are the amps required to turn over the engine at 32°F. Cold cranking amps (CCA) are the amps required to turn over the engine at 0°F. Look on the battery for the letters CA or CCA. The numbers next to it will tell you the number of amps. If you live in an area with extremely cold winters and/or you own a lightweight truck or SUV, you'll want to purchase a battery with a high CCA. The higher the amps, the faster the engine will turn over. Why wouldn't you just want to buy the highest CCA and not worry? The answer is simple— why pay more for something you don't need?

Casing Size and Group Size

The casing size is the dimension of the shelf that the battery sits on. The group size, which is the size of the battery, has two numbers and is listed near the voltage number on the sticker.

Age

You should never buy a battery that is over 6 months old, because when a battery sits for a long period of time without being used it begins to corrode from sulfate (see "Buying a New Battery," page 156).

Cleaning a Battery

Not all batteries are maintenance free, but the one thing you can do to extend the life of the battery is keep the terminals clean.

Terminals, which are located on the top of the battery, are where the battery terminal cables attach. As we've stated, it's vital to keep the terminals clean from oxidation (the white powdery substance) so that the flow of electricity through the terminals is not impeded.

Never clean the battery, the battery terminals, and the battery terminal cables while the engine is running! Always turn the engine off before cleaning.

Note: *Not only is it important to keep the oxidation on the terminals from getting onto your hands and in your eyes, but it's also important to not allow it to get onto the paint of your car. If it happens, flush the area with water.*

Scrubbing off corrosion from the terminals

Put on the goggles and gloves. If there are caps on the terminals, remove them. Disconnect the negative battery terminal cable first, and then the positive cable.

Use the terminal brush to scrub away the oxidation on the terminals, the caps (if applicable), and the cables, if necessary.

To clean the terminals, make a paste of water and baking soda and apply it around the terminals. Let

Tools Needed

Work gloves   **Safety goggles**   **Terminal brush or toothbrush**

Baking soda paste (baking soda and water)   **Jug of water (for safety reasons— if you get it on your hands, in your eyes, on the car's paint)**

Spray bottle filled with clean water   **Rag**   **Terminal protector**

it sit for a little bit and then brush the powdery substance away. Now use the spray bottle, filled with water, to clean away the mess. Wipe it off with a rag, if necessary. Rinse off the terminal brush and let dry.

Preventive Maintenance
A good way to prevent terminals from oxidizing is to spray them, after they've been cleaned, with a protective coating, (a.k.a. terminal protector).

Warning Lights and Gauges

We know a woman whose fuel gauge stopped working so she relied on the odometer to know when to fuel up. And then the odometer stopped working, so she resorted to going to the gas station as frequently as she did her grocery shopping. If only she could serve Slurpees for dinner, she'd be all set.

Did you know that the average new car has more than a dozen computers in it? Don't panic; you don't have to be a computer geek to figure out what's causing a warning light to come on, or a gauge needle to be in the red. The answers are all in your car owner's manual.

On Board-Diagnostics
On-Board Diagnostics II (OBD-II) is a computer system that is designed to give the driver an early warning of an emission control system malfunction so that the issue can be addressed before it turns into a major problem.

Here's an example of how the system works: You forgot to tighten the fuel cap. Behind the scenes, a sensor is letting the OBD-II know that there's a problem with the emissions system, specifically the fuel cap. The OBD-II then records in the computer the specific code for the fuel cap and relays a message to the warning light system, which then displays the words "Check Engine." So even though you may not know exactly what the cause is, your technician will be able to find out the exact code by using diagnostic equipment.

There are about 400 different codes in the OBD-II, all of which are standard throughout the automobile industry.

Warning Lights

The warning lights on the dashboard are often referred to as "idiot lights," but we think you're only foolish if you ignore them. Warning lights are designed to notify you of a problem that may happen or is happening so that you can resolve it before it gets worse.

When you turn the ignition to the "run" position (see "Starting Circuit," pages 12–13) you'll see that all the warning lights turn on. This is a good thing. The system is going through a check of everything—the air bag, the electrical system, the brakes, and so on. When you turn the ignition to the start position, all the warning lights quickly turn off, unless you haven't buckled up or you left the emergency brake on. If any of the warning lights stay on, don't panic; remember that the warning light you see is a *warning*—you're car is not going to break down immediately. Refer to the car owner's manual to see what the problem might be. If you've exhausted all the suggestions from the car owner's manual and a warning light is still on, take your car to the repair shop.

Here's a list of the most common warning lights in vehicles and the problems associated with them (not all cars have all of these lights).

- *CHECK ENGINE.* **The typical cause is with the emission system, possibly a loose or missing fuel cap.**
- *CHARGE.* **The problem is usually not with the battery, but with the alternator or a belt.**

Warning lights

- *COOLANT.* This light can also read LOW COOLANT, which means that you need to fill it, or CHECK COOLANT TEMP, which means that the coolant temperature is too hot.

- *CHECK ENGINE TEMP* or *ENGINE HOT.* If you see this light, pull over when and where it's safe to do so and turn off the engine to let it cool. Check the level of coolant and fill the reservoir if necessary. Your car may need to be towed.
- *CHECK OIL LEVEL.* This will appear if the oil level is too low, so check the dipstick and add oil as soon as possible.
- *CHECK OIL PRESSURE.* This means that the oil isn't flowing through the engine properly. You could be low on oil or another system problem. You may need to call a towing service.
- *ABS.* If you have antilock brakes, this light will come on if the ABS has failed. Don't panic because you still have your regular brakes, but you do need to get the ABS fixed immediately.
- *BRAKE.* This light stays on if the parking brake has not been released or if the brake fluid is low. Check to make sure you have enough brake fluid.
- *AIR BAG.* If the light is on it means that there is a malfunction with the air bag and it will not work properly. You need to immediately take the car in for inspection.
- *SEAT BELT.* This is one of the two lights that you have complete control over. Buckle up!
- *TRANS FLUID HOT.* This means that the transmission fluid is too hot and you may ruin the transmission if you keep driving.
- *SECURITY.* If this light stays on after the engine has started, there is a problem with the security system.
- *DOOR AJAR.* This is a handy sensor that lets you know if a door has not been closed properly.
- *LOW WASHER FLUID.* There's a quick fix for this problem ... just fill the windshield washer fluid reservoir (see "Filling the Washer Fluid Reservoir," page 107).

- *LOW FUEL.* This is probably the one sensor that gets our attention immediately. If this lights up, you should refer to the fuel gauge to get a better sense of how much fuel is left. Just remember to not push your luck, or you may be pushing your car to the nearest gas station!

Now that you may know what's causing the light sensor to turn on, take notes—is it when the engine starts, is it when you're going up or down a hill, is it at a certain speed, or is it when the engine is cold or hot? All of this information will be helpful to the mechanic who's servicing your car.

Gauges

Gauges give you a real-time look as to what's going on with your car. For instance, if you see the needle on the fuel gauge dip below the EMPTY line, you know you've got to get fuel as soon as possible. And if you see the needle going into the HOT area, then your car is overheating right now.

Here are the most common gauges found in cars.

- SPEEDOMETER. This tells you how fast your car is going in miles per hour.
- OIL PRESSURE. This indicates the oil pressure level. The car could be low on oil or it could be another system problem.
- ODOMETER. This is a counter for the miles driven. A trip odometer is sometimes included, as well.

Gauges

- FUEL GAUGE. This gauge won't tell you how much fuel is in your tank, but it will tell you if the tank is full, empty, and anywhere in between.
- TEMPERATURE GAUGE. If the needle is in the HOT area, that means that your car is overheating and you'll need to put the windows down and turn the heater on. Pull over when and where it's safe and turn the engine off. When the engine is cool, check the level of coolant and add more if necessary.
- TACHOMETER. This calculates the speed of the engine in revolutions per minute (rpm).
- VOLTMETER. This shows the condition of the charging system, not just the battery. As long as the needle is in between the low and high areas, then the charging system is in good condition. If the needle is in either the HIGH or the LOW area, turn off the radio and the air conditioner or heater and drive to a mechanic.

Exterior Lamps

Does your car get mistaken in the dark for a motorcycle? If so, you need to replace the burned out bulb with a new one, not only so that you can see the road better, but also so that everyone else can see you . . . all of you.

Every car has exterior lamps and interior lights, but the bulbs and replacement instructions, as well as added features, vary with each make and model. Just another reason for you to be *enlightened* about your car owner's manual.

Note: Before doing any work on headlamps, be sure that they're turned off and the engine isn't running.

How They Work

The exterior lighting system includes headlamps, which are in the front of the car; tail brake lamps, which are located in the rear of the car; side marker lamps; directionals; hazard lamps; and rear license plate lamps. Some cars also have fog lamps.

The size and type of bulb varies with the lamp, but they all have the same distinctive appearance if they've burned out—the glass is smoky or the filament is burned.

DIY: Headlamps

Headlamps are either *sealed-beam*, which means that the bulb and light fixture are one unit, or *composite*, which means the unit has a bulb that can be replaced separately from the light fixture. Newer cars use

It's best to remove any rings, bracelets, or watches you might be wearing prior to working on any lamps so that they don't hit an electrical wire and cause a shortage or spark.

the composite headlamps, which are less expensive to repair because you can just replace a bulb rather than replacing the entire unit.

Some cars use one bulb with two filaments for both low and high beams, and some have separate bulbs and separate headlamps.

Replacing a Sealed-Beam Headlamp

Note: The following instructions apply for replacing a burned-out bulb as well as for replacing a shattered headlamp.

Before you touch the headlamp, buy the replacement part first. You can find the information for the correct replacement part in the car owner's manual, or you can give the make and model of your car to the parts department. Before you leave, ask the clerk which tool is recommended for the project—a Phillips screwdriver or a Torx driver—and remember to double-check that you received the correct part.

Pop open the hood of the car and take a glance at how the headlamps are fastened. Some cars have pins that just need to be pulled out. If so, remove them and unplug the electrical connector. Turn the headlamp counterclockwise to remove. Insert the new headlamp, turning it clockwise to tighten, plug in the electrical connector, and replace the pins.

If your car has a rubber trim around the headlamp, it's probably secured with some screws. Use either the Phillips screwdriver or Torx driver to remove the screws and take off the trim.

Now use the same tool to remove the screws that are securing the headlamp. Be sure to put the screws in a safe place because you may be needing them again. To remove the headlamp, unplug it from the connecting wire.

Tools Needed

New headlamp   Phillips screwdriver or Torx driver

Car owner's manual

Connect the new headlamp to the electrical connectors and push it into place. Insert the screws and tighten. Replace the rubber trim (if applicable) and screws. Before closing the hood, make sure that you didn't leave any items inside. Check the position of the lights and adjust if necessary.

Replacing a Composite Headlamp or Bulb

The majority of new cars use halogen bulbs for the headlamps because they're smaller than regular bulbs, they last longer, and they produce a much brighter light. Be very careful never to touch the glass part of the halogen bulb because the oils from your fingers will cause it to burn out prematurely.

Different cars have different methods of accessing the bulb. Some cars will require you to remove the headlamp to get to the bulb, while others allow you to simply reach behind the headlamp and unscrew a knob and pull out the bulb. No matter which method you have to use, it's easier than you think. In fact, if you just look at the car owner's manual and look at the lamp assembly it will all make sense.

Under the Hood—Method I

Locate the knob that's behind each headlamp. If you see a retaining ring, remove it. Turn the knob counterclockwise to remove the assembly. Pull out the old bulb and insert the new one, remembering to handle it only at its base. Push the bulb into position, turn the

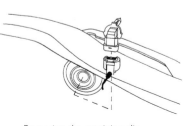

Removing the retaining clip

knob clockwise to tighten, and return the retaining ring, if necessary. Close the hood. Be sure to check the position of the lights and adjust if necessary.

Tools Needed

New halogen bulb or new headlamp

Car owner's manual

Under the Hood—Method 2

Removing the headlamp

If you can only access a bulb by removing the headlamp, remove the locking clips, wing nuts, or whatever locking gear your car has, and pull out the headlamp assembly. The instructions in the car owner's manual may state that you need to disconnect the headlamp from the electrical connector; this may not be required with other cars.

Remove the old bulb by turning it counterclockwise. Insert the new bulb, being careful not to touch the glass, and turn it clockwise to tighten. Plug the headlamp assembly into the electrical connector (if necessary) and push the assembly back into place. Engage the locking gear. Check the position of the lights and adjust if necessary.

Note: Some cars have separate headlamps for high beam and low beam (and therefore separate bulbs), but they're side by side in one glass casing. If so, you may want to replace both bulbs since they're both exposed.

Adjusting the Headlamps

Adjusting the headlamps is necessary so that the light is emitted at the correct angle. This only needs to be done if you've replaced one or both of the headlamps, or you're traveling a great distance with a very heavy load.

Adjusting the headlamps is not difficult, but the problem with doing it yourself is that it won't be 100 percent accurate. You might not be able to notice the difference, but your car may not pass inspection, and it may

Tools Needed

Phillips screwdriver   **Masking tape**

pose a hazard to other drivers. So the next time you take your car in for any repairs, have the mechanic make any necessary adjustments.

Note: This works best at dusk or at night.

Pull the car up to about 1 foot from the garage door or an exterior wall. Turn the engine off, but keep the headlamps on (low beam). Take 2 pieces of masking tape and place them where the light hits the garage door or wall.

Now move the car back about 25 feet (2½ car lengths) and turn the engine off, but keep the headlamps on (low beam). Note the difference in where the light is now hitting the garage wall or door. The optimal position is for each light to be 2 inches to the right and 2 inches below the masking tape. If you have separate headlamps for low and high beams (a.k.a. brights), the high beam's optimal position is for the light to be directly on the masking tape.

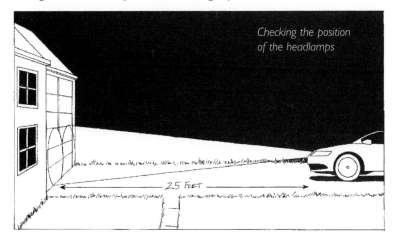

Checking the position of the headlamps

25 FEET

If the lights are completely off-centered, insert the Phillips screwdriver into the vertical adjustment screw located at the top of each headlamp (if your headlamp has a rubber trim, remove it). Turn the screwdriver left or right to adjust accordingly.

Check the lighting and adjust again if necessary.

Daytime Running Lamps

The purpose of daytime running lamps is to provide better visibility of the front of your car to other drivers. These lamps are actually two lights working together—the parking lights or headlamps at 50 percent power. Daytime running lamps are not standard in all cars, especially in older models.

Of all the exterior lamps, these are the ones most likely to have bulbs burn out, because they're used the most. If your car has daytime running lamps, you should always have these on while you drive because anything that you can do to make your car more easily visible to other motorists is always a good thing.

Your daytime running lamps will not run in conjunction with your headlamps—it's always one or the other. Some cars turn on your headlamps automatically when it's dark outside. Check your car owner's manual to see if your car has this feature.

Front Turn Signal and Side Marker

The front turn signal side markers are used as a visual aid for other motorists to better see your car. You'll know you have a problem with them if they're rapidly flashing on and off.

The side markers are located at the sides of the headlamps. Depending on your car, you may need to remove the headlamp assembly (see page 166). If not, push down on the retainer clip and pull out the side marker assembly. Turn the bulb counterclockwise to remove, being careful not to touch the halogen bulb with your fingers. Insert the new bulb, turning it clockwise to tighten. Return the assembly back to its housing.

Tools Needed

Phillips screwdriver

Car owner's manual

New bulb

Other cars may require you to remove nuts with your fingers or screws with a Phillips screwdriver to remove the side markers. Untwist the bulb counterclockwise and replace it with a new one, being careful not to touch the halogen bulb. Return the fasteners and close the hood.

To have access to the front turn signal, follow the directions for the side markers.

Fog Lamps

Fog lamps are effective in providing lighting during foggy or misty conditions because the light emitted is aimed very low at the ground, instead of higher up like the headlamps. When the headlamp high beams are engaged, the fog lamps turn off.

Fog lamps

Not all cars have fog lamps, but if your car does, they're located at the very bottom front of your car. They are typically easy to access for replacing a bulb because all you may have to do is remove the bulb from behind the bumper.

Turn the engine off.

You're going to have to get down on the pavement to remove the burned-out bulb, so use the blanket to kneel on. Reach behind the fog lamp and twist out the bulb and replace it with a new one.

Tools Needed

New fog lamp bulb

Blanket

Taillamps

Note: This works best at night and by backing the car into the driveway so that the tail lights face the garage door or an exterior wall.

Taillamps are lamps that are located in the rear of the car, such as the brake lamp, the turn signal lamp, and the reverse lamp. Older cars may have a separate casing for each of these taillamps, whereas newer cars may have all three lamps under one casing.

To test if the taillamps are working, it's easiest to enlist the help of a friend, or you can always use your side-view mirrors if you don't want to get out of your car.

Back the car into the driveway, leaving a few feet in between the garage door or up to an exterior wall, and turn off the engine, but leave the headlamps on and turn on the parking signal. Now you can either look into the side-view mirrors or get out of the car to inspect both the parking lamps and the turn signals (we prefer to get up close).

To test the brake lamps, you'll need a friend or you'll have to use the side-view mirrors. Turn the engine on and press down on the brake pedal. Now have your friend tell you if the brake lamps are working or look into the side-view mirrors. Remember to check the third brake light (center high mount stoplight) located in the center of the back window, if you have one.

To check the reverse lamps again, you'll need a friend or you'll have to use the side-view mirrors. Turn the engine on and step firmly on the brake, then place the gear in reverse. Have your friend tell you the status of the lights, including the rear license plate lights.

Tools Needed

Phillips screwdriver   New bulb   Helpful friend

Car owner's manual

If any of the taillamps needs a bulb replaced, first refer to the car owner's manual for the correct replacement bulb, as well as how to access the taillamps.

Depending on the car, you'll either be able to have access to the taillamp or bulb from inside the trunk, or by removing screws located on the front of the lamps.

To gain access from inside the trunk, lift the trunk or hatchback. If the taillamps are accessible from the outside, insert the screwdriver into the screws, typically located on the sides of the taillamp. Turn the screwdriver counterclockwise to remove the screws, and place them in a safe place.

Pull out the taillamp assembly and depress the release mechanism if there is one. To remove the bulb socket, turn it counterclockwise. Now pull the bulb out and replace it with the new one. Insert the bulb socket into place and turn it clockwise to secure. Return the tail lamp assembly and insert the screws, turning them clockwise to tighten.

Windows, Windshields, and Wipers

Fixing a Power Window

Molly decided to treat herself and her children to a ski trip to Vermont. But the trek turned *downhill* fast when they went through a toll booth and then couldn't get the driver's window back up. With hundreds of miles ahead of them and snow falling around them, they decided to go *off trail* and head to the nearest car dealership instead.

Molly was lucky that the control panel only regulated the window. In some cars, the control panel regulates the door locks, the windows, and the side mirrors!

How It Works

Windows are operated individually by a switch on each door (powered by a motor inside each door) and by a main control panel located in the front of the car (which also has its own motor). There is one fuse that is designated for all the windows.

If a window isn't working, the first thing to do is to find the origin of the problem.

DIY

If One Window Isn't Working

If just one of the windows isn't working, then the problem could be with its switch. You may have spilled your latte in it, or left the window down on a rainy day, or it may have burned out from wear and tear. Call around to a dealership, as well as to auto parts stores, to get the best price on the part, being sure to have on hand the make, model and year of your car.

Note: Most auto part stores and dealerships will not allow you to return electrical parts; therefore, make sure that you're purchasing the correct part.

Removing the Switch

Use the small flathead screwdriver (or metal nail file) to pry up the switch control. There's not much space to get the tool into, but be patient and don't give up—it will come out! There may be two metal tabs on each end that you can depress to lift the switch out. Pull the switch control out and detach it from the connectors.

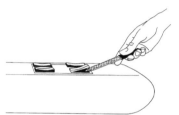
Prying open the switch control

Installing the Switch

Insert the new switch control and attach it to the electrical connector. Push it in all the way and replace the cover. Try to operate the window. If the window doesn't work, there may be an electrical problem and you'll need to have it professionally serviced.

Tools Needed

Car owner's manual 　　New switch 　　Small flathead screwdriver or metal nail file

If All the Windows Aren't Working

If none of the windows are operating, the problem could be a bad motor or fuse. It's best to rule out a fuse first, because it's a lot less expensive to replace.

Locating the Fuse Panel

Fuses are typically located in the front of the car on either the driver's or passenger's side, behind a panel, or under the hood. Some cars have more then one fuse panel, so you'll need to refer to the car owner's manual, which you'll need anyway to locate and replace the specific fuse.

Removing the Panel

Use your fingers to pry off the panel. Sometimes there is a fuse map, located on the inside of the panel, that states which fuse operates certain things in the car. If your car doesn't have one, refer to the car owner's manual to locate the fuse that controls the windows. Depending on the make, model, and year of your car, the fuses will be either cylindrical glass pieces or flat metal.

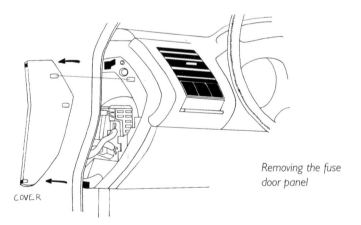

Removing the fuse door panel

Removing the Fuse

Some cars have fuse pullers located in the fuse panel, but you really don't need them because fuses are easy to pull out with your fingers or needle-nose pliers, and you won't get shocked.

Take a look at the fuse. Is the inside of the glass fuse discolored, or is the metal fuse burned? If so, then the fuse has blown and needs to be replaced. Some cars will have spare fuses, which you can locate by referring to the car owner's manual (*yes, again*). If you don't have spare fuses, go to an auto parts store and purchase a replacement of the exact same amperage. While you're at it, you may want to buy some spare fuses of varying amperages to keep on hand in case other fuses blow.

Replacing the Fuse
Insert the new fuse, close up the panel, turn on the engine, and operate a window. If the windows won't operate, then the problem may be the motor, which will have to be professionally serviced.

Tools Needed

Car owner's manual

New fuse

Windshield

Where would we be without the windshield? Probably at the dentist getting our teeth cleaned.

The windshield was originally designed to keep bad weather (and bugs) from getting inside the car. Today, windshields do much more than that; in fact, windshields are designed to reduce glare as well as protect you in case of an accident.

How It Works

You'd never know it, but windshields are made up of two panes of glass compressing a plastic inner layer to create a laminated safety glass. This design acts as a protective barrier in an accident. The other interesting fact about windshields is that they are not clear. Windshields come in assorted colors, including green, blue, bronze, and gray; the only time a clear windshield is used is for TV or movies.

Determining the Damage

Depending on its size and location, a chip or a crack in a windshield can be fixed, but you can't do it yourself—putting clear nail polish on the area won't work like it does on pantyhose. However, you can and should assess the level of damage because 90 percent of your ability to drive depends on visibility; it is vital that your windshield is free of dirt, cracks, and chips.

Chips and cracks should be repaired immediately because they will eventually increase in size over time. Also, it's always better to fix a chip or a small crack, if possible, rather than to have the entire windshield replaced because you want to keep the integrity of the original windshield and maintain its factory seal for safety reasons.

IY

Before you call a glass company, determine if the size and location of the damage will require a repair or replacement.

Take a dollar bill and place it over the chip or crack on the windshield. If the damaged area is larger than the dollar bill, you need to have the windshield replaced. If the dollar bill covers the area completely, it can be repaired.

Determining windshield damage

Many insurance companies will cover the cost of either repairing the chip or replacing the windshield, so you really shouldn't hesitate to have it done. Typically, the glass company will confirm the order with your insurance company before setting up an appointment with you and will even process the claim.

If you don't know of a reputable car glass company, ask your insurance agent for a listing. You want a company that has a door-front location, is licensed and bonded in your area, is in good standing with the Better Business Bureau, the Chamber of Commerce, and members of the National Glass Association, and uses OEM (original equipment manufacturers) or equivalent materials and parts. Last, ask the com-

Tool Needed

Dollar bill

pany how long you need to wait before driving away with the repaired or replaced windshield. If the windshield needs to be replaced, the answer should be 2 hours; for repairs, 30 to 45 minutes. If anyone states that you can drive away immediately, you should look for another glass company because they're not thinking of your safety and the time it takes for the adhesive to properly cure (harden).

Protecting Your Windshield

Behind every pile of snow on a windshield lies a layer of ice. Here are some helpful tips for removing winter's thumbprint, while protecting the windshield.

Snow Broom

The first step is to remove the snow. To do this job, we prefer a large wide broom, which makes it much easier to sweep it off.

Snow broom

The correct way to remove snow is to start at the top and work your way down. Most people just remove it from the windows and windshield, knowing that the snow will fall off the top as soon as they start driving. The only problem is that it can fall onto the car behind, temporarily causing a loss of vision for that driver. So be courteous and clear off all of the snow. Oh, and don't forget to clear off the windshield wipers, the license plates, and the lights, too, so your vision won't be impaired.

Ice Scraper

We're sure you've used very creative objects to clear a windshield like a credit card, a spatula, and even a laminated place mat, but those bad ways are all in the past, right? *Right?!!*

Ice Scraper

Not only should you *only* use an ice scraper for the job, but you should purchase a good quality one as well. What constitutes a good ice scraper? One that has a good comfortable grip, because the size and handle make it easier to put some muscle behind it. Of course, the best solution is to buy an all-in-one-product, such as a snow broom with a removable ice scraper.

Defrosting a Windshield

The best way to defrost your windshield and side windows is to use a good ice scraper and the car's defroster.

Every car has a defroster, which is a part of the car's cooling system. It blows hot air onto the front windshield to help defrost ice and eliminate fog.

To properly use the defroster, adjust the temperature control knob to HOT and select the DEFROST setting; or if your car has a separate defrost control button, depress it. If you're not sure how to start the defroster, check the car owner's manual.

If the defroster isn't working efficiently, the problem could be that there is not enough coolant in the system, the thermostat is not working properly, or the radiator is malfunctioning (see "Cooling System," page 28).

Defogging a Rear Window

If your car has a rear window with thin lines running across it, then it is equipped with a rear-window defogger. The lines heat up to warm the window to defrost or defog it.

Rear-window defogger

If your car has a rear-window defogger, there is a separate button on the dashboard to operate it. If you're not sure where the button is located, consult the owner's manual. The rear-window defogger will shut off automatically when the window has been cleared.

If the rear-window defogger is not working, the likely cause is a broken heating element (one of the lines running across the rear window) or a fuse.

Windshield Wiper System

Sure, Henry Ford invented the assembly line for automobiles, and William Durant started General Motors. *Blah, blah, blah.* **But did you know that it was a woman who invented the windshield wiper? Mary Anderson, a southern belle from Alabama, realized on a trip to New York City that motorists needed a device to clear the windshield.** *Atta girl, Mary!*

Did you know that 90 percent of our driving ability is based on visibility. We'd say that's a pretty good reason for maintaining your car's windshield wiper system and all its windows.

What It Is

The windshield wiper system consists of 4 parts: (1) wiper motor and linkage; (2) wiper blade; (3) refill wiper arm; and (4) washer fluid. The *wiper* motor powers the wiper blade. The *wiper blade* is the device that holds the *refill* and is attached to the arm. The *refill* is the rubber insert in the blade that touches the windshield and acts like a squeegee. The *refill wiper arm* is the piece attached near the base of the windshield and moves the wiper blade across the windshield. It usually never has to be replaced, unless it's damaged in an accident. Last, the washer fluid is the blue-colored cleaning liquid for the windshield located in a plastic reservoir near the engine.

DIY

Checking the Wiper Blades

To properly maintain the wiper system, you need to clean the refills about twice a month, replenish the washer fluid regularly, and replace either the refills or the blades every 6 months. That's right—it's just like changing your clock twice a year for daylight saving time. But don't wait exactly 6 months to the day to replace a part, because depending on where you live, especially in a very hot climate or snowy area, you may need to change it more frequently.

The best time to check your wiper system is after you've washed your car. Manually lift up the wiper arms (being careful not to break them) and check the rubber refills in the blades to see if they're loose, cracked, or worn. If you're not quite sure, spray the washer fluid and turn the wipers on (never use the wipers on a dry windshield because you can scratch the glass). Do you notice any streaks? Do you hear a screeching noise? Those are signs of wear.

Cleaning the Refills

It's important to regularly remove the dirt buildup on the refills so that they can make better contact with the glass and also so that you're not wiping the glass with dirt!

The best product for cleaning refills is windshield washer fluid. Pour it onto a clean rag and gently wipe the refills along the edge that touches the glass—don't forget the wiper on the back of your car. Now is also a great time to check them for cracks.

Replacing the Wiper Blades

Even though you can replace the refills (a.k.a. inserts), we're not going to tell you how to do it because it's a big hassle and it's not worth the

> Never buy cheap wiper blades— you pay for what you get and your visibility is worth more than a few saved dollars.

Tools Needed

Windshield washer fluid

Clean rag

*O*n parts of the country where wiper blades are rarely needed, be sure to operate them (with washer fluid) twice a month to maintain them.

savings. Replacing a blade is a snap—no, really, it is a *snap*—and it takes just seconds to do. The only time we would suggest replacing the refills is if the wipers are still covered under the warranty.

Before purchasing replacement wiper blades, you need to measure each one because on some cars the driver's side blade is longer than the passenger's. Also, the blade on the back of the car is usually smaller than the front ones. The common sizes for wiper blades are 16 inches, 18 inches, and 24 inches. Write the measurements inside the car owner's manual.

Wiper refills come in packages of two, but wiper blades are sold separately. You should never just replace one blade; always replace all of them at the same time. Otherwise, it would be like getting just one shoe instead of a pair!

Never remove the wiper blades until you've purchased new ones, and only remove and replace one at a time just in case you bought the wrong type. We also think it's wise to replace them in the parking lot of the auto parts store, because if you purchased the wrong one, or you're having difficulty installing them, there's help right there.

Lift up the windshield arm, being careful not to break it. To remove a wiper blade, find the release mechanism and either squeeze or push it in or move it up or down and take the blade off. To put in a new one, simply reverse the steps and snap on the new blade. Repeat on remaining wipers.

Wiper-blade release mechanism

Tools Needed

Measuring tape

Pen

Car owner's manual

New wiper blades

Removing Rust from the Wiper Arm

It's important to keep the wiper arms from rusting because they're very expensive to replace. Washing the car often during the winter months will help to keep salt and other corrosive materials from causing rust on the wiper arms. If you see rust, apply any rust-resistant paint, following the manufacturer's instructions, being careful not to get any on the car's paint.

Winter Windshield Wipers and Fluid (Deicer)

Wipers

If you live in an area where you get a lot of ice and snow, you're all too familiar with how it can accumulate at the base of a windshield wiper blade, causing you to frequently get out of your car to clear it. We have a great solution for you—use winter/snow wiper blades. They're designed without openings at the base so that the snow and ice won't get stuck in there. But just because they're listed as "winter" wiper blades, that doesn't mean you can use them in lieu of an ice scraper or car brush. Windshield wipers are not designed to remove snow and ice, only water and windshield washer fluid. These special wipers can be purchased at any auto parts store.

Washer Fluid (Deicer)

Windshield washer fluid gets used more frequently during winter than any other season, so be sure to check the windshield washer fluid reservoir every time you fill up with gas, and replenish if necessary. Also, if the outdoor temperature frequently drops below 32°F, purchase winter-formulated windshield washer fluid (a.k.a. deicer).

Winter-formulated windshield washer fluid (a.k.a. deicer)

If the holes that emit the windshield washer fluid get clogged with snow and ice often, insert a small wire (such as a straightened paper clip) or a sewing needle into the nozzles about ⅛ inch to remove the clog.

> *f you're expecting a snowstorm, a good trick to keep your windshield wipers from freezing is to manually lift them off the glass when the car is parked. Just don't forget to lower them before you drive off.*

Detailing

Detailing is the process of cleaning your car to get it as close to its original condition as possible. **Of course, one woman's *clean* is another woman's *mess*. Our goal is not to teach you how to become a detailing diva, but rather to offer you simple ways to take care of the interior and exterior of your car so you can maintain its value.**

Detailing is in the details. We can't stress enough the importance of using the car owner's manual as a reference guide to buying the correct care products for your car, as well as following the manufacturer's recommendations for using them.

Removing Bugs, Sap, Tar, and Bird Droppings

ap happens. **Yes, you can avoid parking under a tree, but there's nothing you can do to avoid kamikaze bugs, newly paved roads, and the blue bird of happiness leaving her calling card.**

The most important thing you can do to protect the paint on your car is to remove the foreign "by-products" as soon as possible. Bird droppings and insects contain acids, which if left on a car can damage the paint. Tar and sap form a tight adhesive to the paint and over time can become permanently bonded.

There are lots of items on the market that can remove these markings, but you need to make sure that the solvent is eco- and paint-friendly. There's no need in harming the environment while protecting your car's paint.

Diy

Of all the things that can land on your car, tree sap and tar are the most difficult to remove, especially if left for a long period of time. Don't try to pry either off with a knife (even if it's a butter knife) because you'll end up scratching the paint.

Tools Needed

Goof Off

Bucket with warm, soapy water

Clean terry or chamois cloth towels

Never allow fallen leaves to remain on your car, no matter how pretty they are, because they can permanently stain the paint.

Spray Goof Off on the area and let it penetrate the sap or tar for about 5 minutes. For bugs and bird droppings, apply the spray, but let it set for only a few seconds. Use the soft cloth to wipe away the sap. Repeat if necessary. Wash the area with warm soapy water and a clean soft towel to remove any residual solvent.

Removing harmful contaminants

DIFM

If the sap or tar won't come off, then we suggest you take the car to an auto detailing shop.

Removing Bumper Stickers

Are your bumper stickers revealing too much about you, like your age ("I Like Ike") or alma mater ("The Fightin' Blue Hens")? Bumper stickers have always been a unique way for people to voice their feelings about all kinds of things, but when it's time to get rid of your car, the only words that should be displayed are "For Sale."

Some cars have chrome bumpers while others have a metal bumper that is covered with painted plastic. Removing a sticker from a chrome bumper is pretty easy, but you really have to be careful when taking a sticker off a painted bumper. In fact, you may end up paying for a very expensive paint job because you can't use touch-up paint on it. Therefore, if you must declare your political allegiance or tell the world that you have an honor roll child, place the sticker on a window (someplace where it won't block your view).

DIY

Removing a Sticker

Connect the hair dryer to the extension cord and plug it in. Turn the hair dryer on low and heat the sticker for a few minutes (touch it to see if it's warm) to loosen the adhesive. If the sticker is on the paint, be careful not to overheat the sticker because you don't want to ruin the paint around it.

Apply the Goof Off on the sticker and wait about 5 minutes. Use the plastic razor blade or old credit card to loosen one edge of the

Never use a metal scraper or a razor blade to remove a decal or a sticker on a bumper because you may scratch the chrome or paint.

If using an adhesive remover, make sure that it is paint-safe; when in doubt, contact the manufacturer.

sticker. Pull on the edge and try to remove it in one piece. If not, then just work at it in pieces.

Spray the Goof Off onto any residue left from the sticker and remove with a rag. Repeat the process if necessary.

If the sticker was on a window, clean the window using the vinegar and water mixture and wipe off with newspaper.

Removing a bumper sticker

Tools Needed

Hair dryer   Outdoor extension cord

 Goof Off

Plastic razor blade or old credit card

Rag   White vinegar and water
mixture (½ and ½) in spray bottle

Newspaper

Fixing Scratches and Chips

Debra had to park her car in her driveway, and every morning she would notice tiny footprints on the hood. It seems that there were some nocturnal animals having a picnic on her car. It was bad enough to see the muddy tracks and scratches on the paint, but they never bothered to clean up the party nuts.

When you see that your car has received some damage to the body, don't be in denial, no matter how small the problem. Damage to the car's exterior can lead to rusting, which will eventually lead to a serious *dent* in your wallet. Rust (no matter how small of an amount) never confines itself to just one spot, and if left untouched, it will eat away at the surrounding metal.

When you notice damage to the body of the car, first contact your car insurance agent to find out if your policy will cover exterior repairs if you haven't been in a crash. Even if the news is not to your liking, you should have the repair done. While you're talking to your insurance agent, ask her for a list of paint/body shops. (Don't assume that going to your car dealership will be the most expensive alternative. Some dealerships won't charge to rub out a minor scratch, as long as you purchased the car from them.)

If you choose to do the repair yourself, be sure to read the manufacturer's instructions before you start.

Repairing a Scratch

You can fix a scratch, as long as it's not too deep. The rule of thumb for this test is to run your fingernail gently across the scratch. If your nail gets caught in it, then it's considered a deep scratch and you should get it professionally repaired.

If the scratch has not penetrated through to the paint or metal, you can use a car product that acts as a light buffing polish that will remove the scratch.

DIY

Note: Be sure to test the product on an inconspicuous area, possibly on the inside of the door.

Gently buffing a scratch

Pour a little bit of the Scratch X onto the cloth and rub it gently onto the scratched surface. Let it dry completely and then wipe it off with a clean side of the cloth.

If this didn't do the trick, then the scratch is probably too deep and you'll need to have it professionally repaired.

Chips

A chip off the ol' block is not a good thing if you're talking about your car, especially if you see metal. This means that the clear coat and paint layer have been damaged. You will need to have this problem fixed as soon as possible.

DIY

Note: Always wash the car and let it dry before applying the paint. Also be sure that there's no chance of rain for the next 48 hours, and follow the paint

Tools Needed

Scratch X (or something comparable)

100 percent cotton terry cloths (new and soft)

manufacturer's recommendations for exterior temperature, typically above 50°.

Apply the painter's tape around the chip or scratch to protect the surrounding area from any spills. Shake the container vigorously. Pour a little of the paint onto the paper plate—you won't need much.

If you're repairing a chip, lightly dip the tip of the paintbrush into the paint and gingerly apply the paint to the chipped area in one smooth motion. Allow it to dry according to the manufacturer's directions.

Filling a chip with paint

If you're applying paint to a deep scratch, dip the end of the toothpick into the paint and apply a small amount to the scratch in one smooth motion. Let it dry according to the manufacturer's instructions.

N onmetallic paint typically needs one coat, and metallic paint usually needs two or more coats.

DIFM

If you can't afford to have the work professionally done and/or the car is old and you don't want to put too much money into it, have your car serviced at a local technical high school. These schools take cars (typically if they're under 10 years old) and fix them for the cost of materials and parts. Unfortunately, there won't be a quick turnaround and there's no guarantee of the quality of work.

Tools Needed

Touch-up paint

Toothpick or artist's paintbrush

Painter's tape

Paper Plate

Rag

Washing Your Car

on't let Mother Nature be in charge of washing your car. Just remember, she's the one that got it dirty!

Believe it or not, the most important reason for washing your car is *not* to make it look nice. Actually, the most important reason for washing your car is to remove air pollutants, salt, dirt, bugs, grease, tar, and sap, all of which can over time harm the car's paint.

How often you should wash your car depends on the elements where you live. If you live in the Snowbelt, there's probably salt and sand on your car and tires during the winter. If you live in a high-traffic area, there are probably a lot of air pollutants. And if you park near trees, there's probably some sap on your car. If you can relate to any of these situations, then you should wash your car at least twice a month (or even once a week, if you live in a harsh winter climate). On the flip side of the coin, we don't think that anyone needs to be washing their car once a week because we think it's more important to conserve water.

DIY

Getting Ready

Before you start, it's important to contact your water company to see if your area is under any water restrictions because your local government may fine you if you wash your car during a drought.

If you're washing the car in the warmer months, it's always best to do it in the shade with the engine cooled. That's because if the sun is too bright or the car engine is still hot, the water and soap will dry quickly. If it's wintertime, be sure to clean underneath the car to remove any salt,

Water Conservation

Did you know that the Environmental Protection Agency (EPA) states that the typical car owner uses 5 buckets (or about 10 gallons) of water to wash her car. We also bet that you didn't know (because we didn't either) that if you wash your car and allow the soapy water to enter into a creek, a stream, or other body of water, the EPA can fine you $750 for polluting a waterway. Any soapy water that runs into the sewer is treated at a sewer plant, but soapy water that enters a waterway is *not* treated, and therefore can pollute.

How do you prevent this from happening? The EPA suggests that you wash your car on grass, or use your driveway as long as the water runs onto your yard and not into the street. And if that doesn't work for you, then locate a commercial car wash that has a do-it-yourself bay or just use the drive-thru car wash. Commercial car washes use more water than if you do it yourself, but the runoff goes into the sewer. Some newer car washes even recycle the water, which is the optimal choice.

Avoid using hot water when washing your car because it could damage the wax.

dirt, and sand. These materials, which are used to rid the streets of snow and ice, can be harmful to your car.

Always use a car-cleaning product, not dish detergent or any other household cleaner on your car because it can damage the paint and strip the wax.

Washing the Car

Place a piece of painter's tape over the keyhole on the front door to prevent water from entering. (This is especially important to do if you're washing the car in the winter.)

Never wash the entire car at once because the soap will dry before you can rinse it off. Instead, divide it into sections starting at the top of the car and working your way down. For those of you who

If the paint color of the car is coming off onto the sponge, the problem is that the paint has been oxidized. It's best to just stop washing the car.

own an SUV or minivan *and* are not over 6 feet tall, you may need a stepladder to wash the top of the car. Remember to have both spreaders locked, don't overreach, and never stand on the top of the ladder.

Washing a car

Use the spray nozzle to do a gentle rinse to get rid of a lot of the dirt as well as to prepare the car for washing.

When you're washing the car, don't forget to clean underneath the car's body and inside the tire wells. These areas are where dirt and salt collect, which can cause rust.

Once you've washed and sprayed the entire car, remove the spray nozzle and rinse the entire car again. By letting the water flow, you'll have fewer spots. Use the towels to dry off the car, including the windows.

Once the car has been dried off, use one of the wet towels and clean the inside of each door (a.k.a, doorjamb), including the hatch door, if applicable. Use a towel to dry them completely to prevent rusting or to prevent the doors from freezing shut if it's wintertime. Remove the painter's tape from the keyhole.

Cleaning the Tires

Wait a minute . . . you're not done. You still have to wash the tires. Why? Your tires are the only part of the car that touch the ground, so it's important to take good care of them.

Spray each tire and remove any pebbles and debris from the treads. Use the tire brush to scrub the sidewalls of each tire, but not the treads. Let the tires air dry. Don't use a tire preservative because it may crack the sidewalls.

Washing the Windows

Exterior

We recommend that you use a white vinegar and water solution for the exterior of your windows and wipe the exterior dry with newspaper. You may think that there's no way that the newspaper is going to absorb the moisture, but it does—and it won't leave behind any lint or streaks. Remember to clean the side-view mirrors, too.

Interior

For cleaning the interior windows, we suggest you use the old tried-and-true blue-colored window cleaner instead of the vinegar and water, unless you like your car smelling like you've just dyed 3 dozen Easter eggs. Remember to clean the rearview mirror, too.

Tools Needed

Long water hose with spray nozzle

Stepladder (for SUV or minivan)

Clean sponge or sponge mitt

Bucket

Car cleaner (environment-friendly)

Tire brush

White vinegar and water mixture (½ and ½) in spray bottle

Newspaper

Clean towels (soft 100 percent terry or chamois cloth)

Windshield washer fluid

Household window cleaner

Painter's tape

If you are going to use a vacuum to clean the inside of your car, do it before washing the car. Water is a great conductor of electricity; therefore, you need to keep all electrical equipment away from the car when water is present.

Cleaning the Windshield Wipers

Now that you've cleaned the windows, it only makes sense that you clean the windshield wiper blades as well. Pour some windshield washer fluid onto a cloth and wipe the rubber blades clean. Don't forget to clean the wiper blade on the back window, if applicable.

DIFM

A commercial drive-thru car wash comes in very handy, especially during a cold winter. The best commercial car washes recycle the water and are brushless, which prevents the car from being scratched.

Here are some things you should do to your car before entering a drive-thru car wash.

Driving through a car wash

- If your car has a removable antenna, twist if off and place it inside the car so that it won't get bent during the car wash.
- If possible, move both side-view mirrors in toward the car, so that they won't get damaged.
- If you are washing your car during the wintertime, cover the keyhole with painter's tape to prevent moisture from entering. Be sure to wipe dry the doorjambs afterward.
- Remove all valuables, including garage door remote control, title, and registration.

When you leave the car wash, pull over to a parking space so that you can replace the antenna, move the mirrors back into place, and remove the tape. *Now you can show off how good your car looks!*

Waxing Your Car

If you're dreading waxing your car, just think of it as a big piece of furniture. And if that's still too intimidating, then think of it as a great way to work off the box of Little Debbies you just *polished* off.

You may think that the only reason to wax a car is to make it shine brighter and that if a car is brand-new, you don't need to do it. Wrong and wrong again.

Waxing a car is vital to keeping the paint job in great shape for the life of the car. In fact, waxing your car 3 to 4 times a year can increase the life of its paint by 4 to 5 years. Even a new car needs to be waxed, typically 30 days after it was manufactured.

The majority of vehicles have 2-stage paint jobs—a base coat and a clear coat. The clear coat, which is applied on top of the base coat, acts as a barrier against air and moisture getting to the base coat. Clear coats are thin and can be easily scratched or marred. If the clear coat is worn or damaged, the base coat will oxidize and/or rust. This will result in the affected area having to be repainted, which means big bucks.

Have you ever washed your car and had the paint color come off on the cloth? This happens when the paint has oxidized due to the clear coat being worn off over time. It's a crime that your car's paint job is in such bad shape, but we don't need someone from *CSI* to tell us the cause—the car was probably never waxed.

Polishing Up

Car wax is a polishing oil that's applied to the clear coat to protect it from the damaging effects of UV rays, bugs, tar, sap, and leaves that can permanently damage the clear coat.

The average life expectancy of a car's paint depends upon the color of the paint, the climate, and the maintenance. Typically, a paint job and clear coat will last about 4 to 5 years with regular waxing.

Car wax comes in a liquid or paste, and can be purchased at any auto parts store. There are lots of different brands to choose from, but what really matters is that you only choose a nonabrasive wax. An abrasive wax is used on a damaged area of the car to remove the clear coat and paint. So look for a wax that is clearly identified as nonabrasive.

DIY

As we stated, you should wax your car 3 to 4 times a year. But if that's an unrealistic goal, then wax your car when you don't see raindrops bead on the hood, or if the paint is looking dull.

Always wax the car immediately after it has been washed because you don't want to rub dirt, sap, or insects into the clear coat. Never wax the car in direct sunlight because the wax will harden, making it more difficult to rub off. The temperature should be above 50°F and there should be no chance of precipitation in the next 24 hours because moisture causes the wax to streak.

One more thing before you start waxing: We recommend that you use painter's tape to cover areas of the car that you don't want wax

Tools Needed

Car wax

100 percent terry cloths, new

Stepladder

Bucket with warm mild soapy water, if necessary

Work gloves

Painter's tape (for prewaxing step)

Old soft-bristled toothbrush

to get on, such as rubber or plastic parts and the windshield wiper system. Adhering painter's tape to these areas will prevent a big headache for you because wax can be difficult to remove from these parts.

Note: If you need to use a stepladder, be sure that it doesn't hit the car and scratch the paint. Also remember to practice ladder safety and not stand on the top rung.

Put on the work gloves. Remove the sponge that came with the container and apply some wax to it.

Starting at the top, rub the wax in a circular motion, making sure to overlap areas. Remember, you should only work in one small area at a time, probably the width of your body. The reason is that wax dries quickly, so you want to be able to remove it before it hardens.

Waxing a car

Once the wax has dried, remove it with another terry cloth, working in a circular motion again. You'll probably need to use the other side of the cloth and shake it out during the process. Then, using another terry cloth, buff the area. Repeat the process on the rest of the car.

When you're done, step back and take a good look at the car for any places you missed.

Removing Wax

If wax has gotten onto areas other than the paint, use a soft-bristled toothbrush with warm mild soapy water to clean it off.

DIFM

Commercial Car Wash

A commercial car wash with a wax job can cost as little as $5. Is it the best wax job you can give your car? Of course not, but it's better than nothing.

Professional Detailer

A professional detailer will charge under $100 for a wash and wax. But a "deluxe" interior and exterior detailing can cost almost $200. Before you leave your car at the shop, there are a few things you need to do.

1. Find out what kind of wax the staff will be using. Check the container to make sure that it's nonabrasive.
2. Ask to see the shop's state business license and insurance bonding certificate.
3. Get a written estimate. If your car is damaged by a detailer, your car insurance will not pay for it. By getting this information ahead of time, you can make an informed decision as well as being prepared in case of damage to your car.

Interior Detailing

A cluttered car is not the sign of a brilliant mind. It's the sign of a driver who thinks that no one can see inside her car.

Keeping the interior neat and tidy isn't just for aesthetic purposes; it's also for safety reasons. Motorists have been severely maimed or killed by the debris in the car that suddenly turned into lethal projectiles during a crash.

Another important reason for keeping the interior of your car clean is for resale value. Even if your car's engine has been properly maintained and the exterior is in mint condition, if the inside carpet is trashed or there's a bad odor emanating from it, the car's cash value will decrease.

Detailing the interior of your car should be done 3 to 4 times a year, or every time you wax your car.

DIY

Note: Before you buy any cleaning products, consult the car owner's manual for recommended cleaning products and care.

Just like with washing and waxing your car, you're going to start detailing your car at the top (headliner) and work your way down (carpeting).

Headliner
A headliner is the material and insulation that covers the interior of the roof. The majority of cars have cloth headliners, but if the car is old, it may have vinyl. The problem with cloth headliners is that moisture, pol-

lution, and cigarette smoke can deteriorate the adhesive, causing the fabric to loosen, creating big air bubbles, sagging, and humiliation to anyone who has to be seen riding in the car.

If your headliner is sagging, you need to fix it immediately, even if it's just a temporary fix, because it can obstruct your view.

Repairing

You can't really repair a cloth headliner, so don't buy any of the adhesive sprays that promise to work—they won't. You can pay to have the headliner replaced, which can cost hundreds of dollars; but if you can't afford that, then try doing a nip and tuck. Just take a few hatpins, or thumbtacks, and secure the cloth to the insulation. It may look weird, but it sure beats having big air bubbles hanging down!

Cleaning

To clean a cloth or vinyl headliner, just wipe it with a damp rag with mild soapy water. Be careful not to get it too moist, because the water may seep through and destroy the adhesive.

Dashboard

Cleaning a dashboard is a two-part process—you need to remove the dust first and then apply a protective cleaner. You can use a vacuum cleaner with an attachment to remove the dust, or you can use a dashboard wipe, which can be purchased in an auto parts store. Use a long cotton swab to reach any nooks and crannies.

Instrument Panel and Air Vents

Clean this area with a rag and warm soapy water. Use the rag or a long cotton swab to clean the air vents.

Rear Shelf (Deck)

Some people use this shelf to display their collection of Beanie Babies, baseball caps, or bobble heads. We recommend that you don't keep anything there because in case of a crash or sudden stop, those objects can become lethal projectiles.

To clean this area, use the brush attachment on the vacuum cleaner and remove all the dirt and dust. Next, clean the rear window using a paper towel and window cleaner. While you're at it, clean all the interior windows!

Seating

Car owners may change their minds about their favorite car color, make, and model, but they hold steadfast to their preference for leather, vinyl, or cloth seats. No matter which type you have, there are certain things you can do to help the material last longer.

The driver's seat takes the most abuse, so this is the seat that will probably be the one to get a hole or tear first. If a seat gets damaged, you need to address the problem immediately, otherwise the hole or tear will quickly expand because of the person's weight pressing against it. If the driver's seat is too worn, or you want to prevent it from wearing out prematurely, you may want to purchase a cloth or lamb's wool covering.

No matter what type of seating you have, first vacuum using a brush and wand attachment to remove debris from on top of the seat and in between the back and bottom.

Leather

Leather seating can wrinkle and crack over time, which is why it's so important to regularly maintain it.

To clean leather, use a chamois cloth or a soft rag with a mild soap (not antibacterial) or saddle soap and wipe it dry. Do not use a hair dryer to dry it; instead, let it dry naturally. If the stain persists, use a leather cleaner recommended by the dealership or the manufacturer.

If you have a tear in the leather, have it professionally repaired as soon as possible.

Vinyl

This is probably the easiest of the three materials to clean. Just use warm water and a soft rag to wipe down the seats. If there's something stuck on it, use a plastic knife, a plastic spatula, or a plastic putty knife to scrape it off. Then use the warm soapy rag to clean any residue. And for really stubborn stains, use a vinyl cleaner.

If the vinyl is torn, have it professional repaired immediately.

Cloth

The biggest problem with cloth is that if something spills on it, the liquid seeps into the cushion—and then you not only have to deal with the stain, but also a lingering odor. Ask any mother who's had a child knock over a sippy cup filled with milk in her car.

Cleaning up a spill

If something spills onto the cloth seat, immediately address the problem, especially if it's milk. Press some paper towels onto the spot to absorb as much of the liquid as possible. It will take a while for the seat to dry, so if someone needs to sit on it immediately, throw a bath towel over it.

Club soda is the preferred choice of cleaners for spills on cloth. Be careful not to soak the spot because you don't want to be adding more fluid to the area. The other thing you have to be careful of is that when you clean a spot on a cloth seat it may end up lightening that area; therefore, it's best to clean the entire area starting from the seams inward.

Note: If the stain is oil or grease, you need to use the cleaning product recommended by the car manufacturer.

Floor Mats

Cars typically come with floor mats that are designed to protect the vehicle's carpeting from wear and tear. Once the carpeting is trashed, the entire car looks trashed, and replacing the carpeting is costly; therefore, if you see a stain, remove it immediately. To prevent stains in the first place, purchase hard rubber mats (with deep grooves) for the entire vehicle, including the trunk or rear cargo area. These will hold any fluids that spill, which would otherwise damage carpeting.

Carpet Mats

To clean carpet mats, remove them from the car and place them on the driveway or sidewalk. Use the vacuum cleaner to remove any dirt from the mats, and if there are stains, use carpet shampoo and blot dry with towels; if they're too wet, use a wet/dry vac. Let the mats air-dry before placing them back inside the car.

Rubber/Plastic Mats

To clean these mats, remove them from the car (*duh*) and, using the spray nozzle on the water hose, spray off any dirt. Then take a brush that's been soaking inside a bucket with warm soapy water and scrub the remaining dirt and stains. Rinse using the spray nozzle. Repeat on all the mats. Let them air-dry before replacing inside the car.

Note: Be sure to replace any rubber/plastic mats that are cracked or any carpet mats that are frayed because your foot can get tangled in them, causing interference when using the brake or accelerator pedals.

Carpet

Remove dirt from the carpet with a vacuum cleaner and spills and stains with a carpet cleaner. Just be careful not to soak the carpets because too much moisture will create mold and mildew.

Odors

You open the car door and all of a sudden you know where you left the other gallon of milk . . . three days ago. Your car may reek for a week, but there are some odors that make themselves permanent passengers. Here's how to deodorize the demons.

Sprinkle household baking soda on the carpet or cloth seat where the odor is emanating. Let the baking soda sit for a while and then vacuum it up. If the odor persists, try using cat litter. If that doesn't work, you'll need to take it to a professional detailer.

DIFM

You want to get your car's interior professionally detailed, but how do you know who to choose? A good place to start is by asking for a referral from your car dealership or mechanic. Another option is to go online to a chat room and ask for the name of a good detailing shop in your area.

A shop that specializes in car detailing will offer different services at different prices, so be sure to get it in writing before agreeing to anything. You'll also need to know if the owner is licensed and bonded, just in case damage is done to your car. Another thing to check is what type of deodorizing product will be used. Sometimes the product used by commercial detailers to get rid of an odor gives off a smell that's worse than the original one!

Make sure that you remove everything of value before taking the car to be detailed. A good detailing shop will put everything that's not a part of the car into a bag and return it to you, but why take the risk?

Tools Needed

Vacuum cleaner with attachments

Electrical extension cord, if necessary

Scrub brush

Long cotton swabs

Chamois cloth

Soft clean rags

Bucket with warm, soapy water

Plastic putty knife

Water hose with spray nozzle

Baking soda

Club soda

Carpet cleaner

Keys and Locks

Getting a New Set of Car Keys

You're out with the girls and it's your turn to be the designated driver. You'd have no problem taking on this role except that you lost your keys somewhere between the first and second karaoke songs.

Key to Recovery

If you lost your only set of car keys, you'll need to find a car dealership that sells your make of car. When you go there, you will have to have the car's vehicle identification number (VIN) and registration or title.

The VIN is your car's thumbprint. Car manufacturers give each car a number to identify it and no two cars have the same number. You need this number when you register your car with the Department of Motor Vehicles, donate your car, do a background check on a car, and when you have to get a new set of keys made from the dealership.

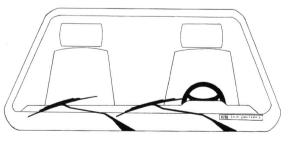

Locating the VIN

The VIN is embossed on a metal plate and is located on the inside of the car on the dashboard. If you're standing outside near the windshield on the driver's side, look for a metal plate with numbers near the windshield wipers. The VIN faces out, so you can only read the numbers by looking from the outside of the car. Write down the VIN and bring it along with the car registration or title to the dealership.

If you lose your set of keys while you're out of town with your car, contact a local car dealership and provide the same information as above. If there's a problem, you can contact the dealership where you bought your car (which has a computer record of your purchase or car repairs) and ask them to contact the other dealership.

Depending on the type of car and its key, the dealership is probably going to charge you anywhere from $10 to $300.

Preventing Theft

Dealerships are not supposed to give you a new set of keys without the registration or title because a thief can write down the VIN on any car, go to a dealership, ask for a new key, and simply enter your car and drive off. Unfortunately, not all employees of dealerships follow the rules, but you can help to prevent this type of auto theft by placing either a piece of masking tape or an index card over the VIN.

Remote Keyless Entry System

*I*t took Leslie 20 minutes to open her car door and it wasn't because she didn't have her keys. It was because the battery in her remote keyless entry was dead and she had never used the key, so the keyhole was frozen in position. So was she.

If you don't have a remote keyless entry, you wonder why would anyone need it. And if you have one, you wonder how anyone could live without it. It's a gadget that's fun to use—but that fun can come at a price if it doesn't work, or if you lose it.

Car key and remote entry

How It Works

A remote entry works by sending out a frequency wave that is picked up by your car, telling it to either unlock one or all of the doors (including the liftgate), or engage the alarm. It works just like your electric garage door opener (by the way, when's the last time you opened that manually?).

The problem with using a remote keyless entry system is that the frequency used by these remotes is not regulated by the Federal Communications Commission (FCC), and therefore can get interference from other objects that emit stronger frequencies. The average distance that a remote will work is anywhere from 3 to 30 feet.

If it's taking you a few tries to open your car with the remote, it may be a sign that the battery is weak and needs to be replaced. It also could be that another car or object is blocking the transmission, the weather is bad, or you're too far from your car. If it's none of the above, have the system checked by your dealership.

IY

Replacing the Transmitter Battery

You can avoid a lot of grief if you replace the battery *before* it dies. The average life span of a battery in a remote transmitter is 2 years, so replace it when it reaches that age.

Open the transmitter by placing the dime in the slot near the key ring hole, or wherever the manufacturer states. Twist the dime to release the covers. Remove the battery and replace it with a new one. Snap the covers closed.

Replacing the battery

After you've replaced the battery, you may need to refer to the car owner's manual to resynchronize the transmitter. With the car doors closed, stand outside of the car and hold down the lock and unlock buttons at the same time for about 7 seconds. Voilà! (Note: These instructions may vary with car models.)

Locked Out

A remote entry will stop working when the battery dies, but you can always use a key to open the door. That is, of course, if you've ever used the key. Sometimes a lock will freeze up if it's never been used, so

Tools Needed
Dime

New battery (typically 3 volts)

Car owner's manual

be sure to open your car the old-fashioned way once in a while—think of it as being very retro. And, of course, replace the battery (remember, the average life span of the battery is 2 years).

Another option, if you subscribe to OnStar, is to call its toll-free number (1–888–4OnStar). Just give the OnStar operator your PIN and a signal will be sent via the cellular network to your car's electrical system, and presto, your car doors will be unlocked. The typical amount of time the process takes is a few minutes.

Lost Transmitter

If you've lost the remote transmitter, and don't have a spare, you'll need to purchase a new one. We guarantee that you'll have sticker shock when you get the bill, but we couldn't live without one either. The typical cost of replacing a remote depends on the type you have, but it can range anywhere from $5 to $150!

If you have one or more transmitters but still want to replace the one you lost, you'll need to bring all of the transmitters to the dealership because they all need to be recoded. The dealership will code all the transmitters so they match each other and will only work with the code in your car, which means that if you find the old transmitter you won't be able to use it.

The panic feature (typically red) on the remote can serve as a deterrent to a potential abductor or thief by triggering the car's horn to blare and the lights to go on and off.

Thawing a Frozen Door Lock

When Cecilia was living in Buffalo, a town famous for its bitterly cold winters, she would wake every morning and boil 2 pots of water—one for her tea and the other for her car's frozen windshield and doors.

We certainly don't recommend Cecilia's unique approach to getting rid of the ice on her car, because it could crack the windshield and damage the keyhole and door. Here's a better option.

Locks

If you try putting the key into the lock and it won't turn, the lock could be frozen. This can happen when freezing rain or snow gets into the keyhole. Don't pour hot water on it because even though it may thaw it, the water is what caused the problem in the first place. Next, don't heat your key with a match or a lighter. Not only is it a fire hazard, but some newer keys come equipped with a microchip inside, which if heated, can become damaged.

Tools Needed

Lock deicer or graphite spray   Rubbing alcohol   Rag

Deicing the keyhole

Dip the key into some rubbing alcohol, and apply lock deicer to the keyhole. Insert the key and try to open the door. Be careful not to force the key, because you may break it. Use the rag to wipe the keyhole dry.

Finding a Great Mechanic

You won't find a definition for the term "great mechanic" in any reference book, but we think it should be defined as "a person who provides reliable car repairs at honorable prices." Maybe we should include this, too: "And someone who refuses to hang calendars of half-naked women in the shop."

Luckily, the vast majority of auto repair shops have evolved over the years. The old pin-ups have been replaced with photos of local sports teams they sponsor. And *Popular Mechanics* magazines share coffee-table space with *Good Housekeeping*.

The Search

You know how you're not supposed to go grocery shopping when you're hungry because you'll buy things you really didn't need? The same principle holds true for hiring a mechanic. Never look for one when your car needs repairs because you'll be more likely to take your car to the first auto shop or dealership you see, and then you'll likely pay for things you really didn't need. An unscrupulous mechanic (a.k.a. technician) can smell desperation ... no matter how much perfume you're wearing.

Take a Proactive Approach
Consider shopping for a mechanic (a.k.a. technician) the same way you would if you were hiring a Realtor to help you find a home, ordering new

kitchen cabinets, or attempting to have your basement finished. With big ticket items like those, you always do comparative shopping, not only to get the best price, but also to hire the best person for the job.

The first step in finding a great mechanic is to ask your friends, coworkers, and family members who they use. If more than one person recommends the same repair shop, then you may have found yourself a winner. But you're not done shopping yet. Call the shop and find out how long it's been in business. If a shop has been around a long time, it's usually a sign that the community has supported it.

Another important qualification you need in an auto repair shop is that the owner is certified by the National Institute for Automotive Service Excellence (ASE) and works on site. You want the owner to be hands-on and in charge so that if there's a problem you can take your complaint directly to him/her.

Check for Certified Mechanics

Next, you need to find out if the mechanic is ASE certified. To be certified by ASE, a mechanic must pass tough industry tests on various automotive repair areas. An ASE-certified master mechanic has passed all 8 tests in the auto series qualifying him/her as a specialist in all parts of the car, and must complete continual education.

Also, look for the American Automobile Association (AAA) logo in the shop. This certifies that the auto repair shop has met stringent criteria set forth by AAA's qualified automotive professionals. You can find a list of certified auto shops in your area by going to www .AAA.com or by contacting your local AAA chapter.

Another important reason to look for the AAA logo is that the Club will investigate any dispute between a member and an approved repair facility. While nonmembers are not entitled to full AAA arbitration, the Club will make at least a conciliatory effort to resolve the differences between the parties.

Don't Overlook Dealerships

When you're looking for a quality repair shop, don't overlook going to a dealership. It's a myth that you'll always get charged more by one. Here are some reasons why the dealership may be a good option for you.

- Some dealerships offer a free rental car while yours is being serviced (be sure to check your warranty package).
- If there's a dispute, you have a better chance of having the claim resolved, because if the dealership isn't fixing the problem you can take your claim further up the ladder—all the way to the manufacturer, if necessary.
- A good dealership regularly trains its technicians in the latest automotive repair and diagnostic equipment.
- If your car is under warranty, the dealership knows exactly what's covered.
- A dealership uses manufacturer parts that are warrantied at any similar dealership.
- A dealership typically has strong ties to its community.

Visit a Qualified Auto Repair Shop and Dealership

You don't have to make an appointment; just walk right in and take a look around. See how the manager or owner acts and is dressed. Someone who wants to make a good impression for his clients will be dressed appropriately and act friendly. Look to see if the bays are clean and tidy, which would show that the mechanics and owner take pride in their working area and take good care of their tools. Notice the way the

Signs of a good repair shop

cars are parked in the parking lot—if they're pulled in a haphazard manner, that's a sign the shop is disorganized. Also look at the condition of the cars that are in the shop. Are they old and beat up, or are they in good shape? People who care about their cars will take them to good repair shops. If you don't see this, keep shopping. Check with your local Better Business Bureau and your county government's consumer department to see if there are any unresolved complaints against the repair shop you've chosen. Note, they will *not* tell you that the shop/dealership is bad and not to use it, and they won't tell you about all the complaints—just the unresolved ones.

Do Your Homework

Very few women feel like they're not being ripped off (even just a little bit) by their repair shop. Why? It's our own ignorance—most of us know nothing about our cars. And because we know nothing, we know we're vulnerable to being ripped off.

Finding a great mechanic/repair shop means that *you* need to be a great consumer, and that means *you* need to know as much as you can about your car and what ails it, as well as knowing in advance what parts will be needed and the costs for those parts, as well as labor charges. This can all be done very easily. Here's how.

- Read up on your car by using the car owner's manual and, of course, this book.
- Regularly maintain your car. This will help you know your car better than your mechanic.
- Know your car's recommended service schedule and follow it.
- Log on to www.edmunds.com and plug in information about your car to get a list of replacement parts and the cost for each, as well as the suggested cost of labor. Also visit your car manufacturer's Web site for more service information.

Once You've Found One . . .

Now that you've chosen a great mechanic/repair shop, bring this book and the car manual, along with the printout from the Web site, and discuss what needs to be done to your car. Did you catch that we said *discuss*? You need to talk through everything that's going to be done to your car, step-by-step, cost-by-cost. Open this book to whatever section relates to the repair and have the mechanic point to the illustration while describing the process. And if you need to, take notes, and

Some counties have laws that require auto repair shops to supply a written estimate as well as to notify the customer if the total bill will be 10 percent more than the estimate. So check with your county government to see if your area has a similar law. Also, make sure that the parts being put into your car are new and not refurbished.

AAA certifies the auto repair shop, not the individual mechanic.

Mechanic-isms

There are two sides to every story, so we decided to talk to some mechanics to hear what they'd like their customer to do.

- Don't assume that they're all crooks ready to steal your money.
- Come with a list of problems about your car. Include the time of day when it happens, the speed you're traveling, and the noises.
- Be patient.
- Don't assume that the mechanic can hear all the noises that you hear. Mechanics work in shops with noisy engines and very loud power tools, so their hearing may not be as good as yours.
- If you're new to the shop or dealership, bring in the car's repair history.
- If you take your car home after it is repaired, and it's still exhibiting problems, don't call the shop screaming and yelling; instead, just state what's going on with the car and bring the car back to the shop or dealership. A reputable shop/dealership will fix the problem for free, if it's the original problem, or if the problem is unrelated, the mechanic will give you another estimate.

don't be embarrassed about doing it—there's a lot of money involved here! If the problem and the repair don't seem to be clear-cut, ask for a diagnostic service to be performed and what it will cost. Heck, ask if they offer free diagnostics for new customers! Don't leave the shop until you understand what will definitely or most probably happen (not every problem is easily diagnosed). And don't leave without a written estimate. Also, be sure to tell the mechanic that you want to be called if there is any unforeseen work that needs to be done.

Disputes

If you believe that the mechanic did not fix your car or overcharged you for the services rendered, don't just take your business elsewhere—*complain!* Go to the manager, and if that doesn't work, talk to the owner. And if the problem still isn't resolved, here's what you can do.

- Put everything in writing, such as the problem, the cost estimate, the final cost, and your complaint. If the auto repair shop is approved by AAA, call, e-mail, or write to the association and provide a copy of the bill. *Note that you don't have to be a member of AAA to voice your complaint.*
- If you paid for the repairs with a credit card, request that the credit card company get involved in the dispute.
- Take your problem to your county government's consumer affairs division or your state attorney general's office.
- If all else fails, sue in small-claims court.

Emission Tests and Safety Inspections

 ou may be done taking tests, but depending on where you live, your car may not. We're going to help you prep your car so that it can pass every time ... without pulling an all-nighter.

Safety and emission inspections not only work to reduce air and noise pollution, but they also help keep the roads safe for everyone by forcing people to make car repairs they might otherwise not do.

Doing Your Homework

The best place to search for any information regarding your state's requirements for inspection and emission tests is your state's official Web site, which will typically have a link to the Department of Motor Vehicles (DMV) and the state police. If you don't have access to a computer, go to the library or to your local Department of Motor Vehicles (also called Motor Vehicle Administration) to request the information.

Some states require that a vehicle be inspected every year, every two years, or only at the time of sale of the vehicle. Where you get your car inspected and tested for emissions also varies from state to state. The most common places are a full-service gas station or a car dealership. However, some states only allow you to go to one of their emission centers or to the DMV.

An emissions or safety inspection can take a long time, depending on the number of cars ahead of you. If you are taking your car to a dealership or auto repair shop, ask if you can drop the car off the night before and pick it up the next day after it's been inspected. And if that's not a possibility, call and find out a good time to have the car inspected. And if that fails, then just bring a good book, stationery for late thank you's, or listen to some music and relax—this may be the only quiet time you get for a while!

Another piece of advice . . . don't even bother driving to the emissions/inspection site if the CHECK ENGINE or SERVICE ENGINE light stays on, because your car will not pass the test(s). Instead, drive to your auto repair shop.

Emissions Tests

Emissions tests are designed to calculate the level of harmful emissions each vehicle emits. These tests can vary according to the age of the car and the state where the car is registered. For cars built before 1996, the test can include checking the fuel cap's pressure, an onboard diagnostic test, a treadmill (dynamometer) test, and a tailpipe test (idle test). For cars built in 1996 and after, technicians use the On-Board Diagnostics II (OBD-II) system to test the vehicle's emissions.

Some states offer a discounted fee for senior citizens who drive less than 5,000 miles per year, and some states give exemptions to handicapped motorists who drive less than 5,000 miles per year.

Some states will accept a current (i.e., 12 months) emissions certificate from another state.

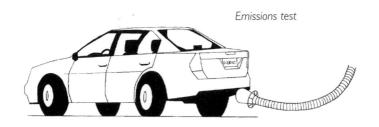

Emissions test

Preventive Maintenance

The most common reason for not passing an emissions test is a faulty or missing fuel cap, or a catalytic converter that's failed. The best way to prevent from failing these tests is to keep your vehicle properly maintained as directed in the car owner's manual; have your car's exhaust system checked for holes and structural damage by the mechanic prior to taking the test; make sure that the fuel cap is on and that it's the correct type for your vehicle; and warm up the car (run it for at least 20 minutes at normal highway speed).

Failing the Test

If your car failed the emissions test, the technician is required by the federal Clean Air Act to give you written notice that the car failed, but is not required to tell you the cause. Also, you will be told the time period you have to get the problem resolved, as well as any limitations on mileage.

Before having your vehicle repaired, check the car's warranties and manual because the repairs may be covered under the emissions performance warranty.

Some states will waive the emissions inspection for an older car if the car has failed the test twice, repairs have been done, and you can provide receipts showing that a certain amount of money has been spent trying to fix the problem.

Safety Inspections

Safety inspections vary from state to state, but sometimes they vary from technician to technician, depending on whether you've gone to a reputable auto repair shop. At first, you may think that you're incredibly lucky that your car passed inspection, even though you know it shouldn't have. The reality is that you don't want to be driving a car that's not fit to be on the road.

Some states require you to go back to the same technician to have the second testing done. Refer to your state's DMV/MVA rules or visit www.dmv.org.

Preventive Maintenance

We wish we could tell you everything that's included in the safety inspection test, but each state has different requirements. However, there are some things that you can do prior to having your car inspected that will help to ensure that it will pass.

1. *Check that the following are all working:*
   - Exterior lamps
   - Turn signals
   - Horn
   - Windshield wipers
   - Brakes
   - Driver's window

2. *Schedule your car for its checkup the month that its inspection is due.* And if your car's technician or dealership performs inspections, have the checkup and the inspection done at the same time; that way, any problems will be caught and fixed.

3. *Have your car at even operating temperature before it's inspected.* It's best to drive the car for 20 minutes so that the fluids have been distributed throughout the engine. If your car hasn't been driven for a significant period of time, you should drive the car 30 to 60 minutes at highway speed.

Failing the Inspection

Depending on what state you live in, if you failed the safety inspection, you may have 2 weeks or 30 days to get the car repaired, or you may only be allowed to drive it to the auto repair shop.

Safety

In our attempt to teach you safety measures, we've had to incorporate a lot of *dos* and *don'ts*. But please don't think of this as an exercise for us in finger-wagging. Trust us when we tell you that we've done some of the *don'ts* (one of us has eaten sushi *with* chopsticks while driving)—that is, before we got on the straight-and-narrow road. So please read this section with an open mind to changing some bad habits and incorporating some good ones, all of which will keep you, and others, safe on your journey, wherever that may take you.

Safety Systems

Air Bags

Blink. Would you believe that an air bag deploys in less time than it took you to do that? For all you mathematicians, that's ⅟₂₅th of a second.

Frontal car crashes are responsible for more than half of all car-related deaths. Air bags reduce the risk of dying in a frontal car crash by 30 percent. The air bag's function is to supplement the restraint provided by the seat belt and to provide a cushion for a motorist's head, neck, and chest so that she won't hit the dashboard or steering wheel. Seat belts are also effective at keeping the motorist from being thrown from the car. Neither one is designed to make the other obsolete; in fact, they're a dynamic duo.

Benefits

By law, every car must have two frontal air bags—typically, one located in the steering wheel for the driver, and the other located above the glove compartment for the front-seat passenger. Today, new cars can also be equipped with knee air bags, door- or seat-mounted side-impact air bags, and roof-mounted side-impact air bags for both front and backseats.

Frontal air bags, located in the steering wheel and the instrument panel (on the pas-

Air bag in a steering wheel

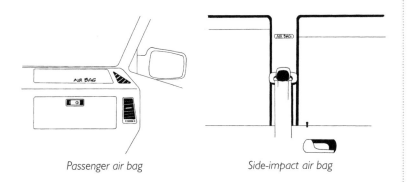

Passenger air bag   Side-impact air bag

senger side), will deploy only when there is a frontal collision. So if you're smashed into from behind or on the side, these air bags will *not* deploy. Side-impact bags are designed to deploy in a side-impact collision. These air bags are typically smaller than frontal air bags, and are usually located in the seatback of the front seats, closest to the door. As of this writing, side-impact bags are not federally mandated; however, more manufacturers are offering them as options, and some are even including them as standard features.

Risks

Air bags are credited with saving 1,500 lives every year. But there have been serious injuries, and even deaths, from air bags. How? Usually the cause is that the driver or passenger was either not wearing a seat belt, was improperly restrained, was positioned too close to where the air bag was located, or was a child under the age of 13 sitting in the front passenger seat.

DIY

Proper Distance
The first 2 to 3 inches from where the air bag is deployed is the area where the force of the air bag is the greatest and is called the "risk

zone." Therefore, whoever is sitting in the front of the car (remember, children under the age of 13 should sit in a rear seat) *must* be properly secured with a seat belt and *must* be seated with the center of their breastbone at least 10 inches from the location of the air bag cover.

Get into the driver's seat and measure the distance between the middle of your breastbone and the steering wheel. To achieve the correct distance, you can move the seat forward or backward, tilt the steering wheel downward, recline your seat,

Achieving the proper safety distance

or, if your pedals are self-adjusting, move them until the distance is reached (if you're not sure whether your car has these features, consult the car owner's manual).

If, because of your size, it is physically impossible for you to achieve the 10-inch distance, then you may need to have an air bag on/off switch installed (see "Disabling an Air Bag," page 231).

Technological Advances

There is a new generation of air bags called "advanced frontal air bags" that act like they are personally tailored for each passenger. Advanced frontal air bags can be designed with sensors that can detect a front seat passenger's weight, seat belt use by the occupant, position of the seat, and the severity of the crash. This is a great alternative to the one-size-fits-all air bag.

Maintaining an Air Bag

How can you possibly maintain an air bag if you can't even see it, or get to it? If your car has air bags, then it's also equipped with an air bag light

Tools Needed

Measuring tape

Car owner's manual

(located on the dashboard panel), which will indicate if there is a problem with the air bag. Take your car to the dealership or to a mechanic that has the proper diagnostic equipment to fix the problem.

Air bags, like other vehicle parts, have a finite life expectancy. You should review the car owner's manual to determine if and when you should have the air bags checked by a dealership. Many manufacturers recommend this when the car is 10 years old.

After a Crash

If you're in a crash and the air bags deploy, they will need to be replaced. Your regular mechanic or your car dealership can do the job for you. The cost incurred from this is typically covered by your car insurance.

Deployed air bag

 IFM

Disabling an Air Bag

The U.S. Department of Transportation requires all car manufacturers to install air bags in vehicles, but under certain circumstances it allows motorists to have their air bags disabled through the installation of an on/off switch.

The only reason to disable an air bag is if you have to transport a child under age 13 in the front seat, you're the driver and you cannot physically achieve the 10 inches between your breastbone and the steering wheel, or your doctor says that because of your health, using an air bag would cause a greater risk than not using one. *Do not have an air bag switch installed unless you absolutely, positively must.*

To do so, contact the National Highway Traffic Safety Administration (NHTSA) to request a form for an air bag on/off switch. Forms may also be available at your car dealership, auto repair shop, or the Department of Motor Vehicles.

Before you have the switch installed, contact the manufacturer of your car and ask if the seat belts were specifically designed to work in tandem with the air bags. If so, the dealership or mechanic will have to make adjustments to the seat belts or install new ones.

Once the switch is installed, the only way you can turn it off is with a key. When the air bag has been disabled, a light will appear on the instrument panel stating which air bag has been deactivated. Do not allow anyone else to use the key, especially a child.

Seat Belts

We don't want to hear your excuses for not wearing a seat belt, like it doesn't fit (use a seat belt extender), that the air bag will protect you (an air bag won't keep you from being ejected), and that you have a perfect driving record (it's the other guy's record you should be worried about). What's next? Your dog ate it?

Benefits of Buckling Up

Let's get real. There is *no* excuse for not wearing a seat belt. The main purpose of the seat belt is to keep you from being ejected from your car. Here are some statistics that really *drive* home our point: of all traffic-related deaths, over 20,000 lives each year could have been saved if the motorists had been using their seat belts.

Risks of Not Buckling Up

One more important fact to know—if you don't buckle up, the odds are that your child won't, either. A nationwide study by the National Safety Council Air Bag & Seat Belt Safety Campaign states that when an adult driver buckles up there's an 87 percent chance that her child will also use a seat belt. However, if an adult does not buckle

Buckling up for safety

up, then there's only a 24 percent chance that her child will use a seat belt.

Wearing a seat belt should be a deal breaker, or we should say a car starter. Don't start the car until you and every passenger is buckled up. And never ride with someone who won't. Here's why. You may think that by not buckling up you're only putting yourself at risk, but a recent study suggests that you need to buckle up to protect the other passengers in the car as well. That's right, a study found that in crashes in which the backseat passenger was not wearing a seat belt, the passenger in the front seat had a 20 percent greater chance of dying. And in accidents in which the backseat passenger was buckled but the front seat passenger was not, the backseat passenger had a 22 percent greater chance of dying. So if you're riding in a car with someone who refuses to wear a seat belt, throw these stats out to her—and then, if you must, throw her out, too!

And if all of these stats are not enough to convince you to wear a seat belt, remember that it's the law.

Anatomy of a Seat Belt

Seat belts look simple, but they're actually complex safety devices. Many newer vehicles have seat belts with a pretensioner that retracts the seat belt after a crash; an upper adjustable belt, which allows the motorist to make the belt fit her size; and an energy management system, which enables the seat belt to move with you when you move the seat because the seat belt is connected to the seat, not to the floor or pillar. And you thought the seat belt was just a piece of cloth and a buckle!

DIY

Proper Use of a Seat Belt

Okay, pretend we're flight attendants and it's time for us to talk to you about safely buckling up . . . but don't *pretend* you're listening.

Get into the driver's seat, close the door, and adjust the seat so that you're sitting up straight and your chest is at least 10 inches from the steering wheel.

Not every vehicle has a height adjuster for the seat belts, but if yours does, it's as easy to use as flipping a switch. In most cars, the height adjuster is located near the top of the shoulder harness. To lower the height, slide the adjuster down; to raise the height, slide the adjuster up.

Height adjuster

Pull the latch plate (a.k.a. tongue) across you and insert it into the buckle. If you've pulled the seat belt too fast, it may lock, so just release it and try again, going a bit slower this time. You'll know the latch plate has been inserted correctly when you hear a *click*. Check that the release button on the buckle is facing up for easy access.

It's imperative that the lap part of the seat belt be worn low and snug on the hips and not the abdomen, because in case of a crash the seat belt will tighten to keep you in place. If it's properly worn, the pressure will be on your hips; if not, the pressure will be on your abdomen, which could cause internal damage to organs. It's equally important to wear the shoulder belt across your breastbone and not under the arms, because it provides greater protection of vital organs.

If your seat belt is constantly getting caught in the door, it's not retracting completely; therefore, take it to a repair shop or dealership for servicing.

During a Crash

When you're in a frontal crash, your body will be forced forward. Seat belts are designed to keep you from going into the windshield or being thrown around the car. Take a look at a crash dummy video and see just how violent a crash can be.

After a Crash

If you are not badly injured and can get out of your car, do so. If your seat belt is jammed, use the blade on the emergency hammer to cut it

A person is not the only thing that needs to be buckled in. Next time you have your briefcase in the car, buckle that in, too. In fact, make sure that all items in your car are secured so that in case of a crash or quick stop, a harmless object won't turn into a lethal projectile.

and remove yourself from the strap. We recommend that you keep this device inside the pocket of the driver's door and not in the glove compartment, so you can easily grab it.

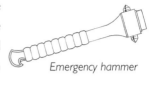
Emergency hammer

If your vehicle has a pretensioner mechanism, you need to know that it is a onetime device, and therefore will likely need to be replaced after a crash. All safety belt assemblies should be inspected by a qualified technician following a collision, and replaced if necessary.

Seat Belts and Pregnancy

You're pregnant and eating for two (heck, we *still* are), but did you ever think that you're driving for two, *too*?

That's right, every time you get in a car you're taking yourself and your unborn baby for a ride. Therefore, it's vital that you protect the two of you by wearing your seat belt, no matter which trimester you're in.

About two-thirds of all pregnancy trauma and about 350 car-related fetal deaths each year are attributed to pregnant women not wearing their seat belts. By not wearing a seat belt, or by wearing it incorrectly, you can seriously harm yourself and your baby. No matter what excuse you come up with—whether you think you're too big to use a seat belt, or it's too uncomfortable, or the air bag will save you—just ask yourself this question: Would you drive around without your newborn in a car seat? We rest our case.

DIY

Wearing a Seat Belt Correctly

First, measure the distance between your chest and the steering wheel, or if you're riding in the passenger seat then check the distance between your chest and the glove compartment. If it's not at least 10 inches, then adjust your seat.

Pull the seat belt and place the lap part under your abdomen

> Do not have your air bag disabled during your pregnancy. The best way to protect yourself and your unborn child is to use your seat belt.

and across your hips. At the same time, adjust the shoulder harness so that it rests diagonally between your breasts. Now make sure that both parts of the seat belt are snug, but not too tight. For more information, refer to the car owner's manual.

Correctly using the shoulder harness and lap belt

Seat Belt Extenders

Cars and everything in them have evolved over the decades, but the seat belt has not kept up with Americans' growth . . . around the waist. Tests on seat belts use crash dummies that were designed based on the body statistics of men and women from 1960! Yeah, and June is still making dinner for Ward.

If you're one of the millions of obese adults in this country, you know how frustrating it is not only to find a car that you can fit into, but also one with a seat belt that you can actually use.

What It Is

To accommodate the changing waistlines of Americans, most car manufacturers have begun offering seat belt extenders. A seat belt extender is a device that snaps into your existing seat belt and expands the length. Seat belt extenders typically come in two lengths—9 inches and 15 inches—but longer lengths can be special ordered. We recommend that you have your dealership measure to ensure that you get the correct seat belt extender.

Tools Needed

Measuring tape   **Car owner's manual**

Remove the seat belt extender when not in use in order to protect another driver or passenger who might not need the additional length.

The *only* reason you should get an extender is if you have tried to lengthen the seat belt (following the car owner's manual) and it still isn't long enough. Don't get an extender to make it easier for you to buckle, or make the seat belt loose, because you could be putting yourself in great danger in case of an accident. The extender changes the position of the shoulder harness; therefore, if you don't physically need it, you will be decreasing the effectiveness of the seat belt. Also, do not use the extender to "double-buckle" children. Every child should have his or her own seat belt.

Finding an Extender

To obtain a seat belt extender, contact your local car dealership and provide the year and model of your car. *You will not be asked for your weight!* If the dealership does not have it in stock, it can be ordered for you. Some dealerships will even give the extender to you for free.

Don't be fooled into buying a one-size-fits-all extender, commonly sold over the Internet, because it won't work. Every model of car has a different length seat belt and a different latch. Which brings us to the suggestion that if you have more than one car in your household, you'll want to get an extender for each car. And if you carpool with someone, call that person's car dealership and get an extender to fit that car, too (seat belt extenders are usually vehicle specific).

Installing a Seat Belt Extender

Before you go to the car dealership, call ahead to see if it has a 9-inch and a 15-inch extender for your car. If not, order both sizes (remember, you need to provide the model and year of the car) in case the 9 inch doesn't fit.

It's important that you try the 9-inch extender before you try the 15-inch extender, because you never want a seat belt to be loose. Also, wear a winter coat to be sure that there is enough room for extra clothing.

Position the seat, whether it's the passenger's or driver's, making sure that your chest is 10 inches from the glove compartment or steering wheel. If you need to recline the seat, that's fine.

Insert the metal tongue of the seat belt (a.k.a. latch plate) into the (9-inch) extender's buckle. Now insert the extender's metal tongue into the car's seat buckle.

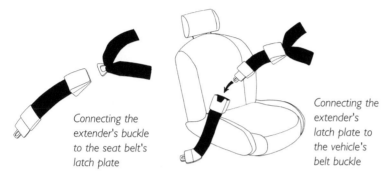

Connecting the extender's buckle to the seat belt's latch plate

Connecting the extender's latch plate to the vehicle's belt buckle

The lap part of the seat belt should rest on your pelvis, not on top of your abdomen. If the seat belt fits, tighten it by pulling the extender's buckle toward the door closest to you. If it doesn't fit, follow the same instructions for the 15-inch extender.

$\mathcal{T}ools\ \mathcal{N}eeded$

Measuring tape

Seat belt extender

Car owner's manual

Head Restraints

*Y*ou can't prevent someone from crashing into the back of your car, but you can do something to avoid getting whiplash and having to wear the big white collar. Not only is it annoying, it doesn't go with anything!

Every year about 2 million rear-end crashes occur in the United States, resulting in neck injuries (e.g., whiplash) that cost insurance companies about $7 billion. That's not including the cost to businesses because their employees are home on sick leave, and it also doesn't take into account the pain and suffering of the injured party. The solution is so simple; in fact, the next time you get into your car, put your head back and think about it for a minute.

How It Works

If you're wondering what a head restraint is, it's the politically correct term for headrest. But, even if you refrain from being PC, this piece of car equipment was never meant to act as a place to "rest" your head. Its main purpose has always been to *restrain* your head in case of a rear-end accident.

Head restraints complete the trifecta of safety devices inside your car: (1) seat belts, (2) air bags, and (3) head restraints. Unfortunately, the importance of head restraints has taken a backseat, so to speak, to the others. In fact, a study by one of the largest insurance companies showed that only 14 percent of drivers knew the correct position for their head restraint.

Cars have one of four different types of head restraint systems:

(1) manual; (2) automatic; (3) dynamic; and (4) fixed. The majority of cars have head restraints that can be moved manually. An automatic head restraint adjusts when the automatic seats change positions. Perhaps the most interesting of them all is the dynamic head restraint because it deploys during a crash, helping to keep the head and torso moving together. Some dynamic head restraints can be adjusted manually. The fixed head restraint is stationary, and therefore cannot be moved.

Whiplash

Whiplash is the involuntary stretching of the muscles and ligaments of the neck and shoulders. It's the most common neck injury for people involved in rear-end crashes. In fact, 1 out of 5 people report a neck injury from a rear-end crash.

When your car gets hit from behind, the seat pushes your body forward. If your head isn't supported, it will lag behind the forward motion of your upper body, causing your neck to toss back, stretching the muscles and ligaments.

Manually Adjusting a Head Restraint

Unfortunately, people think that whiplash is an almost natural by-product of being in a car crash—you get hit from behind, you're going to get whiplash. Case closed. But the reality is that whiplash can be reduced if people just take a few seconds to adjust their head restraints.

When do you need to adjust it? If you're the only driver of your car, then you only have to adjust it once. If there's more than one driver, then you'll need to adjust it every time you get behind the wheel. Also, if your car comes equipped with adjustable head restraints for backseat passengers, make sure every passenger takes a second to correctly alter its position.

We know that you won't start the car until everyone is buckled in, but how about instituting the same plan for head restraints—have everyone adjust theirs before taking off.

The National Highway Traffic Safety Administration (NHTSA) states that the optimal height for a head restraint is for it to reach somewhere between the top of your ears and the top of your head. The optimal horizontal distance between the back of your head and the head restraint should be no more than 2½ inches.

Achieving the correct safety position for the head restraint

Sitting in the driver's seat, feel for the head restraint behind your head. Is it too high, or too low? Adjust the head restraint by either pulling it up or pushing it down for the proper height.

If the head restraint is in the lowest position and won't budge, it may be because it's either an automatic or dynamic head restraint that can't be adjusted manually. If you're not sure, refer to the car owner's manual.

Now buckle yourself in, put your hands on the wheel, and pretend you're driving. Use the tape measure to find the distance between the back of your head and the head restraint. Some head restraints can be adjusted horizontally. If yours has this feature, tilt it to achieve the correct horizontal distance. Otherwise, adjust the seat back to a more upright position.

Tools Needed

Measuring tape

Car owner's manual

Child Safety

Car Seats

Babies don't come with instructions, but car seats do. By following the steps provided below you'll be able to properly install a car seat. And if you start to get overwhelmed, just remember your breathing techniques (*hee, hee, hoo*) . . . you'll be just fine!

The National Highway Traffic Safety Administration (NHTSA) states that 80 percent of infant car seats are installed incorrectly, which means that there's only a 20 percent chance that you did it right. You'd never play those odds in Vegas, so don't roll the dice when it comes to your child's safety.

Installing a car seat does not require you to have a degree in physics. What it does require from you is a commitment to learning how to do it correctly—your child's safety will depend on it for the first 8 years of her life!

Once you've learned this information, take the time to teach it to everyone who may be driving with your child in a car—spouse, a caregiver, grandparents, and friends.

Types of Car Seats

When deciding which car seat to buy, you can choose the color and style, but leave the type of car seat your child needs to the experts.

NHTSA and the National SAFE KIDS Campaign both agree that a car seat should be age, weight, and size appropriate.

There are four basic types of car seats: rear-facing, convertible, forward-facing, and booster.

The laws governing car seats vary from state to state, so you need to be aware of the different laws before you travel out of state, even if you're just crossing a state line. To find the law in your state, go to www.safekids.org.

Rear-Facing Infant Car Seat

A *rear-facing infant seat* can be used to transport your newborn home from the hospital all the way up until the baby is at least 1 year old and weighs up to 20 pounds. However, most infants outgrow this car seat by the time they're about 7 months old because their weight exceeds the 22-pound limitation of the car seat.

If your baby's head is within 1 inch of the top of the car seat or she weighs more than 20 pounds before she turns age 1, don't panic and put her into a forward-facing car seat. There are many manufacturers that make convertible car seats that can accommodate infants up to 30 to 33 pounds in weight for a rear-facing configuration.

Rear-facing infant car seat

The bottom line is that it's always safer for a baby to be seated facing the rear of the car.

Convertible Infant Car Seat

A *convertible car seat* is designed to convert from a rear-facing seat to a forward-facing seat. This is a great option if you don't want to purchase a rear-facing *and* a forward-facing car seat. You can use it as a rear-facing seat until the child is at least 1 year of age and up to 20

If your newborn is under 5 pounds at birth, there are car seats specifically designed for low-weight infants. For more information, go to the American Academy of Pediatrics Shoppers Guide and Preemie Protocol's Web site, www.aap.org, and use the keywords "car safety seats."

pounds or to the uppermost weight limits allowed for rear-facing infants. Read the labels on the car seat or instruction manual to determine this. Today, there are many convertible car seats with an upper weight limit of 30 to 35 pounds.

Convertible car seat

Forward-Facing Infant Car Seat

A *forward-facing (only) car seat with a harness* is typically used for children approximately ages 1 to 4, and 20 to 40 pounds. This car seat should be installed so that the child is facing forward. Many, but not all, forward-facing seats allow the parent to remove the harness and use the vehicle lap and shoulder belt to a very high weight—sometimes to 80 or 100 pounds—to secure the child. Read your car seat labels and instructions to see if your forward-facing combination seat permits this.

Forward-facing car seat

Booster Infant Car Seat

A *booster seat* (a.k.a. belt-positioning booster seat) is for children who no longer fit in their forward-facing car seat, are 4 to 8 years old, and are at least 40 pounds and under 4 feet 9 inches tall. It does just what its name suggests—it gives a boost to the child's height so that the adult seat belt fits her properly. There is no harness on this car seat and the child is fully secured by the adult seat belt.

Note: Some convertible car seats can now be converted to a booster seat by removing the harnesses and will accommodate a child up to 100 pounds.

Booster seat

Purchasing a Car Seat

A higher price does not guarantee a higher level of safety, so buy a car seat that fits your child, as well as your vehicle's needs and your pocket's. And be sure to only buy one that conforms to federal motor vehicle safety standards.

Here are some important safety tips to keep in mind as you buy.

- **Before purchasing any model, contact NHTSA through its hotline or Web site to get a list of car seat recalls.**
- **Never purchase a used car seat at a yard sale or from a resale shop because you won't know if it has been in a car accident, if it has substitute parts, if it's been recalled, or if it's too old, which would mean that its safety effectiveness is no longer up to standard.**
- **If you get a car seat as a hand-me-down from someone you know and who can vouch for its safety record, you can use it as long as it hasn't been recalled.**
- **If you can't afford a new car seat, there are organizations that will provide one at a reduced cost. To find out more information, contact the National SAFE KIDS Campaign to find a coalition in your area.**

Before Installing a Car Seat

Homework

The best way to ensure that you'll be installing the car seat correctly is to read the manual that came with the car seat and the label on it, the car owner's manual, the label on the seat belt, and the information below. Also, visit www.safekids.org and follow its safety test, and attend a car seat inspection station hosted by nationally certified car seat technicians who may be stationed at a local fire or police station.

Why go to all this trouble? Because just having your child in a car seat is not enough. A car seat that is improperly used or secured can lead to serious physical harm or death to your child if involved in an accident.

Critical Criteria

There are five very important criteria to meet when installing any of the four types of car seats: (1) location; (2) direction; (3) harness; (4) seat belt path; and (5) tightness.

Location

Location, location, location. The prime real estate for your child's car seat is the backseat. Every car seat manufacturer, safety institute, government agency, and car manufacturer states that the safest place for a car seat is in the back. Why? The impact of an air bag is too great and can cause severe injuries or death to a child in a front seat. Another reason is that most crashes are head-on collisions, and therefore the safest place for a child to be is in a car seat that has been correctly installed in the back of the car, farthest from any impact.

Direction

The direction of the installation of the car seat varies with the type of car seat. Rear-facing car seats should always be installed so that the baby who is under 1 year of age and up to 20 pounds is looking out the back window of the car. Forward-facing car seats and booster seats should always be installed so that the child is facing the front of the car. The direction of the convertible car seat depends on whether it's being used for an infant under 1 year of age and up to 20 pounds (rear-facing) or for a toddler over 1 year of age and 20 lbs. (forward-facing).

Harness Straps

Infant-only, convertible, and forward-facing car seats come equipped with harness straps. Be sure the harness straps are threaded through the correct harness slots for the direction your child faces: straps are at

For a listing of car seat inspections in your area, visit www.nhtsa.gov.

or below the shoulders of the rear-facing infant; and at or above the shoulders of the forward-facing child. You *must* read the car seat instructions and labels to know which harness slots are correct for your child. Also, the harness straps must be tight. The best way to test that the straps are correct is to assure that they lay flat and are taut enough so that they can't be pinched.

Harness slots

Seat Belt Path

Every car seat is secured in to the vehicle by either a seat belt or the LATCH system (see the sidebar). The location where the seat belt goes is called a "belt path." Car seat manufacturers tell you exactly where to place the seat belt based on design and crash test results. Follow the car seat manufacturer's instructions and the labels to know exactly where to secure the seat belt.

Newer car seats used in vehicles (built after 2002) utilize the LATCH system, which does not employ a seat belt to secure the car seat to the vehicle.

Cars manufactured from 1996 on do not need locking clips for their seat belts.

LATCH System

The LATCH (Lower Anchors and Tethers for Children) system allows adults to attach newer rear-facing or forward-facing car seats equipped with lower anchor hooks and a top tether hook. This method does not require the use of a seat belt. Your car seat and vehicle must both be equipped with LATCH to use this system. Vehicles and car seats manufactured after September 1, 2002, should have this federally regulated feature. Check to be sure!

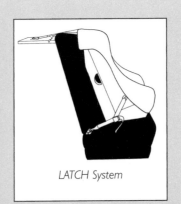

LATCH System

Tightness

The tightness test requires that once the car seat has been installed, it can't be moved in either direction by 1 inch or more. The test must be done at the seat belt path.

DIY: *Installation*

Rear-Facing or Convertible Infant Car Seat

In addition to meeting the above criteria, there are some other things you need to do to ensure a successful installation of a rear-facing car seat: (1) the car seat needs to be at about a 45-degree angle so that the baby's head won't drop forward, blocking the baby's airway; and (2) the baby's head should be at least 1 inch below the top of the car seat.

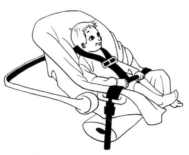

Achieving the required angle

Most rear-facing car seats have an adjustable foot that raises the base to get a better angle. If your car seat does not have it and you're not able to achieve the required angle, place a tightly rolled-up towel or pool noodle on the backseat, and then place the car seat on it. If the car seat has a handle, lower it completely.

Installations are easiest when 2 people work together. Place your weight (a knee works well) into the car seat to remove the plush from the vehicle's seat cushion. Thread the seat belt through the belt path as directed by the manufacturer and have your friend pull it out from the other side. Tighten the seat belt. Now lock the seat belt, following the instructions in the car owner's manual.

Once the seat belt is locked, you can test its tightness. Using one hand, grab onto the car seat at the seat belt path and give a hearty tug on the lap portion of the seat belt. If it moved more than 1 inch either way, then you need to release the seat belt and try again.

Practice makes perfect, so by the second or third time you have to install the car seat, you'll find it easy to do.

It's important to always keep the car seat installed, even if the child is not in it, because in case of an accident or a short stop, the car seat will not become airborne and cause injury.

Installing a Forward-Facing Car Seat

Installations are easiest when 2 people work together. Place your weight (a knee works well) into the car seat to remove the plush from the vehicle's seat cushion. Thread the seat belt through the belt path as directed by the manufacturer and have your friend pull it out from the other side. Tighten the seat belt. Now lock the seat belt, following the instructions in the car owner's manual.

Once the seat belt is locked, you can test its tightness. Using one hand, grab onto the car seat at the seat belt path and give a hearty tug on the lap portion of the seat belt. If it moved more than 1 inch either way, you need to release the seat belt and try again.

Wait, you're not done! Now it's time to check that the harness straps are positioned correctly. For a forward-facing car seat, the harness should be at or above the shoulder level and placed over the reinforced part of the car seat.

Properly Using a Booster Seat

How will you know if your child is ready to stop using a car seat and start using a booster seat? A child can usually stop using a car seat when she is about 8 years of age and is at least 4 feet 9 inches tall. The shoulder belt must fit the child properly across the collarbone and the lap belt should fit snugly over the lower hips (not the abdomen). The child's knees should bend over the seat with feet touching the floor when sitting with her back completely against the vehicle's seatback cushion.

There are two kinds of booster seats—backless and high-back. They're equally safe, but a child can only use a backless booster seat if there is a head restraint for the vehicle seat.

Pull the shoulder belt so that it goes across the child's chest, letting it rest comfortably (but not loosely) against the shoulder. The lap

Tools Needed

Car seat manual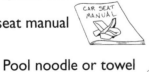

Car owner's manual

Pool noodle or towel

Helpful friend

Backless booster seat

High-back booster seat

belt should come low across the child's hip; be careful that it doesn't rest on the child's abdomen. Also make sure that the child's ears are not higher than the backseat of the car and/or the booster seat, if it's a high-back model. Use the shoulder belt guide if it is provided with your booster seat. This adjusts the shoulder belt for safety and comfort.

We know that every child wants to stop using a car seat, especially when she starts grammar school, but don't let your child's embarrassment overrule her safety.

Fill out the registration form that came with the car seat. Why? Because the manufacturer will contact you if there is a safety recall for that product.

If you have been in an accident, you may need to replace the car seat because the forceful impact may have weakened some parts or all of it. If the accident was a minor fender bender and you're not sure if you still have to replace the car seat, contact the car seat manufacturer. Also check to see if your car insurance will cover the cost of a replacement. Go to www.nhtsa.gov to see if your car seat meets the criteria established by NHTSA for avoiding replacement in very minor crashes. There are basic questions listed, and if you can answer no to all of them you may not need to replace your car seat. When in doubt, err on the side of safety and replace the car seat.

*E*very vehicle is different, so don't assume that because your seat belt locks one way in your car that it will lock the same way in the babysitter's car. There are several ways to lock seat belts, and you must follow the instructions for the vehicle being used.

Door and Window Safety Locks

Kathy was late picking up her children from school and was going a little too fast in the parking lot, causing her to take the turn a little too sharply, which caused her little 3 year old to fly out the car door. Feeling blessed that her son was not injured, she decided to take a turn for the better when it came to car safety. Now Kathy's first thought is securing the car doors instead of securing a good spot in the car-pool line.

Doors

Most cars have child safety locks located on the inside of the edge of the back passenger doors to prevent children from opening the doors from inside. The child door safety locks work independently of the car's door lock system; therefore, if the safety lock is engaged, the only way for the child to exit is for someone to open the door from the outside.

This locking system is great if you have a precocious child that wants to act like Houdini and escape. The downside is that it keeps a child from exiting quickly, if necessary.

If your car does not have child safety locks, or even if it does, always drive with your car doors locked.

Tool Needed

Car owner's manual

Engaging and Disengaging the Lock

To locate the safety lock, open the back passenger door and look at the inside edge. There should either be a button or a switch that can be pushed or moved to the desired position—locked or unlocked.

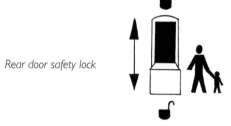

Rear door safety lock

Windows

Power windows are a great convenience, but they can also be harmful to children. Cars have child lock switches (a.k.a. lock-out switches) that disable the rear passenger windows from moving.

Some new cars have what is called an "antipinch" feature that is designed to prevent children from being caught between the window and the window frame. This system is activated when an object is in the path of the movement of the window. If your car does not have this feature, we recommend that you control the movement of the rear windows by using the lock-out switches until your child is of a responsible age.

Children Left Unattended in Cars

Remember to not leave a child inside a car in the garage with the engine running, even if you have the garage door open (see "Preventing Carbon Monoxide Poisoning," page 319).

There's a parking spot right in front of the dry cleaners. Pay dirt! Your baby is sleeping and it is freezing cold outside, so now you can leave her sleeping in her car seat and keep the engine running because you'll only be a minute. Nothing will happen to her, right? Wrong.

Never leave a child inside a car unattended, especially with the engine running! We completely understand the temptation of leaving a sleeping child sleeping in the car instead of removing her, putting her into a stroller, and schlepping her into the grocery store or dry cleaners, but you could be endangering her life from possible heatstroke, carbon monoxide poisoning, and carjacking. Also, a child can accidentally put the car into gear. In fact, a 4-year-old child recently took his mother's car out for a spin. And if that doesn't put fear into you, then think about this—if you leave your child unattended in a car and it's reported to the police, you could be arrested.

Heatstroke

We've all entered our car on a hot day and sat on a seat and realized where the term "hot pants" originated. You almost feel like you'll get a burn if you sit on it. That's because the temperature in a parked car, which has its windows up, will always be much higher than the external temperature.

Well, imagine a child being buckled into a car seat that she cannot undo and left in a car that she cannot unlock, and the temperature is rising. In a 4-year period of time, more than 100 children died of heatstroke from being trapped inside a car. And it didn't just happen in the summertime. A warm spring or fall day with temperature in the 80s will produce a temperature of around 120°F in a car in about 30 minutes. So don't risk it *any* time of the year.

Child left unattended in car

Trunk Entrapment

"Trunks Are for Elephants, Not for Kids" is a safety outreach program sponsored by the National SAFE KIDS Campaign and General Motors that teaches parents the dangers posed by children playing inside cars and trunks.

Some children think that a car trunk is a great place for playing hide-and-seek, but what they don't realize is that for cars built before September 1, 2001, once the trunk is closed it can only be opened from the outside. If your car was manufactured before that date you may be able to have the trunk lock retrofitted with a release mechanism that allows a person to escape from a closed trunk by turning a glow-in-the-dark handle. Contact your car manufacturer for more information.

No matter how old your car is, teach your children not to play in or near parked cars and keep the car locked and the keys out of reach.

Child playing in trunk

Children are more susceptible to heatstroke than adults because their bodies cannot regulate their temperature as well, and consequently will go into shock, causing their organs to shut down, within 10 to 15 minutes.

Keep the car cooler by installing static-cling window shades on the back windows and placing a towel over the child's seat and seat belt so she won't get scorched when entering. (Window shades that attach by static, not rods, are preferable because rods can become projectile hazards in a crash.)

Rear-End Blind Zone

You're thinking that because you're sitting up high in your SUV or minivan, you have a bird's-eye view of everything behind your car. The reality is that you're basically driving backward with your eyes wide *shut*.

A blind zone is the area that cannot be seen either through your windows or rearview mirrors (including the side-view mirror). A rear-end blind zone is the cause of at least 2 children every week being killed and 48 children injured by a motorist backing out of a parking spot, driveway, or garage, states the nonprofit foundation Kids And Cars. In about 70 percent of these incidents, the motorist is a relative of the injured child.

Unfortunately, the number of back-over incidents is on the rise. Why? It's not that motorists are becoming more careless; it's that more of them are driving bigger cars, and the bigger the car the larger the blind zone. Another factor you need to take into account is not only the size of the car you drive, but also your size, too. That's because the smaller the driver, the bigger the blind zone.

Consumer Reports® tested rear-end blind zones in four types of passenger vehicles: a sedan, a minivan, an SUV, and a pickup truck. The sedan, which was the smallest vehicle of the group, had the smallest blind zone, about 12 feet; the minivan's blind zone was 15 feet 4 inches; the SUV's was 15 feet 10 inches; and the pickup truck's was 30 feet! Don't just take Consumer Reports®'s word for it. Take this simple blind zone test for yourself. We guarantee that you'll be shocked at your own findings.

Some larger vehicles have blind zones in the front as well as the rear.

Blind Zone Test

To perform this test, you'll need to purchase a traffic cone, which replicates the size of a toddler. You can buy the traffic cone at a hardware store for less than $10, and after you're done with it we recommend that you give it to a friend to let her take the test, or donate it to your church, synagogue, or school—their cones are always getting run over!

Try this in your driveway or the parking spot in front of your home. Get into your car but don't turn the engine on. Have a friend place the traffic cone a couple of feet behind the center of the back of your car, but don't watch where she's placing it!

Assessing the blind zone

Now look in the rearview and side-view mirrors to find the cone. If you don't see it, yell to your friend to move the cone another few feet back. Now look in the mirrors again to find the cone. Keep repeating the process until you see it. Have your friend measure the distance from the back of the car to the location of the cone. This distance is the size of your blind zone.

Tools Needed

Measuring tape (25 feet)

Helpful friend

Traffic cone

Preventive Measures

There are a wide range of items on the market that are designed to aid a driver in not only seeing everything behind the vehicle, but also emitting a warning sound for others. The products are as simple as a convex mirror and as sophisticated as a rearview camera with a reverse sensor system. The prices vary widely, too, from $20 up to $1,200. And if you're looking to purchase a new vehicle, there are a few that now come with rearview cameras as standard equipment.

Perhaps the best preventive measures are the simplest. Just walk around your car the long way to make sure there are no children and animals close by. Teach your children never to play near a car and take a

Playing in a car's blind zone

head count of children whenever entering or leaving your car. There have been many back-over cases caused by a child who ran out to see a parent who was driving away.

Responsible Driving

Cell Phone Safety

Tori was shopping for the sports car of her *dreams*, only to have it turn into a *nightmare* when she found out that the only ones on the lot had manual transmissions. The sales rep asked her if she knew how to drive a stick, to which Tori replied, "Yes, but it would be too difficult to shift gears *and* talk on the phone."

For women, owning a cell phone may have started out as a safety-only device, but for many it's evolved into a body part. Deals are going down, playdates are being brokered, and Christmas presents are being ordered, all while driving.

Car Talk

Look, we love our cell phones just as much as you do, but let's be honest here, none of us should be multitasking while driving. Everyone's number one task should be to pay full attention to the road and not to increase our productivity by making and returning phone calls.

Using a hands-free device

New Rules for the Road

Most states do not require police to cite any crashes caused by a motorist using a cell phone while driving. However, that didn't stop New York from being the first state to pass legislation banning the use of hand-held cell phones while driving. New Jersey and the District of Columbia have followed suit.

But it's not just state governments that are instituting change for safety reasons. Companies are now realizing the legal ramifications of having their employees make business calls while driving. There are cases of businesses being sued when an employee was involved in a car crash while making a call for work. This has prompted businesses to institute policies stating that workers cannot make business calls on cell phones while driving.

Cell Phone Gadgets

If you can't drive without talking on the phone, then at least purchase a cell phone product that will enable you to talk hands-free. And no, this doesn't mean that now you can talk, apply makeup, and drive all at the same time.

Cell Phone Holders

It seems that there are as many cell phone holders as there are cell phone plans. Cell phone holders are sold everywhere, from computer stores to kiosks in malls, and they all look so promising, but here's what we found works and what doesn't.

Any product that has an adhesive backing that you press onto a part of the car will work temporarily. After a short period of time, your cell phone may fall off and land at your feet. *(If this happens, do not bend down and pick it up; instead, wait until you can pull over safely.)* The most effective way of keeping your cell phone in place is to install a permanent cell phone holder. The downside to this solution is that you need to place screws into the console of your car, which means that it's a permanent fixture ... or at least the holes are. While your cell phone is resting in its holder, use the speaker feature, if available, to enable you to talk hands-free.

Headsets

Isn't it tempting to go up to someone who's wearing an earpiece and speaker microphone and ask them for a large fry and shake? All joking aside, if you are attached at the cord *(hee-hee)* to your cell phone, then a hands-free device is exactly what you need, especially while driving. There are so many options that there's surely one to fit your needs.

Safety Tips

Here are some safety suggestions that should be common sense but unfortunately are not, yet:

- Be familiar with all the phone's buttons, especially the REDIAL and DISCONNECT features.
- If the weather is bad or traffic conditions are hazardous, don't use the phone.
- If there's a passenger in the car, have her dial for you.
- If you have a cell phone that also acts like a computer (PDA), don't respond to e-mails while driving.
- Don't thumb through your address book or take notes while you're talking on your cell phone and driving.
- Save any serious/emotional phone calls for later. If you can't suspend the conversation, pull off the road, find a safe place to park the car, and resume talking.
- Let the person you're talking to know that you're driving and that you'll have to keep the conversation short.
- Teach your teenager the importance of not using the cell phone while driving. Young drivers get easily distracted and therefore should not be multitasking.

What's in the Future

Automobile manufacturers know that cell phones are here to stay, so they're adapting their cars to provide a safer way for motorists to use their cell phones while driving. Soon your car will be able to detect a high-stress driving situation and put any calls you receive on hold, or block any unimportant ones, until the conditions have improved. Until then, let's just hang up and drive!

Aggressive Driving

*I*f you're assuming that young male drivers make up the majority of aggressive drivers, you'd be correct. To find out who the other perps are you may only have to look no farther than your mirror.

Aggressive Drivers

The National Highway Traffic Safety Administration (NHTSA) estimates that about one-third of traffic crashes and about two-thirds of the deaths associated with them can be attributed to aggressive driving.

Not all aggressive drivers have long rap sheets or drive fast cars. In fact, it's often law-abiding people who've had a bad day at the office, or have a screaming child in the car, or are worrying about an overdue bill, or are suffering from holiday stress. They meet up with another motorist who is doing something stupid, and presto, they've transformed from upstanding citizens to *raging road warriors*!

Before you give a judgmental "tsk, tsk" to such offenders, try taking the following test to see if *you* can live in a glass car.

Aggressive Driver Test
- You have blared (not honked) your horn at a driver.
- You've refused to let a driver pass.
- You've refused to let a driver enter your lane.
- You've made an obscene gesture to a motorist.
- You've cut in front of another car.
- You've tailgated a car.

- You've flashed your lights repeatedly at the car in front of you.
- You've deliberately slowed down to anger the motorist behind you.
- You've yelled at a motorist.
- You deliberately took a parking spot someone else was waiting for.

If you do any of these things more than 2 or 3 times a year, then you can be classified as an aggressive driver.

Avoiding Trouble

To avoid escalating a traffic offense into a road war, you need to decide if you want to be right or *dead* right. In other words, you can choose to know you're right and not participate in the battle, or you can choose to be right and get revenge.

If It's Not Your Fault

If someone cuts you off, flips you off, or rides your bumper, the best thing for you to do is to not take it personally—if it wasn't you, it'd be someone else. The angry motorist wants to get into a power struggle and he can do it anonymously in his car. It's normal to want to react in a less than adult way, but take a deep breath and remember that this fool is not worth it.

Instead of getting angry, get even by using your cell phone and call 911, or if you're traveling on an interstate, contact the state police. Give the operator your location and direction of travel along with the make and model of the aggressive driver's vehicle, and, if possible, the license

An aggressive driver riding your bumper

plate number. Once the other driver sees you talking on the cell phone, chances are he'll speed away. Most states have aggressive driving laws, which can result in jail time for a violator.

If You're Being Followed

If the road rager is following you, drive to a police station, hospital, or other very public place and lay on your horn. If that's not possible, then lock your doors, put your windows up, and keep driving. Do *not* pull over and do *not* get out of your car.

If It Is Your Fault

If you were wrong and accidentally cut someone off on the road, or didn't notice that you took a parking spot that someone had been waiting for, or were going 35 mph in a 50 mph lane and were holding up traffic, immediately apologize out loud to the driver or mouth "I'm sorry" and wave. If it's not too late, you could back out of the parking spot and offer it to the other driver.

Easy Rider

Whether you're commuting to work or running errands, there are lots of interesting ways you can keep your anger in check and actually enjoy the ride.

Books on Tape

For those of you who belong to a book club but never seem to find the time to finish one, books on tape is the answer. They can be purchased at any bookstore, or online at www.booksontape.com. And, of course, you can borrow them for free through your local library. You can't stretch your legs while you're driving, but you can stretch your mind.

Share a Ride

If the only way for you to control your anger is to be around people you know, then commute with someone. Not only will it keep your mind off the other drivers, but it will save you money. In most major cities, you'll also be able to use the HOV (high-occupancy vehicle) lanes.

The Road Less Traveled

If you live in a metropolitan area, there is no road that's less traveled. However, there are times that are, so run errands at nonpeak periods of the day, and see if you can change your schedule at work so that you're not commuting during rush hour.

Tickets

*I*s the only blue-light special you're familiar with the one that's trying to pull you over? If so, don't *cop* out on reading all of this important information.

Getting Pulled Over

It's a sickening feeling, isn't it? You're driving along and you see the blue light flashing in the rearview mirror and you think, "No way, it can't be me." But the police car is still behind you, and now you know it's you. You have no choice but to pull over . . . or do you?

Getting pulled over

Unmarked Police Car

You see a blue flashing light on the car behind you, but it looks like a regular car, not a police car. How do you know if it's an unmarked police car and not an imposter?

An unmarked police car will have multiple antennae, a spotlight, and lights inside the grille, not on the top of the car. The lights are sometimes placed inside the windshield toward the top of the window. It's very expensive to outfit a car with a siren and flashing lights, so if an imposter has rigged his car to look like an unmarked car, it probably will only have one light. Another clue is that unmarked police cars won't have ornate grilles, whitewall tires, or any other fancy packaging.

Trust your gut. If the car doesn't seem kosher, then it probably isn't, so don't pull over. If you have a cell phone, call 911, report the situation, and request a uniformed officer to respond to the scene. The operator will be able to verify whether it is a police officer behind you—and if it's not, then a police officer will be dispatched to your aid.

Continue to drive at a normal speed and turn your flashers on, which will indicate to the motorist (if it is a police officer) that you are aware of the situation and will pull over when you feel it's safe to do so. If this occurs at night, turn on the interior dome light and signal with your hand that you will be pulling over. If possible, drive to the nearest hospital, police station, or public place, and if you feel you're in danger, blare your horn.

If you have pulled over, don't get out of your car and don't turn the engine off until you know for sure that the person is a police officer. Every police officer must show you his or her identification card *with* a badge—not just the badge. If there is no ID card, the person is definitely an imposter. Drive away as quickly as you can to the nearest public place and call 911.

Pulling Over

Now that you're certain that the police officer is legitimate, there are rules to follow to make the process less painful.

- Don't cry . . . it doesn't work anymore.
- Admit your guilt if you know you're wrong, and if you have no clue as to why you were pulled over, ask.
- Don't argue—save your arguments for court.
- Don't even think about loosening a button or hiking your skirt because that puts the officer in a liability situation, which means you will absolutely, positively get a ticket—and if you stoop that low, then, *sister,* you deserve it!
- Don't ask the officer how many doughnuts he's eaten today or why isn't he getting the *real* criminals out there.
- Never, ever, get out of the car unless the officer requests it. Instead, roll down the window and present the officer with your driver's license and registration.

Traffic Violations

The most common traffic violations are speeding, moving violation, drunk driving, and failure to pay full time and attention to your driving. We all know what the first three are, so we're going to skip right on down to the last.

Driven to Distraction

What do reading a book, shaving your legs, putting on makeup, using a fax machine, and watching TV all have in common? These are all things that police officers have caught people doing while driving their cars. And those are the ones we can print!

It's disgusting and obnoxious behavior, but there's no law saying that you *can't* do these things in your car, right? Well, yes and no. Yes, there is no law expressly prohibiting someone from shaving her legs in the car while driving, but there is a law called Failure to Pay Full Time and Attention to Your Driving that basically states that if you're doing anything other than paying full attention to your driving, you can be ticketed. And shooting the bird at another motorist does fall under this category.

Talking on the cell phone can also fall into this category; in fact, some states only allow motorists to use hands-free cell phones, and some states are considering banning cell phone use in cars.

Police cars and emergency medical vehicles never share the same color lights. For example, if police cars have blue lights, emergency medical vehicles will have red lights. It's important to note that the colors vary from state to state.

Safety Tips for Teens and Elders

The leading cause of death for people 15 to 20 years of age is car crashes. Older drivers (ages 75 to 80) are 4 times as likely to die in a crash than middle-age drivers. Here are some ways to *reverse* these statistics.

Teen Safety

As parents, we thought the scariest day of *our* lives was sending our children off on their first day of school. That was until we handed them the keys to a car.

About 6,000 teenagers die each year from car crashes, and it's worth stating again that it's the number one cause of death for children 15 to 20 years old. And it's no longer just a teenage male problem. In fact, girls are more likely to have friends in their cars and are more apt to talk on the phone while driving than boys—two situations that raise the likelihood of a crash. (Having three or more passengers in a car increases the risk factor fourfold.)

Common Problems

Your child can be an honor roll student and editor of the yearbook, but when she gets behind the wheel of the car, she turns into a person you wouldn't recognize. She's on the phone while driving with three of her friends in the car, missing stop signs and making illegal turns without a care in the world.

She's not alone.

Here are some typical teenage driver problems.

- They overcompensate when turning the steering wheel.
- They lack experience behind the wheel, so they react poorly when the unexpected happens.
- They tend to be risk takers, especially when they first get their licenses.
- They lack the emotional and physical maturity needed to process information quickly.
- They're less likely to wear seat belts.
- They're uninformed about car maintenance.

Preventive Measures

Here are some ways to keep your child safe on the road.

- Seek a quality driving school with classrooms, professional instructors, and a serious focus. Get recommendations from other parents.
- Enroll your teenager in a defensive-driving course. Contact your local police department or Department of Motor Vehicles (DMV) to see if it offers one for teens. These courses may cost a couple of hundred dollars, but the learning experience is invaluable.
- Pay for private driving lessons *in addition* to driver's education classes, if such classes are offered at your child's school.
- Visit www.roadreadyteens.com, a Web site sponsored by the National Safety Council, the American Automobile Association (AAA), and Mothers Against Drunk Driving (MADD) to help teens understand the risks involved in driving and how it takes years of experience behind the wheel to become a good driver.

Safety measures for a new driver

- Visit www.aaapublicaffairs.com to locate a state-by-state listing of regulations governing teenage drivers, including minimum hours of supervised driving, passenger limitations, and curfews for unsupervised driving.
- While your teenager has her permit, create a chart and log every hour of driving she does. Determine a set number of hours behind the wheel that has to be reached before she can get her license.
- Don't allow your child to drive with more than one other passenger in the car. Teen crash rates rise sharply as additional passengers are added.

Now, let's say you did massive research on finding a safe car for your child to drive, you enrolled her in multiple driving courses, and you've set rules. Hold on; you're not quite ready to hand over the keys to the car until you've taught your teenager how to maintain it. She needs to know how to check the air pressure in the tires, change a flat, check the fluids, and so on. Okay, now you can give her the keys.

Elder Safety

No matter if you're 16 or 86, driving is all about freedom—the freedom to come and go as you please so you don't have to rely on the kindness of friends and family, or a schedule for mass transit. And the older you are, the less you want to give it up. But freedom comes with a price, and unfortunately sometimes the price is someone's life.

AAA states that by the year 2020, some 50 million Americans will be 65 years of age and older, and most of them will be driving. Here are some ways to help you or your elderly parent acquire better driving skills.

Helping Yourself

You're trumping like "The Donald" at bridge. You're taking Intro to Physiology at the community college. And you're teaching water aerobics three times a week. But you're getting lost while driving in once-familiar areas, you're becoming nervous on highways, and you're having difficulty

Drivers over the age of 50 get distracted 2 to 3 times more often than younger drivers.

judging distances. Cars seem to be coming out of nowhere and people seem to be honking at you more. These are typical problems for older drivers, but just because they're universal to people your age, it doesn't mean that they should be ignored. Instead, you need to address them by having your driving skills professionally evaluated *and* by having your health checked.

Cleo in her classic car

Here are some other common driving dilemmas.

- Failure in perception, causing the driver to not notice signs or signals and not yield the right of way
- Inability to properly make a left turn
- Illness that comes on quickly and unexpectedly while driving
- Misplacement of the right foot onto the wrong pedal
- Driving too slowly
- Difficulty in paying attention
- Too many fender benders or near crashes
- Difficulty in backing up the car
- Family and friends don't want to ride with you

Preventive Measures

You can't prevent yourself from aging, but there are ways to improve your driving skills. The following information is provided to aid you in motoring into your twilight years safely; you just have to be willing to get on board.

- Take a driving course offered through the American Association of Retired Persons (AARP), AAA, or the National Safety Council.
- Purchase a car that has factory-installed pedal extenders, an adjustable steering wheel, larger rearview and side-view mirrors, and a fully adjustable driver's seat.
- Have your eyes checked regularly by an ophthalmologist.
- Don't drive when you're tired or feeling ill.

Thirty-six states (plus the District of Columbia) offer insurance discounts to senior citizens who take driver's education courses specifically geared to elderly drivers. Check with your car insurance company for more details. Helpful Web sites to visit are www.seniordrivers.org and www.aarp.org.

- If you find yourself losing your concentration, turn off the radio and temporarily stop talking with your passenger.
- Allow extra time to arrive at your destination.
- Plan your travel schedule to avoid rush hour and other busy times.
- Adjust your travel route to avoid uncomfortable roadways and driving conditions.

Driving courses offered for seniors can be found by visiting those organizations' Web sites or calling their 800 numbers (see "Finish Line: Resources," page 326). The courses are designed to help you to determine if you are a safe driver, as well as to point out problems so that you can improve your driving skills. If it's time for you to retire your license, driving courses such as these can help you decide (no one will make the decision for you).

If you're about to have your license renewed, contact your state's DMV to find out what will be required of you to pass the test. One of the AAA's Web sites, www.aaapublicaffairs.com, has a link to senior licensing laws. Even though the standards for passing the driver's test vary from state to state, every state will require you to take a vision test. If you don't pass the vision test, then you may be asked to have an eye examination by your physician or take additional tests.

Helping Your Parents

You can't assume that because your parents are in their 80s that they're a menace on the road. Instead, you need to see for yourself. Have them drive you around and assess their driving skills. Check their cars for excessive dents in the front or rear, which would indicate that they may be having problems pulling in and out of parking spots. Ask to speak with their doctors about any health concerns that may cause problems while driving. And talk to them about when in the future they foresee themselves voluntarily giving up their licenses. "Voluntarily" is the key word here. Your parents don't want you to take their licenses away, and you don't want to have to be put in that position. So have the discussion way before you need to, so that everyone's on the same page when the time comes.

Your parents also may wish to consider getting an evaluation by a certified driver rehabilitation specialist (see the Web site for the American Occupational Therapy Association, www.aota.org). It can run about $300, but it's as important as any other type of checkup.

On the other hand, don't be in denial when it's time for your parents to give up their licenses. It may be easier on you to have your mom drive herself to doctors' appointments, and your dad to drive himself to meet his buddies for coffee, than for you to have to take them everywhere. But they may only be driving so as not to be a burden to you. The bottom line is that their safety—and the safety of others who will be on the road with them—should be the deciding factor.

If your parents have been the cause of numerous crashes and are not physically capable of driving safely any more, but refuse to give up their licenses, here's what you can do: call the DMV or office on aging in your parents' state. Some states have provisions for people to anonymously report someone whose driving abilities have diminished to the point of causing harm.

Alternative Transportation

If you live in New York City, giving up your driver's license is not an extreme sacrifice. But if you live in a rural area, not driving can alter your social life, as well as limit trips to doctors and the grocery store.

Before a driver's license is retired, voluntarily or not, there needs to be a Plan B for transportation. The best sources of information for finding alternative modes of transit in your area are the public library, the county government, or the mayor's office. Some cities even offer free or discounted bus services for senior citizens.

Honing Your Own Driving Skills

Now that you know how to help the senior and teenager in your life become better drivers, how about doing the same thing for yourself? Sign up for a defensive driving course in your area (check with the DMV or your local police station), or attend a winter driving course, such as Bridgestone Winter Driving School in Steamboat Springs, CO (www.winterdrive.com).

Road Trip

When Amy was growing up, she and her four siblings always looked forward to family vacations: sun, sand, and . . . someone's suitcase falling off the top of the station wagon. The most exciting incident was when her own suitcase fell off onto an 8-lane highway and her mother insisted on stopping traffic so she could pick up Amy's socks and underwear.

In this section, we're going to teach you how to prepare your car for a trip—everything from packing a car to doing preventive car maintenance—so that you can save the excitement for your destination.

When you start financially planning for a vacation, be sure to include a line item in there (above cute clothes and great books) for pretrip car maintenance and possibly membership in an auto club to help keep you safe on the road.

Pretrip Maintenance

Car Checkup

The most common roadside problems are flat tires, broken belts, over-heating, and running out of fuel, all of which are easily preventable.

We've divided this pretrip maintenance into two checklists—one for your mechanic and one for you.

DIFM

Mechanic's Checklist (1 to 2 Weeks Prior)
Don't wait until the last minute to get a checkup because mechanics get very busy during the holidays and summertime, and you may not get an appointment. Another important reason to do this ahead of time is that you might need a replacement part that has to be ordered and will take awhile to arrive. Therefore, schedule an appointment at least 1 to 2 weeks before your trip for the following items:

- All belts and radiator hoses
- Air and oil filters (or you can do these yourself)
- Brakes
- Battery
- Exhaust system
- Radiator

DIY

Here are some pretrip maintenance projects that you can easily do yourself.

- Clean all windshield wiper blades, check them for wear, and replace if necessary.

Be aware of the additional height of the cargo box before going into a parking garage or tunnel. And be sure to remove it before entering a car wash.

- Test exterior and interior lights, including turn signals.
- Check all tires, including the spare, for air pressure, uneven wear, bulges, and tread. Replace if necessary.
- Check all fluids and replenish, if necessary.
- Change engine filters (air and oil).
- Check that all seat belts are visible and not underneath a seat.
- Locate all items needed for changing a flat (see "Flat Tire," page 132).
- Check all items in your emergency car kit.
- Check mirrors and windshields for cracks and have replaced, if necessary.

Roof Luggage Carrier

When we grew up, there was no such thing as a luggage carrier. You loaded the suitcases on top of the station wagon, threw a tarp over them, tied it all down, and said a Hail Mary that it would stay put.

Luggage carriers offer a great solution to overcrowding the inside of your vehicle, as well as transporting items safely. Any items that are not properly secured can be lethal projectiles if you have to make a fast stop, or if you're in a car crash. It's estimated that 3,000 car crashes occur each year from items falling off of vehicles onto roads.

Types of Carriers

Typically, there are two reasons why women hesitate buying a luggage carrier: (1) the cost; and (2) they don't think they can install it themselves. Carriers range in price from under $100 and up—way up—so if you can't afford to buy one, borrow one from a friend. Or, since it typically only gets used once or twice a year, you may want to share the cost and the carrier. With regard to reason number two, we've installed a few carriers by ourselves and together—and if we can do it, you can, too.

Purchasing a Roof Luggage Carrier

There are two types of luggage carriers—a cargo box and a cargo bag. A cargo box comes in two distinctly different styles. One you may know as a "turtle" (or as the industry comically refers to it, a "hamburger box"), because of its shape and opening. The other type of cargo box is long and sleek, and therefore much more aerodynamic than the turtle. A cargo bag is typically square in shape and is made of waterproof material.

You can purchase luggage carriers at some hardware stores, but for the best selection, go to a bicycle or ski shop. Before you go shopping, you first need to see if your car has a roof rack *with* crossbars.

Crossbars

If your car has a roof rack, it may not have crossbars. Crossbars run across the width of the roof and attach to the roof rack. Their job is to keep the luggage carrier from scratching the paint of the roof, as

Crossbars on a roof rack

well as to provide a more secure foundation for the luggage carrier.

If your roof rack doesn't have crossbars, you can purchase them at a bicycle or ski shop and install them yourself. If your car did not come with a factory-installed roof rack, you can purchase one through a car dealership or at a bicycle or ski shop—just make sure that you buy one *with* crossbars. It's best to have the new roof rack professionally installed.

Note: Crossbars come in stationary and adjustable models. For the following instructions, we used stationary crossbars.

Installing a Cargo Bag

There are two ways you can install a cargo bag—prefilled or empty. It all depends on if you have a friend to help, and how heavy the bag will be when full. We prefer to prefill it when it's on the ground because

Cargo bag

It's very important not to exceed the car manufacturer's weight guidelines because driving the car could be dangerous and the warranties may be voided.

you can get so much more in it. Of course, if you're putting really heavy objects inside, then it's best to fill the cargo bag *after* it is on top of the car.

There may be two ways to install it, but there's only one way to remove it—and that's with the cargo bag empty. Also, never leave an empty cargo bag on top of the car. If you're not using it, take it down and store it in its tote bag.

Before you begin, be sure to read the manufacturer's instructions.

Place the cargo bag on top of the roof rack and position it so that the zippered opening is at the rear of the car and the bag is centered.

This is where you're going to need to either open a front or back door and step up onto the doorframe, or use a stepladder to reach the roof. Open up the zipper and gently lay the flap onto the roof. Fill the cargo bag, being careful to evenly distribute the contents and to not overload (follow the guidelines from both the car and the cargo bag's manufacturer regarding weight limitations). Zip the bag completely shut.

Loosely fasten the belts to the front and rear crossbars, center the cargo bag, and then, once that's done, go back and tighten each one. Now tighten the side belts to compress the contents of the bag.

Protecting the car's paint

Installing a Cargo Box

Note: These instructions are based on installing an aerodynamically shaped cargo box.

Tools Needed

Manufacturer's instructions

Helpful friend

Stepladder

If you are going to install a cargo box yourself, the aerodynamic style is much easier to lift than the hamburger style.

Before you begin, be sure to read the manufacturer's instructions.

To protect the car's paint, place the large towel over the door and onto the roof rack. Open the back door and tuck one of the top corners of the towel inside the door and then close the door to keep the towel from slipping.

Before installing the cargo box, empty it of any contents, excluding the mounting hardware. Lock both sides with the key.

Installing a cargo box

If you're doing this with a helpful friend, each grab an end of the cargo box and place it on top of the roof rack with the nose facing the front.

If you're doing this yourself, lean the cargo box against the door that's covered with the towel. Grabbing from the bottom, push it up until it's on top of the roof rack with the nose facing the front.

Lifting the cargo box

Refer to the car owner's manual for guidelines on how to adjust the air pressure in your tires according to the additional load, especially if you're driving an SUV, which already has a high center of gravity.

Tools Needed

Manufacturer's instructions   Large beach towel

Stepladder   Helpful friend

Adjust the cargo box so that its mounting slots are positioned correctly over the crossbars. Remove the towel.

This is where you will probably need to either open a front or back door and step up onto the doorframe, or use a stepladder to reach the roof. Use the key to unlock one side of the cargo box and lift it open. Reach inside and pull out 1 of the hardware mounting sets (there will be 4). Place it over the holes so that it will straddle the crossbar. Insert the U-bolt from underneath so that it goes directly into the holes and into the mounting

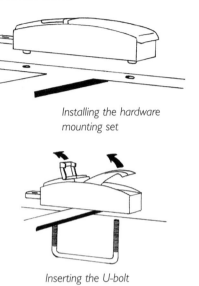

Installing the hardware mounting set

Inserting the U-bolt

hardware. Make sure that the U-bolt is in completely before locking the interior lever and safety lever into place. Repeat this process on the other mounting set on the same side. When completed, lock it. Then repeat the entire process on the other side.

Note: It may seem like such a hassle to remove the cargo box once it's been installed that you may decide you're just going to leave it there. But having a cargo box installed on top of your car will cause you to use 1 to 2 gallons per mile of gas more than without it. With gas prices today, you can't afford not to take it off!

Safety on the Road

According to NHTSA, about 13,000 Americans are killed in car accidents every year from Memorial Day through Labor Day. Here are some tips to get you safely to your destination.

Driving Tips

The best driving tip we can give you is to go the speed limit. You may think you'll be losing time on the road, but in reality you're saving time and money. If you drive the speed limit, you won't use as much fuel, which means you'll save money; you won't get a ticket, which means you'll be saving time *and* money; and you'll have more control of your car, which means that you will be less likely to get into a crash.

Cruise control is a feature in many cars that allows the driver to set and keep the car traveling at a constant speed. This is great if you're driving a long distance and have a tendency to drive a bit too quickly sometimes. To engage cruise control, follow the simple directions in the car owner's manual.

AAA recommends that you keep at least a 2–3-second following distance (we like using a few more seconds) behind the car you are following. This distance will allow you to safely make a quick stop without crashing into another car. On wet or snowy roads, leave additional room between you and other vehicles.

Unless your car comes equipped with daytime running lamps, keep your headlights on all the time. Any extra visibility that you can provide other drivers is always good. And don't worry about the battery dying if you have the headlights on all day—as long as the engine is running, the alternator is recharging the battery.

If you're driving a long distance, take a break every 2 hours to avoid drowsiness. If you find yourself drifting off into sleep, find a hotel and get a good night's rest. And, of course, always wear your seat belt.

Foul Weather

Flash Flood

We've all seen vehicles being swept away by rushing water and wondered, "What was that driver thinking?" We can pretty much guess that the driver assumed that her heavy car could easily get across the road because there wasn't that much water. But what she didn't know is that it only takes 2 feet of water to sweep away any car. It doesn't seem like much, but rushing water is lethal.

The best thing to do is to never put yourself in that situation. Listen to the weather reports on the radio and TV, and don't travel during flash-flood warnings (which usually occur during the summer months). If you *do* get caught on a road that is under water, put a window down, unlock the doors, and turn off the engine. If the water is moving your car, do not try to swim to shore because the current is too strong and you won't make it. Instead, open your window and climb on top of your car. Wrap your legs around the pillar (frame between the front and back seats of the car), pull out a seat belt, and hold on.

Tornadoes and Hurricanes

If you see a tornado heading your way, don't try to outrace it; instead, get out of your car and run for cover into a building. If there's no building nearby, then find a ditch, taking caution to protect your head from flying debris. Also, never drive your car under an overpass because it will not protect you during a tornado.

Once a hurricane warning has been issued, be sure to fill up your tank; gas pumps fail to operate when there is no electricity. You should never try to outstay a hurricane, but if you're unable to leave, do not stay in your car or mobile home. Hurricanes can produce flash floods that can carry you and your car away. Instead, wait to drive until the warning has been lifted.

Lightning

It's much safer for you to be in your car during a lightning storm than outside because if your car gets hit, the rubber tires will diffuse some of the electricity and the exterior of the car acts like a shell that absorbs most of it. Keep your windows up.

If you're driving your car in a storm and lightning is occurring, safely pull over to the side of the road, turn on the emergency signals, and turn the engine off. Do not touch anything metal in the car, such as a door handle or radio knob. Just sit there with your hands in your lap to keep you from accidentally touching anything you shouldn't. If your car is struck by lightning, don't try to leave your vehicle because you'll risk getting shocked; instead, wait for help to arrive.

Blizzard

If you're ever stranded in your car by snow, the rule of thumb is to never abandon your vehicle. Why? A vehicle offers shelter from the harsh weather conditions, it's easier to spot than a person, and you may get lost or hurt if you venture away.

If you're wondering whether you should call 911 or your auto club service, it depends on the situation. If you are in a populated area and not in any foreseeable danger, you should call your auto club service. If you don't belong to an auto club, call a towing company. If, however, you are in a remote area, call 911 for help and give as much detailed information as you can on your whereabouts, and ask for an estimated time of arrival. Don't leave your cell phone on because it's best to save the battery.

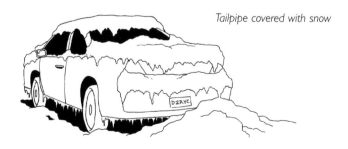

Tailpipe covered with snow

Your main goal in a situation like this is to prevent hypothermia from setting in, so you need to keep your body warm and dry.

Now that you've called for help, let's assume that you have the winter emergency kit (see page 325) inside the car and the gas tank is at least half full. Turn the engine off to conserve fuel.

The next thing to do is to remove the red rag from your emergency kit and tie it to the top of the antenna or to the highest point on the top of your car, like a roof rack. Take out the shovel and dig away any snow that's around the tailpipe.

Turn the engine on to heat up the car and put the window down a bit to get fresh air inside, but don't run the engine and heater for too long. In fact, AAA recommends that you run the engine for only 10 minutes per hour.

If help has not arrived in the time you were told, call again. Just be aware that if there is a major snowstorm in the area, you are probably not the only person stranded—but you're probably the most prepared.

General Car Problems

If, after you've done everything right, something goes wrong with your car, follow these safety guidelines.

- If possible, don't pull off onto the side of the road; instead, get off at the nearest exit and find a safe place to park.
- If you must pull off on the side of the road, carefully exit your car and put as much distance between you and the road as possible.
- Never park on a bridge, an overpass, or a curve in the road.
- If you're a member of an auto club membership service, call it. If not, call the police or the highway patrol. Don't call 911 unless it's a true emergerncy.
- Pop open the hood and place a safety triangle 200 feet from the car in the direction of traffic.

Traveling with Pets

Okay, so we told you at the beginning of the "Safety" chapter that we wouldn't be finger-wagging at you for any bad habits. Well, we thought that since we're dealing with pets in this section, a little wagging would be acceptable.

Whether you're running errands or taking a long road trip with your pet, there are things you can do to provide a safe journey for your four-legged friend.

Probably the most important thing you can do for yourself and the passengers in your car—both humans and those who think they are—is to use common sense. Common sense should tell you that if you're traveling with your pet, the animal should be wearing a collar with an ID tag that displays up-to-date information in case the pet gets lost.

Another commonsense practice is to *never*—and we mean *never*—drive with your pet on your lap. There is no circumstance that would make this an okay thing to do. We don't care that you've been driving with Mr. Toodles on your lap for 10 years and nothing bad has ever happened. If you can't see that you're endangering your life, your passengers' lives, and other motorists' lives, then consider what would happen to Mr. T if the air bag was deployed. Enough said.

Transporting

The Humane Society of the United States recommends that the safest way to transport your pet is by using some type of restraint system, either a crate/carrier or a harness.

A harness, which can be purchased at a pet store or possibly your car dealership, is worn by the animal and then attached to the seat belt latch.

When purchasing a crate/carrier, there are some things you need to consider. First, make sure that it's of adequate size for your pet. Another important feature to look for is the quality of the latch on the door.

Once you've purchased a crate/carrier, be sure to insert a soft padding on the interior base to provide comfort, as well as cushioning in case of a car crash.

Safely transporting your pet

Running Errands

It's hard to find a shopping center parking lot that doesn't have at least one unattended car with an animal in it. The pet owner leaves the animal in a car, cracks the window, and runs some errands thinking that all is well. What the owner finds out too late is that in the 30 minutes she's been away, the interior temperature of the car has risen to 120°F, causing her pet to get heatstroke or die.

Some signs that your pet is experiencing heatstroke are vomiting, excessive panting, stupor, seizures, or a deep-red or purple tongue. If any of these symptoms occur, immediately remove the animal from the car, apply cold rags or ice packs to your pet's chest, head, and neck, or let her lick an ice cube or even ice cream, and take her to a veterinarian or an animal hospital.

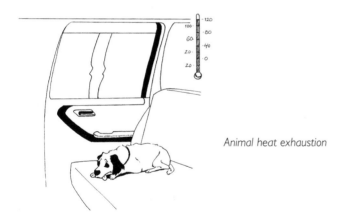

Animal heat exhaustion

If you are a passerby and see that an animal in a car is in distress, go to the nearest store and alert a manager or call 911. Most states have animal protection laws for just this kind of situation. Some locales will even incarcerate the pet owner.

Traveling Out of Town

Remember, the safest place for your pet is not in the car, but at home.

If you're taking Max to Maine or Whiskers to Wisconsin, you'll want to be sure to check off everything on the following list.

- Be sure that your pet is wearing its collar with up-to-date information on the ID tag.
- Be careful when you're exiting your car that your animal won't run out.
- When making a reservation at a hotel, be sure to ask if pets are allowed.
- Find a vet or an animal hospital in the area where you'll be staying, in case your pet becomes ill.
- Create a first-aid kit for your pet (see below).
- Double-check the items in the car kit for your pet (see below) before you put it in the car.

Car Kit for Cats and Canines

- Pet's medicine
- Water bottle
- Bowls
- Pet food
- Photo of pet, in case of disappearance
- Record of pet's vaccination history
- Scooper and disposable bags for animal refuse
- Pet's first-aid kit (medicine, gauze, bandages, thermometer, emergency information for the veterinarian, and a first-aid book that includes CPR information)

For more information about safely traveling with your pet, consult your veterinarian or visit the Humane Society's Web site at www.hsus.org.

Happy trails!

Car Calamities

Stolen Car

You come out of the mall, hands full of packages, and can't find your car. After searching long and hard for it, you realize that you weren't having a senior moment ... your car was stolen.

The FBI states that a vehicle is stolen about every 24 seconds in this country. That adds up to 150 per hour or 1,314,000 a year. Don't think you're off the crook's radar screen if you own an older car. Cars aren't just being stolen for joyrides; in fact, most cars are now being stolen for parts that are shipped overseas.

If Your Car Was Stolen

When you come to the realization that your car has been stolen, call 911. Give the police the make, model, year, VIN, and license plate number of your car, along with your location. Do it as soon as possible, so that the police can input the information into a national database to which all law enforcement has access.

If you are a member of OnStar or LoJack, notify the company next and let the person assisting you know that you've already contacted the police. OnStar is able to pinpoint the exact location of the stolen vehicle by using the Global Positioning System (GPS), thus helping the police trackdown your car. LoJack is a recovery system. Its computer interfaces with the National Crime Information Service (NCIS) by sending a signal to a satellite that emits a homing device and the police will get a code to track the location of the vehicle. An added feature of LoJack is that its signal can penetrate buildings, which allows a car to be found even in underground parking garages.

If you have comprehensive coverage, contact your insurance agent/company and give her the file number of the police report (if you own more than one vehicle insured by that company, let her know which one was stolen, as well). Don't assume that your insurance company will cover the cost of a rental car for you—this will only happen if your policy includes rental car insurance. If you have it, you should be able to get a rental car immediately. Just be sure to ask how many days the policy will cover the cost of the rental.

If you had any important items in your car, such as credit cards, car registration, and checkbook, immediately contact your bank, credit card companies, and the DMV.

Preventing Theft

Car thieves can steal your car in less than a minute. And those who aren't quick use a tow truck which only takes them a couple more minutes. Thieves love it when they see a door unlocked (50 percent of all cars stolen had their doors unlocked), an extra set of keys left on the car (e.g., a magnetic key holder under the bumper), a window down, or a car running without the driver in it. Here are some dos and don'ts for you to follow.

Parking Your Car at Home
- Always lock your car and keep the windows up.
- If you have a garage, park your car inside.
- If your garage door is manual, not electric, be sure to lock it.
- Never leave your car key in the ignition, even if the car is inside the garage.
- Avoid parking your car on the street; but if you must, turn the front wheels toward the curb and engage the emergency brake to make it difficult for a thief to tow it.

- If you do not park in the garage, avoid leaving the automatic garage door opener in the car. If you do, keep it out of sight.
- Don't leave your car running outside your home while you go inside for something.
- Rear-wheel-drive cars should be backed into a driveway and front-wheel-drive cars should be parked front end first in a driveway.

Parking Your Car in a Shopping Center, a Parking Garage, or a Lot

- Always leave your car in an attended parking garage or lot so that at least there's a possible witness should your car be stolen.
- Keep all windows up and be sure to lock the car.
- Avoid leaving any valuables in sight. Put them in the trunk or underneath a blanket or a coat.
- Park in a well-lit area, preferably near the stores.
- Engage the parking brake because it makes it more difficult for a thief to tow the car.
- If you're uncomfortable walking alone to your car, ask the parking attendant to accompany you.
- Avoid walking to your car with your hands full, which makes you an easy target.
- Only give the parking attendant the key to the car, not your full set of keys.
- Make sure that the key ring that holds your car key does not have your name on it. Don't keep your keys in your purse; instead, keep them in your pocket. Keys with a chirp alarm could aid a thief in locating your car should your purse be stolen.
- Avoid leaving your garage door opener in your car.

Theft Prevention Accessories

Back before there was LoJack, OnStar, and car alarms, a thief could jimmy a metal clothes hanger through the window frame, pull up the round door lock, open the door, and hot-wire the engine, all without much fuss. Nowadays there are new automobile security gadgets that are making the criminals sweat a little.

Using some of the security devices and services available today, here's what you can do to protect your vehicle.

- Purchase the OnStar service, which is available on some GM, VW, Honda, and Acura models.
- If you own a car that is rated among the most stolen vehicles in the country, invest in a LoJack system for your car. The company claims a 90 percent recovery rate.

Steering wheel lock

- If your car currently does not have a factory-installed alarm, consider having one professionally installed. Ask your insurance agent if doing so will decrease your monthly insurance rate.
- Purchase a steering wheel lock, which you can install yourself.
- Install an engine ignition kill switch, which cuts power to the starter when activated.
- Have a fuel kill switch or a fuel cutoff valve professionally installed. These will shut down the fuel supply from the fuel pump.
- Use a steering wheel shield in combination with a bar lock. This makes it more difficult to cut the steering wheel, thus preventing air bag theft.

Brake pedal lock

- Brake pedal locks (floorboard locks) make the vehicle undrivable.

- Use a VIN etcher to imprint the number on windows and car parts to deter theft and reduce insurance premiums. This can be purchased at any auto parts store.

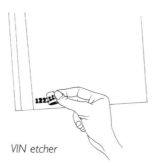

VIN etcher

Preventing Carjacking

Carjacking and car theft both involve a vehicle being stolen, but carjacking means that you or other people are in the vehicle while it's being stolen. Here are some ways to prevent this from happening to you.

- Drive with all the doors locked.
- At intersections, put all the windows up and leave enough space between you and the car in front so that you can pull around and escape.
- Never leave your child in the car with the engine running.
- If a carjacker is trying to force you into the car, throw the keys as far as possible, then run away and scream.

Crashes

We all know the emergency number for the police is 911, but do you know the emergency number for the state highway patrol? The number varies with each state, so to find out, contact your state highway patrol or look for the highway patrol signs on the highways. Keep this important number in the car owner's manual and in your address book.

Helene stopped at a red light, but the young motorist behind her didn't. After the driver begged Helene not to call the police, they exchanged the necessary information and left. Helene later realized two things: (1) that her injuries didn't exhibit themselves until days after; and (2) because there was no police report, it was her word against the other driver's. And that was a crime.

Car crashes account for 43,000 fatalities each year, or approximately 115 a day, which is the equivalent of a plane crashing every day. If there was a plane crash every 24 hours, there would be pandemonium and our government would shut down all airline traffic. Unfortunately, car crashes have become a way of life for us.

After a Crash

You've just been in a crash with another car, and everyone is physically fine but emotionally shaken. It's hard to think clearly, which is why so many drivers make mistakes with *after-crash* protocol. Mistakes made now may end up costing you dearly later.

To Move or Not to Move the Car
The rule of thumb for moving a car after a crash is this: If it's a fender bender *and* you can move it safely to the side of the road, do so. If you're on a highway and can safely move the cars to the next exit, then definitely do it. However, if people are injured, or there's a big dispute

over who's at fault, do *not* move the cars. Also, if you see fluids leaking, or a car is emitting smoke or is on fire, leave it where it is and get away from the car.

Calling the Police

No matter how big or small the crash, the first thing you need to do, after you've checked the physical welfare of all involved, is to call the police. If you're on a highway, then contact the state highway patrol. Yes, even if you have multiple traffic violations and your insurance company wants to dump you. And yes, even if the other motorist begs, pleads, and offers you money not to place the call. Here's why.

A police officer who arrives on the scene of the crash must take both parties' license and insurance information, write a report on the circumstances of the crash and the crash site, and determine who's at fault. However, it's up to the officer's discretion whether to file the report with the Department of Motor Vehicles. Typically, if the crash is severe, or was caused by alcohol or drugs, the officer will report it.

But if you choose not to call the police and a few days later begin feeling aches and pains and contact your insurance company, the case would no longer be considered a traffic case. It would then be a civil case, because there would be no police report and, therefore, no evidence. It would be your word against her word—that is, if you can even locate the other driver.

Securing the Area

Turn on the emergency flashers. Pop open the hood (if it hasn't been smashed), put out safety triangles behind the cars, and stand away from the scene in a safe location.

Exchanging Information

We recommend that you never exchange driver's license and insurance information with the other motorist until a police officer arrives on the scene. Too many times drivers have fallen victim to false information, which means that they have nothing to pass on to their insurance companies. This, in turn, means that your insurance company can

Keep a disposable camera in your car or use your cell phone to take a photo of the crash or fender bender.

After-crash protocol

Most car crashes happen within 25 miles of home, and the majority of serious injuries and deaths happen at speeds under 40 mph.

not file a claim against the other driver's insurance company, leaving yours with the entire bill for repairs and expenses.

If the police officer does not have the proper forms to fill out, request that she call for assistance. Never allow the officer or the other motorist to leave the scene until a report has been written.

This is where having a cheat sheet comes in very handy. In fact, you can request a form from your insurance agent/company that you can keep in your glove compartment. It's helpful to record the names and phone numbers of witnesses, information about the crash, and information about the other driver, including any injuries and her insurance data.

What Happens to the Car

If your car has been badly damaged to the point where it is unsafe to drive, it will have to be towed. Either you or the officer can place the call to have your car towed, but it's your decision where to have it towed.

Remember to remove any important items from your car, such as the garage door opener, the car seat, the registration, and so on, before having it towed.

Towing

The next time you're waiting for a tow truck to arrive and you start getting angry, remind yourself that you've waited longer for a pepperoni pizza to be delivered . . . and you tipped that guy!

There are two ways that cars get towed—one in which you're a willing participant and one in which you're not. Here are some ideas to make both processes less painful.

Having a Car Towed

Don't drive a car unless you have an exit strategy, that is, how to get it towed. Here are some options—in addition, of course, to calling a friend.

Auto Club Memberships

Although auto clubs offer many different services to their customers, the main reason people join them is for the towing services they offer. If you are a member, all you have to do is call the auto club, provide your membership number, and wait for a tow truck to arrive. What you need to be aware of are the typical restrictions, such as the limited number of towing services allowed each year (4 times) and towing mileage (a regular membership entitles you to 3 miles; a premium membership, 100 miles). If you go above the contracted number for towing services, the auto club will still send a towing truck, but you will have to pay for it. And if your car has to be towed over the restricted mileage, then you will have to pay a certain amount per mile.

Car Warranty Package

If you purchased your car with a warranty package, a free towing service may be included. Be sure to refer to the warranty before purchasing an auto club membership or calling for a tow truck.

Car Insurance

Car insurance companies offer towing policies for a modest yearly fee. The benefit of purchasing a towing policy is that there are no limitations on towing services or mileage. The downside is that you have to pay the towing company for the service and then get reimbursed by the insurance company, and you also need to have the number of a towing company ahead of time.

Finding a Towing Company

If you don't belong to an auto club and you need to have your car towed, you can call a towing company yourself—that is, if you know of one to call. What happens to a lot of motorists is that they don't plan ahead and get the name of a reputable towing company and keep it on hand.

The best way to find a good towing company is through your mechanic, car dealership, or car insurance agent. Then call up the company and find out its rates and hours of operation—needless to say, you'd like one that offers 24-hour service.

You can also call a taxi. Most people don't have a taxi company's number on hand, so call 411 for assistance. Or if you see or know of a hotel or store nearby, call or walk there and tell an employee about your situation and ask if she or he can call a taxi for you. It's worth spending the money, rather than to be stuck on the road with no help in sight. Also ask the hotel or store manager if he or she knows the name and number of a reputable towing company.

If you're stranded late at night in an unfamiliar area and none of the above options are available to you, call the nonemergency number for the police. A police officer will come to your location and determine if you need to have the car towed. If yes, the officer will then call for a tow truck and remain with you until the car is towed.

Leaving the Car

If you need to take off before the tow truck arrives, tell the towing company where you will be leaving the key. If you want to leave the car unlocked, put the key under the driver's floor mat. If you want to lock the car, put the key either in the tailpipe (believe it or not, this is the first place towing companies look) or on top of a tire.

If the car has an automatic transmission, place the gear in PARK and engage the parking brake. If it's a manual transmission, place the gear in NEUTRAL and engage the parking brake.

If you have to leave your car stranded on the side of the road because you can't get a tow truck to come out, pop open the hood of the car as a distress signal, lock the car, and *take the key with you*. When you arrive safely at your destination, locate a towing company and arrange to have the car towed as soon as possible. If you don't, either the police department or the state highway patrol will have the car towed and impounded.

Just the Facts

Towing companies say the biggest mistake drivers make is not paying attention to their surroundings. Motorists call to get towed but have no idea where they are! Pay attention, especially at night, to exit signs, mileage markers, and other landmarks, while you're driving so that you can give quality directions. If you have OnStar, its GPS can pinpoint your exact location.

Getting your vehicle towed

No matter whether you've called your auto club service or a towing company, the information you need to provide is the same:

- *The make, model, and year of your car.*
- *If your car is a 4-wheel, all-wheel, or 2-wheel drive.* If you don't know, check the car owner's manual or provide the VIN. This is really important because all-wheel-drive and 4-wheel-drive vehicles can only be towed on a flatbed; otherwise, the transmission will be destroyed.
- *The number of passengers.* If there are too many people to ride in the tow truck, then the towing company will have to call a taxi.
- *The problem with the car.* Let the towing company or auto club know if you've had a flat tire, the car stopped running, you're out of gas, or the radiator is steaming.
- *If you need a spare.* Tow trucks do not carry spare tires, so if yours is not functional, let the auto club or towing company know. Also, don't expect that a tow truck driver is going to change the tire for you. Most prefer to tow a car to a service station rather than to change a tire on the side of the road, which can be very unsafe.

Things to Remove from the Car

While you're waiting for the tow truck to arrive, make a list of everything in the car that you need to get out. Things you may not think of may include:

- A car seat
- The garage door opener (some people only enter and exit their home through their garage and therefore may get locked out)
- Smart Tag devices or EZPass (get you through toll booths faster)
- Valuables
- The car's registration

Note: Don't bother removing a seat belt extender because it's usually vehicle specific.

Where It Should Be Towed

If you're near home, you can have the car towed to your mechanic or dealership. If you're out of town, ask to have the car towed to the nearest dealership that sells your make of car, instead of an unknown mechanic's shop. If your car is under warranty, it's best to have the car repaired at the dealership so that any repairs will be covered by the warranty.

Your Car Has Been Towed

You've been looking for your car for a long time and you're reminded of the funny *Seinfeld* episode, but this time you're not laughing.

Your car is missing for one of three reasons: (1) it was towed by a repo man; (2) it was towed for a traffic violation; or (3) it was stolen.

Repossessed

If your car was towed away by a repo man, it was because you were delinquent with your payments and the bank or leasing company has hired a repossession company to get the vehicle back. To resolve the situation, contact the financing institution immediately and try to work out a payment plan. Of course, you should have done this *prior* to having the car repossessed.

Traffic Violation

If there's no way that it was repossessed, look for any parking signs that may say "TOWING ZONE," "DO NOT PARK," or "NO PARKING." We know they weren't there when you parked your car, but look anyway. If you find such a sign, it's likely that the car was towed either by the police department or a private towing company. Call the non-emergency number for the police. Notice how we didn't say to call 911—that's because 911 should be reserved for life-endangering situations, and this isn't one of them.

When you call, you'll need to provide the police with the make, the model, and the year of your car and where you parked it. Towing companies are required by law to report to the police every car that they tow. Therefore, if your car was towed, it will be on file with the police department.

Impound Lot

Towing companies have impound lots where they keep cars until the owners come to claim them. To get your car out of "towing jail," you must bring your driver's license, registration, and cash or a credit card; checks are rarely accepted. Not only will you have to pay a towing fee, but you will also have to pay a daily storage charge. Some towing companies even charge by the hour. So if your car gets towed, get it back immediately or you'll be paying big bucks.

Don't get into a verbal fight with the towing company because your words will fall on deaf ears. A towing company towed your car for a reason, not on a whim. They get paid by motorists who call for help, through contracts with the police department, or by an auto club service. Therefore, if you believe that your car was wrongly towed, don't shoot the messenger. Instead, take your case to civil court.

Stolen

If the police department has no record of your car being towed, then it was stolen. Ask the police to investigate immediately; then, if your car has OnStar or LoJack, contact the company so that it can assist the police in locating the car (see "If Your Car Was Stolen," page 291).

Insurance

Roberta scraped together her waitressing tips to buy a car, and didn't have a lot of money left for insurance, so she bought the least amount of coverage possible. As luck would have it, her car was stolen, and her insurance policy didn't cover auto theft. So now Roberta is giving out tips to all her customers—don't short-change yourself when buying car insurance.

We're not car insurance salespeople, and we don't play them on TV. But we do feel it's vital to relay to you what we've learned from the top insurance experts in the country. It's dry and it's boring, but hey, at least we're not cornering you at a party with it.

This is a primer, not a full lesson, on car insurance. When it's time for you to buy car insurance or update an existing policy, you must do more research yourself.

Even if you're not buying car insurance, it's really important that you understand what kind of coverage you have. In fact, we recommend that you don't let your child get her driver's license until you've explained to her the kinds of policies that she's covered under, how much they cost, and how much the cost will increase with every speeding ticket or crash.

Determining Your Needs

First, you should determine your needs. Are you buying car insurance just for yourself, or are you adding dependents onto an existing policy?

Are you shopping around because you have too many speeding tickets or crashes and you've been dropped by your insurance company? Are you recently divorced or widowed and need to alter the policy? Are you insuring an old car, a new car, or a leased car? How much insurance can you afford? If you know the answers to these questions, you'll be less likely to overbuy or underbuy insurance.

Don't assume that because your driving record is impeccable you won't need much insurance. You need to think of car insurance as being just like health insurance: you can't assume that you'll never get sick, and you can't assume that your car will never be in a crash. Also, you may never even get a speeding ticket, but your car could get totaled by a fallen tree or an act of nature that's not within your control. What you don't want is to be caught without—or without enough—insurance.

Most people will get a car insurance policy from the same company that handles their life and homeowner policies. This isn't a bad idea, because insurance companies will offer discounts for multipolicy customers, as well as long-term clients. Another benefit to having the same agent for all of your insurance policies is that the agent is less likely to drop you if you have more than one policy with that company. The flip side to this is that you may be able to get a better deal for car insurance if you shop around.

If you choose to look elsewhere for car insurance, it's a good idea to ask friends and family what company they use and if they've ever run into problems filing claims or receiving payments, or if they've ever been unfairly dropped. Next, go online to do a comparative analysis of coverage and costs. Once you've narrowed the playing field to three companies, meet with a local agent from each. After meeting the agents and comparing the offers, the choice is up to you.

Note: Most insurance companies use an underwriting score, which is based on your motor vehicle record, your credit history, and the number of insurance claims you've submitted, to determine if you should be accepted as a new client, if a new claim will affect your score, or if you should be considered a nonrenewal client.

Types of Insurance

Insurance is bought in layers, and you buy each layer based on needs and costs. What may work for your neighbor will probably not work for you, so don't panic if someone has different insurance coverage than yours. Buy tailor-made insurance that will fit you.

You may think that it's best to have a low deductible, and it can be, depending on your situation. However, the lower the deductible, the higher the rates; and the higher the deductible, the lower the rates. Therefore, when you choose the amount of your deductible, you should base it on your driving history and your finances.

Liability

Liability insurance is the first layer of car insurance. It's the most basic, and 47 out of the 50 states require every motorist to have it. Your insurance company is liable (responsible) for any injury—personal or property—that you caused to a motorist or vehicle via a car crash. This includes paying the other motorist's medical bills, loss of salary, and any cost incurred from repairing or replacing the car. Remember, liability insurance only takes care of the other person's needs, not your own. If you are the injured party and the crash was not your fault, then it's the other motorist whose liability insurance would pay for your needs.

Some states require no-fault insurance, which is a liability insurance, but each motorist's insurance is only responsible for their claim, not the other motorist's. For example, if we were in a car crash with you, it wouldn't matter who is at fault (i.e., no fault) because each of our insurance companies would pay our own claims.

Collision

Okay, so you've learned who pays whom after a crash, but who pays for the damage to your car after you've backed it into a fire hydrant? Collision insurance covers any damage to your car that you caused. It will even cover damage from a minor fender bender, as long as both motorists agreed to call it a day because no one was hurt and there was minimal damage. The catch is that collision is an expensive insurance to carry. One way to lessen the monthly payments is to opt for a higher deductible.

Comprehensive

Another layer of insurance is called comprehensive. This type of insurance covers natural disasters (floods, hail, etc.), theft of your car, vandalism, and hitting a deer. Don't hesitate to file a comprehensive insurance claim for hitting a deer because it may not affect your driving history, depending on your underwriting score. Comprehensive insurance may also require a deductible.

(If you need to take a break now and get a cup of coffee or stretch, we understand. Just don't forget to come back and finish this section.)

Uninsured Motorist

This insurance covers you in case you are in a crash and the other motorist has no liability insurance, or you're involved in a hit-and-run accident and have no way of filing a claim against the other motorist. Most states require all motorists to carry this type of insurance. Even if you're not required by law to carry this insurance, it would be a wise investment, especially if you live in one of the states that does not require motorists to carry it!

Underinsured Motorist

If you were paying attention during the liability insurance section (you didn't know there'd be a test, right?), you know that some motorists do not carry enough liability insurance to cover all costs incurred from a crash. Underinsured motorist insurance covers the difference. This type of insurance is covered under the *uninsured motorist insurance*.

Gap Protection

Gap protection is always required when you lease a car, and it is recommended for anyone who is taking a loan with little or no downpayment. But it can also be a financial lifesaver if your car is stolen or totaled. Gap protection does exactly what it says it's doing—it provides insurance for the gap between the loan balance and the car's cash value. Here's an example: Let's say you have a $25,000 loan with a balance of $23,000. The original price of the car was $25,000, but after 2 years, its value is down to $20,000. If your car was stolen or totaled, your insurance company would only pay the loan company the actual cash value of the car, which is $20,000. You would be responsible for the difference between the present balance and the cash value of the car, which in this case would be $3,000. Gap protection would cover the difference, minus a deductible of a few hundred dollars. It's a onetime purchase and it's not that expensive, but there is a catch—you can only purchase it at the time of the sale of the car. Your insurance agent or credit union (if it provides car loans) typically will charge less for the policy than a dealership, so shop around.

Finally, you must have collision comprehensive coverage on your car in order to qualify for gap insurance. Therefore, if your car is stolen or totaled, and you only had liability insurance, you will not be covered for any loss.

Rental Car Insurance

Insurance for renting a car is different than car rental insurance. When you rent a car for personal use and you have comprehensive and collision insurance, then you are covered while driving a rental car. However, if you're renting a car for business, your personal car insurance will not cover you. Therefore you need to check with your company to see if it carries a policy for its employees that will cover them under such situations, or that they will cover the cost of obtaining insurance from the car rental company.

Insurance If You're Driving Someone Else's Car

If you're driving someone else's car and you're involved in a crash, most states have the same rule: *the insurance follows the car*. Therefore, the liability is with the car owner's insurance company, not yours. However, if the loss is severe and a lawsuit develops, your insurance company may then become involved as a secondary insurance.

Supplemental Coverage

This is the final layer of insurance, and it is the one that most people do not purchase. There are pluses and minuses to buying this coverage, but first we need to explain the different options.

Towing

This is wonderful if you're not a member of an auto club. The cost is a minimal once-a-year payment, you get to choose the towing service, and it's cheaper than a yearly auto club membership. The disadvantages? If you're out of town and you need to be towed, you have to find a towing company yourself and pay it, or the repair shop where your car was towed, out of your own pocket. The insurance company will then reimburse you in full.

Rental Reimbursement

The typical amount of time a car is in the shop after a crash is two weeks, which means that it can be very costly to rent a car while yours is being fixed. Rental reimbursement is a minimal charge that you pay yearly, and it covers the cost of a rental car only if it's claim related, not service related. This means that your insurance company is *not* going to pay for you to rent a car while you're on vacation, but it will pay for a rental car after you've filed a claim after a crash.

Auto Replacement

Of the three supplemental coverages, this is the one you're least likely to purchase. This insurance will completely cover the cost of repairs or replacement for a car at the price you paid, even if the cost is more than the blue book value. Basically, you're paying for your car to never be deemed "totaled" by your insurance company. The only reason to purchase this insurance is if you own a very (and we mean *very*) expensive car or a classic that's not replaceable. You can probably guess that this insurance is extremely expensive.

Paying for Insurance

Now that you have an agent, know what your needs are, and understand the different types of insurance coverage, it's time for you to write a check. But wait. First, we need to tell you something that your insurance agent may not have shared with you. If you are 30 days late with a payment, or you bounce a check, your policy can be instantly terminated. Do whatever it takes to keep your payments current.

What Will Drive Up Your Rates

Crashes

People are afraid to call 911 after a crash because they're concerned that their insurance rates will go up. What most people don't know is that police officers are not required to report crashes to insurance companies, but they are required to file a report with their department, and it's up to their discretion to file a report with the DMV. This is to your benefit, because if you don't call a police officer, and no report is filed as a result, and later on the other motorist claims injury, it will be your word against hers. Therefore, instead of the case being heard in traffic court, it will now have to go to small-claims court.

Car crash

Points

Points are accrued every time you have a traffic violation. (The point system is regulated by your state's Department of Motor Vehicles, not your insurance company.) The bigger the offense, the more points awarded. The DMV can decide to put you on probation or take away your license based on the number of points you have on your record and the reason for them. Points may stay on your driving record for 3 years.

Tickets

The number of tickets for speeding or other moving violations may cause your insurance rate to increase. The magic number of tickets is usually 2 in a 36-month period. Of course, the increase in your rate depends on your underwriting score.

But that's just for minor traffic tickets. There's another category of tickets that's referred to as major. Major traffic tickets include reckless driving, driving under the influence, hit and run, and racing. An insurance company can cancel your car insurance if you have just one of these offenses, or it may increase your rate twofold.

Stolen Vehicle

If your car is stolen, your insurance company will cover it only if you have comprehensive coverage.

Age and Sex

It's true—if you're male, single, and under the age of 30, your rates will be higher than a woman who is your age and single. Why? Because studies have proven that young men have a greater risk of being in a crash than women their age.

Make and Color

While the make of the car matters, it's a myth that owning a red or black car drives your rates up. The more expensive the car, the higher the rates, because the insurance companies estimate how much it will cost to repair or replace the vehicle. Therefore, driving a foreign sports car is going to cost you more in insurance premiums than if you drive a minivan. Fun will cost you.

Where You Live

Each state determines its car insurance rates. If you have a car registered in New Jersey, you will pay the highest insurance premiums in the country—no matter what type of car you own. New York and California also have high rates.

How to Improve Your Rates

Good Student Rates

If you have a young driver in the family who is an A or B student, send a copy of her report card each quarter to your insurance agent. Studies have shown that kids who get good grades are usually good drivers;

therefore, insurance companies will give discounts to students who have As and Bs.

Over-50 Rates

If you're 50 or over, ask your insurance agent for an age-related discount. You can get an additional discount if you take a certified driving class that tests your skills and tells you where you need improvement. For a class near you, contact your local police department. If you're a member of AAA, contact your local chapter for a listing.

Get Married (Just Kidding)

If you're male, single, and under the age of 30, car insurance will cost you more. We know of a young man, 24, single, who got his first speeding ticket and his rates doubled. He got married a year later, switched insurance companies, and lowered his rates.

Trade in Your Expensive New Car

If you really need to cut down on your insurance rates, then go as no-frills on a car as you can. The more expensive the car, the higher the rates. You didn't want to make those high car payments anyway, right?

Choose Higher Deductibles

Remember, higher deductibles mean smaller rates, and smaller deductibles mean higher rates.

Stay with the Same Agent

As we stated previously, insurance companies will offer discounts to multipolicy holders as well as long-term clients.

What To Do If You've Been Dropped

Be humble. Don't panic. Be humble. Get the picture? Don't throw a tantrum and scream and yell. Agents just don't cancel a client on a whim. Actually, your situation has to be pretty bad for it to happen. It's definitely

If you like the insurance company's product, but not the agent, you can switch agents without being penalized.

If you own a car that is rated as one of the top two stolen cars, or if you live in a heavy crime area, we recommend that you buy gap protection to cover your loss in case of theft.

your fault, or your child's, so take ownership of it (wait, that sounded like Dr. Phil) and move toward finding a solution.

The number one reason a client is dropped is because of major traffic violations, such as racing, driving under the influence, hit and run, and reckless driving. And it can only take one violation to ruin your underwriting score.

Another major reason for being dropped is not paying your bill on time. It just takes missing one payment to lose your coverage. No matter the reason—say that you simply forgot to pay, or that you don't have the money—just be honest with the agent and get the money to her as soon as possible.

If you have a good relationship with your agent and you have multiple policies with her, you stand a better chance of working out a deal. The agent may keep you on as a client, but she will increase your rates.

When an insurance company decides to drop you, you will be given a nonrenewal notification that will state exactly when the coverage will stop. Typically, you'll get 45 to 60 days prior notice. This is not like health insurance, in which you're given a grace period. No, sister; when they say it's over, it's over. So you'll need to do some serious insurance shopping.

When you find an insurance company that will take you as a client, be up front and honest. Don't try to hide anything, because the agent will have your driving record as well as your payment history—so actually there's nothing to hide. Just be grateful that you're getting coverage.

Garage Safety

Installing a Parking Spot Marker

Colleen hadn't used her garage in four years. Neither rain, nor sleet, nor snow, nor hail could get her to drive her car into the garage. It wasn't because it lacked space; it was because she had no sense of space. In fact, it didn't matter what size car she drove—she'd hit the wall. Now, after installing the tennis ball, Colleen hits *it* every time and is off to a *non*smashing start.

There are plenty of products on the market, ranging from bumpers to electronic gadgets, that can keep you from driving too far into the garage, but we like the good-old tennis ball to do the trick. It's inexpensive and easy to install. All you have to do is keep your eye on the ball!

Stopping when the ball hits the windshield

Tools Needed

Tennis ball   String   Eye screws (2)

Scissors

Ladder or stepladder

In a 2-car home with a 2-car garage, each car usually has a designated bay. Unless both cars are identical, you'll want to do this project for both bays, using the car that's "assigned" to each one.

DIY

The objective is to have the tennis ball hit the windshield instead of the car hitting the wall!

If you have more than one bay (spot) in your garage, choose the one that you'll use for your car every day. Park your car in that bay and turn the engine off.

Take the string and tie each end to an eye screw (a.k.a. fastener), knotting them tightly. Insert one of the eye screws into the tennis ball, twisting it clockwise until only the eye is showing.

Place the ladder near the car, close to the windshield. Climb up the ladder with the tennis ball in one hand. *Never stand on the top rung of a ladder or stepladder.*

Place the end of the eye screw with the string attached to it against the ceiling above the windshield of the car. When you have the right spot, screw the fastener into the ceiling.

Climb down the ladder and move it away from the car. Now it's time to test your handiwork.

Back the car out of the garage and then drive back in, stopping when the ball hits the windshield. Adjust the location of the string if necessary.

Safely Storing Items

*I*f you're like us, you store everything in the garage except your car. The size of the car has nothing to do with it. It's the amount of stuff—sports equipment, bins of holiday decorations, the extra refrigerator—that leaves little room for the garage's original purpose. In fact, the only vehicle you can get inside is a tricycle.

No matter if you have a large or small storage area in the garage, you need to make sure that the space is a safe location for car products and that they're stored properly.

Two great sources of safety information are the manufacturers of the products and your local fire department. Most products list a consumer hotline number and the manufacturer's Web site on the label.

Just about every car product can be classified as a hazardous material—even windshield washer fluid. A hazardous material is a product that has one or more of the following properties.

- *Toxicity.* Substances that are toxic are lethal if absorbed, inhaled, or ingested. Examples include antifreeze and brake fluid.
- *Flammability.* Flammable items can be easily ignited. Gasoline is such a substance.
- *Volatility.* Volatile substances can explode. Again, gasoline is an excellent example.
- *Corrosiveness.* Caustic substances, such as battery acid, can burn skin.

Because of the potential danger of these products, they need to be stored out of reach, especially from children. Pets can also be poisoned by ingesting antifreeze (it has a sweet smell), so never leave an open container on the floor and clean up any spills immediately.

Here are other important safety suggestions:

Properly storing car products

- **Read the labels on each product for the manufacturer's directions for proper storage.**
- **Never use a different container for a product other than the one it came in.**
- **If a product's container is becoming corrosive, set it inside a larger plastic container and pour cat litter around it. Dispose of it properly.**
- **Make sure that all lids are properly secured onto the containers.**

The following items should *not* be stored in your garage; rather, they should only be stored inside a metal shed that's not attached to the house.

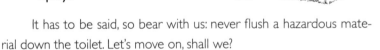

Safely storing gasoline

- **Paint**
- **Gasoline**
- **Pesticides**
- **Sprays**

It has to be said, so bear with us: never flush a hazardous material down the toilet. Let's move on, shall we?

By disposing of hazardous materials properly, you're doing your bit to help protect the environment, as well as provide a safer home for yourself and your loved ones—and it also will keep you from receiving a hefty fine from the Environmental Protection Agency (EPA). Check with the appropriate local government agencies to receive information about proper recycling or disposal.

Preventing Carbon Monoxide Poisoning

*I*f you're freezing your tailpipe off and want to warm up your car, make sure that its tailpipe is sticking outside the garage before starting the engine!

More than 500 people each year in the United States die from unintentional (nonsuicidal) carbon monoxide poisoning. One-third of these deaths are caused by a car engine left running in an enclosed garage.

What It Is

Carbon monoxide (CO) is a silent but deadly killer. It is an odorless, highly poisonous gas that is created by fuel-burning household appliances, lawn mowers, grills, and cars. Poisoning occurs when cars and fuel-burning appliances are not working efficiently or are improperly ventilated. For example, you won't get CO poisoning if you're grilling outside on your deck, but no garage is vented enough to be safe for grilling—with either charcoal or gas.

Don't assume that it's okay for you to warm up your car in the garage as long as the garage door is open. What most people don't realize is that it takes awhile for a car's catalytic converter to warm up; therefore, it's unable to convert carbon monoxide into carbon dioxide. Carbon monoxide fills up the garage quickly, even with the garage door open, and if the garage is attached to the house, it can seep inside, sometimes lingering there for up to 2 hours. You can drive out of the garage all toasty warm, never realizing that you're leaving everyone in the house in harm's way.

> *If you drive an older car that does not have a catalytic converter, you run a higher risk of carbon monoxide poisoning.*

> *It's important to have your car's exhaust system checked for leaks during its scheduled maintenance checkup. An exhaust system that is not working efficiently can be harmful to your health.*

Warning Signs

Exposure to high levels of carbon monoxide can cause flulike symptoms: headaches, dizziness, muscle weakness, and vomiting. If untreated, exposure to carbon monoxide can cause coma or death. If you think you or anyone in your family is exhibiting signs of CO poisoning, get everyone out of the house immediately. Don't wait to call 911 from your home phone; instead, get out and call from your cell phone or a neighbor's phone.

Preventive Measures

If you need to warm up your car, pull it out of the garage and let it idle outside. We know that having your car outside in the cold seems to defeat the whole purpose of warming up the car, but the reality is that *you* need to warm up, not the car. A car really doesn't warm up until it's been traveling for 10 miles.

Also, never leave anyone in a car while the engine is running. There is a tragic story of a woman who left her children inside her car with the engine on while she shoveled the snow from around it. By the time she was done, the children had died of CO poisoning. What this woman did not realize was that the tailpipe had been covered by snow, thereby allowing the CO to enter the car. Leaves can also cover a tailpipe, leading to the same problem. So never turn on the engine of your car until everything has been cleared away from your car's tailpipe, and keep children inside the home until you're all done. One other word of caution: be sure to leave a window down a quarter of the way for fresh air to enter until you're on the road.

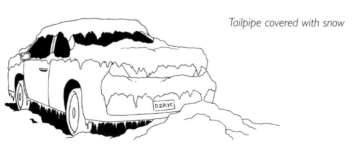

Tailpipe covered with snow

Installing a Carbon Monoxide Detector

There are many different types of carbon monoxide detectors, but the kind we like the most is the one that can be plugged into an electrical outlet. Do not install it inside your garage, whether attached or detached to your home, because it will  frequently go off and then you'll be tempted to remove it. Instead, plug it into an electrical outlet in the hallway on the first floor near the garage, following the manufacturer's instructions.

(Don't forget to install carbon monoxide detectors on every level of your home and maintain them every month.)

Parking Garage: Clearance and Safety Measures

All parking garages have a clearance height sign that hangs in front of the entrance. The height reflects the pipes and beams found in garages.

You've finally found a parking garage that's not at full capacity, but you can't bring yourself to drive in. It's not because you care about the hourly rate—you just don't want to turn your **SUV** into a convertible!

It seems that every parking garage, car wash, and tunnel has a different clearance height for vehicles. There's no one-size-fits-all, so how do you know if your SUV or minivan can *clear* the clearance? Here's a simple way to avoid playing car limbo.

All you need to do is measure the standing height of your car, which is the distance from the ground to the roof—and don't forget to include the roof rack.

Go to the middle of the side of the car and measure the distance from the ground to the roof of the car. Use the stepladder, if necessary. Write down the actual height of the car inside the car owner's manual so that you'll always be able to reference it when you see a clearance sign.

Determining your car's height

Tools Needed

Measure tape (12 feet)

Car owner's manual

Pencil

Stepladder (if necessary)

Now that you know the standard height of your car, refer to it when you see the clearance height painted on the outside of a tunnel, or posted on a car wash, or printed on a hanging beam at the entrance to a parking garage. If you don't see a posting, ask an attendant before entering.

Never let a parking garage attendant wave you in if you know that your car won't fit, especially since you will be the one responsible for any damage to your car.

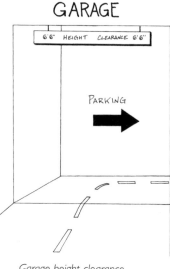

Garage height clearance

Safety Measures

Now that you've driven your car safely into the parking garage, it's time to practice some personal safety measures.

- Always park your car near high-traffic areas, such as an elevator, an entrance, or an exit.
- Park in a well-lit area.
- Don't leave valuable items visible in your car.
- Avoid getting into a fight over a parking spot.
- Only leave a valet key, not your entire set of keys, with an attendant..

Be aware that your cell phone may not be able to get a signal in a parking garage. Therefore, if you're uncomfortable walking to your car alone, request an escort from the building's security.

Glove Box, Trunk, Winter Emergency Kit, and Garage Essentials

Glove Box

Car owner's manual
Emergency window breaker
Tire gauge
Fuses

Trunk

Safety goggles
Fix-a-Flat
Jumper cables
Flashlight
Rags
Bottled water
Work gloves
First-aid kit
Waterless hand cleaner
Safety vest
Safety triangles
Cheater bar
Plastic bag
Lubricating spray
Wheel chock
Duct tape
Towel

Winter Emergency Kit

Red rag

Blanket

Flashlight with extra batteries

Shovel

Nonperishable food

Bottled water

Cat litter

First-aid kit

Candle and matches

Snow broom (foam rubber)

Ice scraper

Garage

Funnels

Rags

Work gloves

Wire brush

Fire extinguisher

Automotive hand cleaner

Lubricating spray

Oil pan

Motor oil

Windshield washer fluid

Battery charger

Cat litter

Oil absorbent

Finish Line: Resources

AAA
1000 AAA Drive
Heathrow, FL 32746
407-444-7000
www.AAA.com

AAL-MATIC Transmission Service
11611 Lee Highway
Fairfax, VA 22030
703-273-8192

AAMCO Transmissions, Inc.
1 Presidential Boulevard
Bala Cynwyd, PA 19004
800-GO-AAMCO
www.AAMCO.com

AARP
601 E Street, NW
Washington, DC 20049
888-OUR-AARP
www.aarp.org

1-A-Auto
888-844-3393
www.1aauto.com

American Petroleum Institute
1220 L Street, NW
Washington, DC 20005-4070
202-682-8000
www.api.org

BP
www.bp.com
www.amocoultimate.com

Consumer Reports®
www.ConsumerReports.org

Department of Motor Vehicles
www.DMV.org

Fix-A-Flat
www.fixaflat.com

Insurance Institute for Highway Safety
1005 North Glebe Road
Arlington, VA 22201
703-247-1500
www.highwaysafety.org

Jim Coleman Automotive
10400 Auto Park Avenue
Bethesda, MD 20180
301-469-7100
301-469-6600
www.jimcolemanautomotive.com

Johnson Controls, Inc.
Automotive Group
5757 North Green Bay Avenue
PO Box 591
Milwaukee, WI 53201-0591
414-524-1200
www.johnsoncontrols.com

Meguiar's, Inc.
Corporate Headquarters
17991 Mitchell South
Irvine, CA 92614
800-347-5700
www.meguiars.com

National Highway Traffic Safety Administration
NHTSA Headquarters
400 Seventh Street, SW
Washington, DC 20590
888-327-4236
TTY: 800-424-9153
www.nhtsa.dot.gov

National Institute for Automotive Excellence
101 Blue Seal Drive, SE
Suite 101
Leesburg, VA 20175
703-669-6600
877-ASE-TECH
www.ase.com

National SAFE KIDS Campaign
1301 Pennsylvania Avenue, NW
Suite 1000
Washington, DC 20004
202-662-0600
www.safekids.org

National Tire & Battery
Corporate Headquarters
Tire Kingdom International
823 Donald Ross Road
Juno Beach, FL 33408
800-926-8473
www.NTB.com

Oil Dri Corporation of America
914 Curie Drive
Alpharetta, GA 30005
www.oildri.com

Pohanka Chevrolet, Inc.
13915 Lee Jackson Highway
Chantilly, VA 20151
800-322-4396
www.pohanka.com

Prevent Blindness America
211 West Wacker Drive
Suite 1700
Chicago, IL 60606
800-331-2020
www.preventblindness.org

Thule, Inc.
www.thule.com

Valvoline
www.Valvoline.com

Index